PEARSE'S PATRIOTS

Pearse's Patriots

St Enda's and the Cult of Boyhood

Elaine Sisson

For Oisín and Éle
My morning and evening stars

First published in 2004 by
Cork University Press
Youngline Industrial Estate
Pouladuff Road, Togher
Cork, Ireland

Reprinted 2005

British Library Cataloguing in Publication data
A CIP catalogue record for this book is available from the British Library.

ISBN 1 85918 325 5 HB
ISBN 1 85918 395 6 PB

A CIP record for this publication is available from the Library of Congress.

Typeset by Redbarn Publishing, Skeagh, Skibbereen, Co. Cork
Printed by ColourBooks Ltd., Baldoyle, Co. Dublin

www.corkuniversitypress.com

Contents

Acknowledgements

This book started life many moons ago as a doctoral thesis and I have many debts of gratitude to the following people who have helped me at all stages of its production. In particular I would like to thank Professor Terence Brown of the English Department, Trinity College, Dublin whose excellent, exacting and meticulous advice has been invaluable. Dr Antoinette Quinn saw me through the first stages of this project and I am appreciative of her guidance also. Dr Nicola Gordon Bowe of the National College of Art and Design has been extremely generous with her knowledge of Celtic Revivalism in the arts and I owe her an especial debt of gratitude as well as one of friendship.

I am grateful for the courtesy and attention I have received from the archivists and librarians at the National Library of Ireland, at Trinity College Library, at the National College of Art and Design Library, the Hugh Lane Gallery and the Brother Allen Library in Richmond Street, Dublin which has a wonderfully eclectic collection of ephemeral material. I am especially indebted to Pat Cooke of the Pearse Museum for permission to reproduce visual material and to the late Turlough Breathnach for his enthusiasm and his knowledge especially in relation to the work of Willie Pearse. I would also like to thank Lady Davis Goff for her kind permission to reproduce Beatrice Elvery's painting *Éire Óg*. The Institute of Irish Studies provided me with valuable financial assistance at a time when such help was much needed. I am fortunate to have wonderful colleagues at the Institute of Art Design & Technology, Dún Laoghaire and am grateful for the insights that arose from the Institute's research seminars in Irish Cultural Studies. I would like to acknowledge the commitment of Sara Wilbourne and Caroline Somers at Cork University Press in bringing this book to fruition. Thanks particularly to Bill Darlison, a great friend and mentor, who performed the arduous task of reading the book at proof stage.

Families play a vitally important, if often invisible, role in the production of any kind of project that drags on for years. To my parents, George and Betty, brothers Ray, John and Niall and sister Lynda and their extended families I say thank you for their unflagging support which has accompanied me on this journey from doctoral thesis to published book. Never last or least, I would like to say *buíochas mór* to my beloved husband Denis Conway who never thought he would be living with Pearse for so long. For his longsuffering commitment to this book, his occasionally firm insistence on its completion and for services rendered to the thankless tasks of childminding and housework I share this book with him.

Elaine Sisson
May 2003

Illustrations

Introduction

Between August and September 2000 a heated argument on the legacy of Patrick Pearse was played out on the letters pages of the *Irish Times*. For a number of weeks readers vigorously contested the status of a man perceived either as an honourable Republican patriot or a misguided conservative fanatic. It was evident on reading this daily debate that, more than eighty years after his death, Pearse continues to exert a fascination of some kind today. Eventually the editor of the newspaper called the debate to a halt and refused to publish any further letters on the subject. It was clear from his decision that otherwise the correspondence might easily have continued for months, if not years.

If nothing else, the passion and ferocity of the contents of the letters signalled that Pearse's legacy is troublesome and that it is perhaps telling of contemporary Irish society that his historical place within Irish history is far from secure. As Ireland pulls away at high speed from the past towards a modern global identity, the subject of Pearse stands as a disruptive and troubling indication of our relationship with history. Does he represent part of a proud tradition on which the modern state is founded or does he signify the narrowly proscribed socio-political Irish identity of Catholic and Gael which is rapidly being shrugged off?

Perhaps surprisingly for an Irish audience there are times when Pearse sounds very modern. His indictments against the brutality of colonial systems, the subjugated positions of the self under colonial rule and the internalized self-hatred of degraded peoples resonate through the writings of more recent postcolonial critics: Frantz Fanon on the psychology of oppression, Albert Memmi on the subjugation of the self and Paolo Freire on the use of education as a tool of power and degradation. But these men were writing about other countries – Algeria, India and Brazil – and in different times, the 1960s, the 1970s and the 1980s. Through the echoes of the past Pearse's voice becomes connected to a broader intellectual argument about the way in which oppressive systems teach subjugation and complicity. The position of the *seonín* – the person who does not know what he is and who apes the manners and affectations of others – does not only have currency within Pearse's world but in our own also. Given the number of correspondents to the *Irish Times*, it seems that most people know enough about Pearse to have an opinion but perhaps not enough to offer a critique, and so he remains in a form of no man's land suspended between veneration and vitriol.

One of the telling absences from the letters pages was a careful consideration of Pearse's legacy as a social reformer and headmaster of St Enda's. His reputation was almost entirely considered in terms of politics rather than his other achievements as a cultural nationalist, writer and educator. The aim of this book is not to redress this imbalance: it is not a biography, as Ruth Dudley Edwards has already written an excellent life of Pearse which has informed much of this publication. Nor is this book a political history or an appraisal of Pearse's political legacy. Indeed the subject of Pearse remains so contentious that to admit to writing on Pearse presupposes that the idea is either to debunk the myths of martyrdom or to reinforce him as an icon of the past. This book seeks to do neither, instead as a cultural history of St Enda's school between 1908 and 1916 it explores the visual and literary myth-making discourses of national identity and masculinity which the school so successfully promoted. Therefore this book falls outside the vast majority of publications which address the political consequences of the life of Pearse and is, perhaps, a small contribution to less well-debated considerations of Pearse's ability to appropriate cultural discourses on history, masculinity and citizenship from imperial sources and to reinvent them as national traditions.

Pearse was born in 1879 in what is now, of course, Pearse Street. His father, James, was from England, and Margaret, Pearse's mother, was his second wife. James had been widowed the previous year and he had two children by his first marriage. James had been brought up as a Unitarian and freethinker but had converted to Catholicism on the occasion of his first marriage. James and Margaret had four children: Margaret Junior, Patrick, William and Mary Brigid. The children grew up in a noisy, happy household nurtured by their mother's imaginative tales of the Irish heroic past and their father's dedication to natural justice, independence of thought and social reform. It made for a heady combination and is one whose roots can be traced throughout Pearse's life.

Patrick and William were educated by the Christian Brothers in Westland Row and, before entering University College Dublin (UCD) and the King's Inns to study law, Pearse taught Irish for a period, while becoming increasingly involved in the Gaelic League and the new literary societies that were beginning to spring up around Dublin at that time. He wrote extensively for the new Irish language newspaper *Fáinne an Lae*, which eventually became *An Claidheamh Soluis* and which Pearse later edited for almost five years. The study of law did not really interest Pearse and as he became more and more involved in the Gaelic League he took up the full-time editorship of the newspaper. He used the paper to highlight his concerns about the nature of education and the importance of teaching culture and history to a generation of schoolchildren who had been forced through the grind of a colonial education system. At this time he also published poems, plays and short stories, in Irish and in English. Increasingly *An Claidheamh Soluis* became the mouthpiece for Pearse's educational philosophies and it was only a matter of time before he established a school of his own along nationalist lines. In 1908 St Enda's opened its doors to the public and Pearse resigned all his other duties to become its headmaster.

Pearse's commitment to cultural nationalism gained a more military and political edge after 1913, when he became a member of the IRB – the Irish Republican Brotherhood. From then on even his closest friends observed that his worship of military discipline became fanatical and a private obsession with Napoleon was deemed to be excessive. By 1916 Pearse's involvement led him to the GPO, where there were over thirty St Enda's boys, past and present. Indeed the toll for St Enda's was high overall: out of the fourteen men executed in 1916, five of them – Pearse, Willie Pearse, Joseph Plunkett, Thomas MacDonagh and Con Colbert – had taught at the school. Pearse was executed by firing squad on 3 May 1916. He was thirty-six years old.

The Indian postcolonial theorist Partha Chatterjee's study of the emergence of nationalism in India presents a very compelling argument about the importance of nationalist schooling as a conduit for ideas about nationhood.[1] He argues that, as literary and cultural nationalism gains significance within a society, new forms of communication become available in vernacular forms. By this he means nationalist newspapers, a seeking of new forms of theatre, expressions of nation in art, the revival of sports and so on, thereby putting a whole cultural revival into place. However, it is, argues Chatterjee, educational reform that allows all of these different forms of cultural expression to be explored in the one place. The emergent forms of cultural nationalism in literature, language, music, art, drama and sport come together and are most powerfully articulated as an inter-dependent web of ideas in a school environment. St Enda's is a perfect example of how these fragile and emerging forms of national revival were condensed, taught and then redisplayed to a wide nationalist community who understood the school as a microcosm of what a nation state could be.

Studies of cultural nationalism have assigned a marginal place to St Enda's within the history of modern Ireland. For this reason it is often difficult to estimate the significance of the school for contemporary writers. There is also a dearth of written reminiscences by men who attended the school during Pearse's time. On the one hand this seems surprising, since those few who did recall their schooldays have emphasized their sense of being involved in something wonderfully innovative. On the other hand, given that the generation of men who passed through the gates of the school between 1908 and 1916 formed part of a pioneering and revolutionary generation, it is perhaps not too difficult to understand how their schooldays were merely the precursor to a much more exciting period in Irish history. Therefore the almost total absence of detailed accounts of what it was like to be a St Enda's boy is understandable when set against the turbulent political climate of those days after leaving school.

However, during its heyday St Enda's captured the imagination of the wider nationalist population in a particularly overwhelming fashion. Roger Casement praised it as a school 'of a distinctively national character' which interested boys 'in their own country' and made them 'good and useful citizens of it'.[2] Many years later, after the school's closure, W. P. Ryan reported that at its zenith 'Sgoil Éanna . . . became something of a watchword, a symbol, a national achievement, a culture-ideal in manifestation and realisation' which at first 'seemed to many [to be] a sort of fairy-tale, a dream of what Irish education ought to be' and contributed to 'the formation of character, the kindling of imagination [and] the creation of interest in Ireland'. What St Enda's stood for may be standard educational practice in some countries, he claimed, but in Ireland it was revolutionary.[3] Ryan's son Desmond, Pearse's friend and biographer, commented fifty years after the founding of the school that St Enda's had been one of the lessons that Pearse had taught 'not only his pupils but a nation'.[4] In a 1918 edition of *The Irishman* Lord Alfred Douglas went so far as to praise 'the holy beauty of the educational system of Pádraig H. Pearse' and, quoting William Bulfin, maintained that St Enda's 'was the most important thing in the interests of Gaelic Nationality that had been done in Ireland since the foundation of the Gaelic League'.[5]

This book suggests that St Enda's was more than a radical experiment in schooling; it was, in Pearse's words, 'an educational adventure' which operated as an instructional training ground in national identity and masculinity.

1

Beginnings

When the gates of St Enda's opened in September 1908, its headmaster and founder, Patrick Pearse, dreamed that the school would be 'an educational adventure' in nationalist schooling. It was a vision long cherished by Pearse, who had been publicly advocating nationalist-run schools as early as 1903. At St Enda's, Pearse's objective was to provide a modern, child-centred, bilingual education for Irish boys. From the very beginning St Enda's held a special place in the nationalist imagination and was an important crucible of ideas on national identity, masculinity and education in the years from 1908 until the time of Pearse's death in 1916, although the school itself did not close until 1935.

Expectations for St Enda's were high; the week the school opened, the Gaelic League newspaper, *An Claidheamh Soluis,* predicted that St Enda's 'will be a nursery of character, intellect, patriotism, and virtue, which may eventually exert a benign influence on the private and public life of our country'.[1] Optimism for the success of the school was based on the reputation of the highly respected Pearse. Pearse had from his earliest years been involved in many aspects of the Irish language and cultural revivalist movement. Pearse became the editor of *An Claidheamh Soluis* in 1903 and used the pages of the bilingual newspaper to argue persuasively for changes to the educational system. He gained a reputation as a journalist, writing extensively on education matters, and was considered to be perhaps a pedantic, but always passionate and hardworking, advocate for the League. By 1908 he was a well-established figure amongst nationalist circles and his credentials for running a project like St Enda's seemed impeccable.

Pearse's high profile within Gaelic League circles would always have ensured publicity for St Enda's amongst Irish speakers. However, the League's broad appeal as a social and cultural organization secured an amount of attention for the school that extended beyond the Irish-speaking community. For most parents, St Enda's offered an opportunity to provide their sons with a good-quality, broad-based education, a grounding in nationalist history and culture, a chance to learn Irish and Irish games and customs and a feeling that they were supporting an experiment surrounded by an aura of history.

The St Enda's roll-call reveals the appeal of the school to committed 'Irish-Irelanders'. The first pupils to enrol were drawn from some of the most eminent nationalist families in Ireland. Pearse noted that 'nearly every boy in the Boy Corps of Sgoil Éanna is the son or brother or nephew or cousin of some man or woman who is graving a mark in the history of contemporary Ireland'.[2] Among them were Eoin MacNeill's three sons and a nephew; the MP and Gaelic Leaguer Stephen Gwynn enrolled his son Denis; William Bulfin's son Eamonn attended as a boarder, as Bulfin lived in Argentina and was the editor of the League paper, *The Southern Cross;* George Moore's nephew Ulick attended, as did W. P. Ryan's son Desmond. James Larkin's sons joined later in the school's history, while relations of Agnes O'Farrelly, Mary Hayden, Stephen Barrett and Padraic Colum also attended. 'In no other school in Ireland', said Pearse in the school magazine *An Macaomh,* 'can there be, in proportion to its size, so much of the stuff out of which men and nations are made. There is rarely a boy of all our seventy who does not come from a home which has traditions of a literary, scholarly or political service.'[3]

Yet support for the school extended beyond parental enthusiasm. In the early years St Enda's attracted the attention of most of the significant cultural nationalists of the day. Douglas Hyde, Standish O'Grady and W. B. Yeats were regular visitors and lecturers. Constance Markievicz, Maud Gonne, Ella Young and other women associated with cultural and political life were also keen supporters. Roger Casement and Sean O'Casey signalled their approval of what Pearse was trying to do. There was unlikely support from international figures: Rabindranath Tagore, the Indian nationalist, Lord Baden Powell, the founder of the Boy Scout Movement in England, and Lord Alfred Douglas (Oscar Wilde's Bosie) were all aware, and admiring, of St Enda's. The commitment of the teaching staff to nationalist politics was well established and five of the staff, including Pearse, were executed for their part in the Rising of 1916: William Pearse, Joseph Plunkett, Thomas MacDonagh and Con Colbert.

St Enda's boys were a regular fixture in Dublin social and cultural life in the early years and were considered, without exception, an emblem of the potential of Irish manhood. The authority of the St Enda's boys as an imaginative symbol for Ireland, past and present, is evident in the many ways in which St Enda's was understood as a type of national spectacle. Between 1908 and 1912 the boys performed in seven different plays at the Abbey Theatre and numerous others in the school; they also acted in at least six open-air pageants of Irish history at St Enda's, Jones' Road and *feiseanna* around the country. However, a larger cultural influence is also evident in the promotion of Gaelic games for boys, the need for an Irish contemporary popular literature in the form of boys' adventure stories and juvenile tales, and the distribution of many images of the boys at work and play which were sold as picture postcards. The sense that St Enda's represented the future of Ireland is reiterated over and over again by those who watched the boys perform in plays at the Abbey Theatre, at the colourful and publicly staged pageants on mythology and history; who saw them marching through the centre of the city in the costumes of ancient Ireland; who bought pictures of the boys as Cúchulainn and Fionn; who admired their skill at hurling and Gaelic football, and who watched them drill in military formation in the uniforms of the Fianna Éireann.

In this exploration of the cult of boyhood as an imaginative and cultural project I want to address the question: what made St Enda's so distinctive? It required a peculiar mix of educational *nous* and sentimental vision, both of which were amply provided by the imagination and passion of Patrick Pearse. One of Pearse's innovations at St Enda's was to recognize *imperial* pedagogical and cultural forms and reinvent them for an Irish audience. Pearse was interested in the way in which imperialist understandings of history, mythology, popular literature and masculinity had proved a very potent mix for generations of English schoolboys. Seamus Deane has commented on the similarity between Pearse's brand of chivalric nationalist heroism and contemporary ideologies of empire.[4] From the standpoint of cultural history, St Enda's provided a training ground for the teasing out of a new definition of Irish masculinity – as yet unformed in the bodies of its young pupils. Schools offer opportunities for experiment, not only in pedagogical terms, but also in the realm of ideas and history. Ideas on physical fitness and the perceived relationship between manhood and patriotism were under constant revision in the early years of the twentieth century. Anxieties about the decline of British manhood were commonly expressed across a range of social and political discourses at this time. Irish nationalism had reasons of its own to be more anxious than most about the possible physical degeneration and 'feminization' of men. To understand the particular anxieties of Irish nationalism an understanding is needed of how Irishness, in the broader discourse of Celticism, had been consistently portrayed as feminine since the middle of the nineteenth century. Initially it was not Pearse, but D. P. Moran, who tackled the complexities of masculinity and Celticism. Moran, a considerable influence on Pearse, is one of the first of what is now understood as a 'post-colonial' voice to emerge from Ireland. His analysis of the debilitating effects of imperialism on the psychology of masculinity predates, by almost eighty years, the now established post-colonial critiques of Albert Memmi, Frantz Fanon and Ashis Nandy.[5]

D. P. Moran's *The Philosophy of Irish Ireland,* based on a series of previously published essays, was printed in 1905. The self-styled Irish-Irelanders, spearheaded by Moran, understood themselves to be the 'authentic' Gaelic-speaking voice of nationalism. In particular Irish-Irelanders saw themselves in opposition to the more suspiciously anglicized aspects of Irish revivalism such as literary clubs and theatres, whose members, such as Yeats and Synge, continued to write in English. *The Philosophy of Irish Ireland* is a scathing and often vindictive critique of contemporary literary figures and the emergence of Irish Celticism as a powerful imaginative force within art and literature. Moran considered Irish Celticism as an insidious anglicized invention and argued vociferously that it was responsible for perpetuating a relationship with English culture that was harmful and subjugating. He maintained that the invention of Irish Celticism alienated Irish people from recognizing their older, Gaelic heritage and that the literary movement of the Celtic Twilight (with particular savagery reserved for W. B. Yeats) was embracing Celticism to the detriment of the enormous body of literature in the Irish language. This, to Moran, was not only copperfastening imperial cultural dominance but was a form of self-hatred which sought to 'hibernicize' English conventions in literature rather than reviving a genuinely 'authentic' Gaelic culture which was dying away. Moran's disappearing Gaelic Ireland was coined 'Irish-Ireland' and was at odds with Celticism, which he distrusted as anglocentric.

The division between the Gaelic and the Celtic, as persuasively argued by Moran, disguised a deeper chasm than that between 'authentic' and anglicized Irish identities. On a deeper psychic level Celticism was viewed by Irish-Irelanders as suspiciously urban and feminized, somehow less robust and vigorous than rural Gaelic culture. This was not merely a form of class snobbery but was closely linked to the late Victorian fascination with Celticism and, within imperial discourse, with the 'feminine' virtues of the Celtic nature. Therefore Moran's distaste for Celticism was not merely occasioned by the popular elevation of 'drawing room literature' but with a more insidious colonizing discourse which emasculated Irish men by turning them away from the natural hinterland of Gaelic, Irish-speaking culture.

Victorian perceptions about the 'feminine' aspects of Celtic culture were popularized through the writings of Matthew Arnold. By the time Arnold's influential study of Celtic literature was published in 1866 the vogue for Celtic antiquities and cultures and the stereotyped notions of 'Celtic character' were firmly in place.[6] Arnold's writings promote the Celt as a sensitive artist and the Celtic impulse as one of refinement and civilization. His argument that the Celtic races are 'keenly sensitive to joy and to sorrow' and 'aspire ardently after life, light, and emotion' was bound to appeal to the vanities of Irish Celticists.[7] In fairness, given the amount of anti-Irish material in circulation, Arnold's enthusiasm for Celtic culture was refreshing. However, his appraisal of the Celtic character was framed within a gently chiding paternalistic voice. While the Celt is sensitive and artistic he is also emotional and intemperate, argued Arnold, and although imaginative, energetic and touched by genius the Celt lacks the rigour of application and the strength of character to see his ideas through.

It is not difficult to see how critics of Arnold, like Moran, felt that Victorian Celticism was an imperial discourse which emasculated Irish men while praising them for their flighty tales about fairies and twilights. Moran's critique of the mentality produced under imperialism makes for a surprisingly modern commentary on the psychology of the colonized subject. His anger is not directed at imperialism's desire to colonize (which he understands as a means of eradicating cultural difference) but at the acquiescent Irish who enter into a master–slave relationship as cultural and economic slaves. He considers Celticism as the cultural equivalent of cap-doffing, indicating the internalized contempt of a bleating, spirit-broken race.[8] For Moran, Celticism held nothing 'masculine in its character' and produced a cultural politics which was effete and impotent.

Moran's insistence on the masculinity of the Gael as a role model for Irishness rather than the feminized Celt is tied up not only with imperial representations of Ireland but also within the mesh of social and psychological narratives which constructed mid- and late-Victorian womanhood. The implications for the Irish of being a 'feminised' race must be understood within social discourses which suggested that women were not capable of political responsibility. Imperial iconographies of Ireland as passive and female are consolidated by the prevailing stereotyping of suffragists, feminists and activists as 'defeminized' women. Representations of 'disorderly' women suggested that women could occupy either a 'natural' domestic role or a public, masculinized position.[9]

When Arnold aligned the Celtic with the feminine he was therefore, directly, or indirectly, suggesting that public life, self-government, rationality and autonomy were not available or desirable for the Irish. Studies of female iconography suggest that Ireland is gendered as female in order to make certain points about the nature of Irishness. Yet Ireland is not always gendered as female within imperial discourses; as L. P. Curtis has argued, it is often gendered as male in brutalized depictions of Fenianism.[10] Belinda Loftus has shown that Ireland is gendered as either male or female, according to prevailing social and political conditions. She suggests that imperial representations of Ireland as female tended to focus on Ireland's weakness, ineptitude, youth and beauty and, in the nineteenth century, the desire to be shielded from sexually rapacious and socially uncouth male Fenians. Therefore the representations of acquiescent and obliging Ireland and of politically rebellious Ireland became split along gendered lines.[11] This is confused somewhat by the nationalist tradition of representing Ireland as female, which, although reflecting a different set of political values, nevertheless draws on prevailing ideologies of femininity. The female image of nationalist Ireland is largely an image of dispossession, of disenfranchisement, of marginality and of victimized oppression.[12]

Since imperial representations of Ireland were not only organized along gendered lines but also along social and class lines, the figuring of Ireland as female became further polarized between, for example, the noble and imperial Hibernia and the ineffectual and pretty Maid of Erin. Male representations inscribed in discourses of power and domination (because of men's associations with public life and political agitation) remained overwhelmingly barbarian. In the nationalist tradition the gendering of Ireland was also produced across a number of different figurations of the female: Mother Ireland, Cathleen Ní Houlihan, the *Sean Bhean Bhocht* and *Roisín Dubh*, amongst others, occupied different social and ideological positions within nationalist discourse. The point to be made, however, is that male representations of Ireland were generally used to debase or belittle actual political protest and social agitation; in other words the representations of simian-like men were meant to be read as representations of actual male subjects.[13] Female representations on the other hand were more abstracted allegories of Ireland and Irishness and were not meant to represent women in any real socio-political sense. Contemporary iconographies of the female, whether nationalist or imperial, were dependent on prevailing notions of femininity to illustrate a psychic rather than a political state of mind.

The implication, therefore, of Arnold ascribing a 'feminine' sensibility to Irishness is double-edged. On the one hand it fed into a pre-existing nationalist system of representation which allowed for an apposition between Irishness and femininity; on the other hand it reinscribed many imperial ideologies already in place about the suitability of the Irish for self-government. It would seem that to accept one meant accepting the logic of the other.

For Moran, the figure of the elemental Gael offered an alternative model of Irish masculinity to the enervated, emotional, feminized Celt of Arnoldian Celticism. Moran contended that the cerebral and scholarly pursuits of the Celtic intellectual served to illustrate the extent of Irishmen's alienation from the land and the manly benefits of manual labour.[14] He maintained that, in the days of the warrior princes, scholarship and learning formed an integral part of everyday life and was inspired by a vigorous and raw relationship with the landscape and with the natural world.[15] Moran argued that the inspirational and originary figure of the Gaelic man had been cast aside in the rush towards pluralism and modernization and that Celticism had debased Irish manhood so much 'that not one in a thousand Irishmen believes in his heart that we were [ever] anything but savages' before colonization.[16]

The concept of a hypermasculinized[17] Irish-speaking Gael may have been introduced by Moran, but it was Pearse who constructed an educational philosophy for 'remasculinizing' Irish-Ireland. Pearse's bold and visionary move was not to dismiss Celticism but to recuperate it as a powerful literary and visual discourse into the philosophy of Irish-Ireland.[18] Seeing Celtic and Gaelic masculinity as complementary rather than contradictory identities, Pearse's contribution to the 'remasculinization' of Ireland was to expand an understanding of the Gaelic into the broader pan-European discourses of Celticism. At St Enda's Pearse's vision created a prototype of the distinctly modern Irish male subject by mapping many of the perceived 'feminized' attributes of Celticism onto a masculine ideal of pagan Gaelic civilization. Seeking indigenous male role models for his boys, Pearse rifled through the antiquities of bardic history and the annals of the early Celtic church to find models of manhood that were both pagan and Christian, warrior and scholar. Pearse's great imaginative achievement at St Enda's was to produce an Irish boy who was educated to believe himself to be the natural inheritor of the bardic and Christian traditions in Ireland.

Pearse was astute enough to realize that it was not Celticism that had enervated Irishmen but an education system which kept children in ignorance about their own country. For Pearse, the scholastic and artistic achievements of the early Celtic Christian church were something to be admired and the supposed emotional sensitivity of the Celtic scholar-artist a virtue to be celebrated by nationalist men. He condemned the educational values of imperial England, which had produced an Irish race of 'mental castrates' and 'eunuchs' who had no understanding of the greatness of its literary or artistic history.[19] Instead of inspiring its children the modern education system was taming them; it contributed to their ineptitude and highlighted their weaknesses by alienating them from what they knew and understood. Pearse considered the English educational system to be an imposition on the 'natural' order of things: a pre-existing system of fosterage that had existed in both pagan and early Christian Ireland which had been dismantled and subjugated after the fall of the Gaelic clan system in 1601 and the subsequent flight of the Earls. The unnatural English system is the 'murder machine' to which Pearse famously makes reference: it is an engine, a series of cogs, a depersonalized institution.

Pearse's original vision for St Enda's was focused on the possibility of establishing a school in the Aran Islands. Pearse had first visited Aran in 1898 and his sister Margaret breathlessly records how he formulated his dream 'of founding a school for boys . . . which would also be – a *home!*'[20] According to Margaret, Pearse's trip was an epiphanic pilgrimage wherein 'on Aran's holy isle . . . [where] St Enda . . . raised the banner of Christ, a vision of St Enda's school' rose before him.[21] The significance of Aran to cultural nationalists was not only in its association with early Christian monastic settlements but with an older, pre-Christian, civilization.[22] The remains of Christian settlements on Aran coupled with the island's mystical pagan history fed into Pearse's burgeoning desire for the masculine appropriation of Ireland's mythic and heroic Christian and pagan past.[23] For Irish-Ireland and for literary revivalism the islands offered a landscape of multiple meanings associated with Ireland's cultural heritage. More importantly Aran was able to provide two models of Celtic masculinity: the cultured monk scholar and a more ancient (and more elemental) pagan man, both of whom occupied the 'natural' western terrain of Irish-Ireland.[24]

Irish-Ireland's embrace of the west as a site of elemental Irishness and its belief in Gaelic culture as the authentic voice of the Irish people situates it within a discourse of the primitive in which the 'peasant' is privileged over the urban. Irish-Ireland's appropriation of the primitive 'within' not only defined Irishness against non-Irishness, and rural against urban, but in privileging the male body as epitomizing the national character it suggested that masculinity was a more authentic or normative gender role than femininity. Although the female body continued to have currency as a literary and visual metaphor for Ireland, it was the 'real' male body which was seen to 'embody' Irish identity and social and political reality. By implication the male body was considered to represent a 'natural' and 'native' Irishness.

Recent work in the area of gender studies suggests that gender, like national identity, can never be 'owned' but is continually collectivized in order to create social definitions of what it means to be male or female.[25] As a cultural narrative rather than a 'given' identity, gender identity, like national identity, is 'imagined'. Historically and culturally masculinity is understood as a naturally occurring shared identity, yet the meaning of masculinity varies from culture to culture and norms of masculine behaviour are almost always temporally and culturally specific. Male social power is displayed not only through social roles but through cultural representations which reinforce deeply held beliefs about the nature of masculinity. Graham Dawson argues that, while 'masculine identities are lived out in the flesh', they are 'fashioned in the imagination' and that the imagining of masculinities 'indicates the process by which norms [of behaviour] are subjectively entered into and lived in, or "inhabited" by men'.[26]

The American scholar Eve Kosofsky Sedgwick has argued that the most important social bonds between men are forged in all-male institutional communities, such as, for example, the public school, the military, the gentlemen's club or the cloister, which are closed off from the world of women and family life.[27] It is through such bonds, which she calls 'homosocial', that a consensually agreed form of masculinity emerges. The homosociality of men is vital to producing the 'right' kind of masculinity while at the same time indulging, in a socially acceptable fashion, an outlawed emotional need to be close to other men. This concept of masculinity as a consensual rather than a 'given' identity suggests that what is understood to constitute 'manliness' and 'manhood' may be culturally unstable. For late Victorian and Edwardian culture 'manliness' was understood as the social identity of maleness, but the concept of 'manhood' was something altogether more precarious. 'Manhood', unlike the fact of being male, was a complicated process of learning 'manliness' through different homosocial and cultural codes.

Nineteenth-century narratives about 'manhood' expressed anxieties about the depletion of the male life force, suggesting that 'manhood' was constantly in danger of being undermined or lost. The fragile state of 'manhood' or the difficulties in attaining 'manhood' were necessarily threatened by any behaviour or emotional life which was considered to be feminine and thereby emasculating. In the light of this perception of the precarious nature of 'manhood' it is not difficult to understand why Moran was so agitated by the effects of Celticism on Irish men. Studies on English masculinity have shown how concepts of 'manliness' underwent a series of changes in the latter half of the nineteenth century and in the years before 1914.[28] Emphasis on the virtues of moral earnestness and purity of feeling made way for the values of athleticism, physical prowess and moral courage.

The ancient bardic culture of Gaelic Ireland provided models of physical strength, patriotism and heroism that were in keeping with contemporary conceptions of manliness. In Germany Richard Wagner's cult of Romantic hero-worship used Celtic and Norse mythology to create powerful statements about the relationship between masculinity, national identity and cultural regeneration. Wagner's explorations of the regenerative power of myth and language were hugely influential in articulating the concept of *zeitgeist* and deeply affected Pearse's vision of the pedagogical relationship between patriotism and male heroism. In Ireland Standish O'Grady's 1878 *History of Ireland* had introduced the possibility of cultural renewal through Irish heroic literature and bardic 'men of action' to a generation of intellectuals, like W. B. Yeats, who rejuvenated Irish mythology in new literary forms.

The cult of boyhood at St Enda's engaged the influences of Christian Celticism and Gaelic warrior pagan culture in the formation of a particular concept of Irish 'manliness'. The search for authority led Pearse back to the clan-based systems of fosterage which were common in pre-Christian Ireland and whose form had been adapted and reworked by early Christian communities after the arrival of St Patrick in the fifth century. Early hermitages and monasteries functioned as self-sufficient social units: they were estates, small farms, publishing houses, schools and homes and in turn they had assimilated and superseded pre-existing druidic and bardic social patterns. Both societies shared a belief in the importance of nature as evidence of the existence of the supernatural; both, as privileged and aristocratic communities, placed great store on the importance of learning, genealogy and memory and both invested significance in geography or what is known in the bardic tradition as *dinnseanchas*: a recognition of the importance, knowledge and love of place. The practice of fosterage involved the sending of sons from aristocratic families to be educated by druids and, later, monks. The social insularity that such schools offered meant that learning was intensive and the school or scholastic community was given the responsibility of parenting the adolescent boy into manhood.

'It is not merely that the old Irish had a good education system', argues Pearse in his pamphlet *The Murder Machine*, 'they had the best and noblest that has ever been known among men . . . which in pagan times produced Cúchulainn . . . and in Christian times . . . produced Enda and the companions of solitude in Aran'.[29] 'To the old Irish', says Pearse, 'the teacher was *áite,* fosterer; words which we still retain as *oide, dálta, oideachas* or educator, pupil and education'.[30] 'Is it not the precise aim of education to foster', he enquires, 'not to inform, to indoctrinate, to conduct through a course of studies but, first and last, to "foster" the elements of character native to a soul, to help to bring these to their full perfection'.[31]

The figures of Colmcille and Cúchulainn were held up by Pearse as examples of the excellence of the Christian and pagan systems of education, which provided 'the Christian ideals of love and humility' as well as 'the pagan ideals of strength and truth'. These ideals, according to Pearse, made one man a saint and the other a hero.[32] Freedom for the individual lay in a child-centred curriculum which sought to 'discover the hidden talent that is in every normal soul'[33] and which copied the schools of early Christian Ireland, which were 'less a place than a little group of persons, a teacher and his pupils' and where philosophy was not learned from textbooks but was 'learned at the knee of some great philosopher'.[34]

Monastic schools were renowned for their excellence in philosophy, astronomy, mathematics, art and literature, especially poetry.[35] By all accounts the curriculum was extensive, covering Greek, Latin, Hebrew, rhetoric, the natural sciences and poetry, all taught through the medium of the Irish language. The monastic system had been mapped onto the pre-existing bardic tradition, an incidence of cultural co-operation which greatly impressed Pearse.

St Enda's tried to emulate the foster-school model, with its emphasis on the importance of interdisciplinary learning, the primacy of the pupil over the curriculum, the importance of the outdoors, the significance of place and the school as a home-spun university of life. The importance of the home as a place of learning highlighted the disparity between a child-centred home environment and contemporary schooling. What the monastic and bardic models offered was an intellectual engagement with all aspects of life.

At St Enda's the exemplar figure of the Christian boy was augmented by a model of boyhood and adolescence drawn from Ireland's pagan and heroic past. As a model of masculinity the Christian Celt offered a world where men might be sensitive and artistic. Bardic pagan culture, on the other hand, offered a world where men pass on the codes and rules of masculinity to the boys in their care. Unlike the Christian codes of behaviour, which are organized around the principles of humility, passivity, humankindness and intuition, the 'warrior' rules of masculinity delineate a military world of physical prowess, honour, duty, courage and chivalry. Within the school these narratives of pagan maleness co-exist (at times more easily than others) with discourses on Christian manliness and manage to produce a contemporary figure of the Celtic boy warrior. Pearse was able to bring into being a form of manliness which embodied the virtues of the Christian Celt and the pagan warrior and produced a vision of a contemporary Irish male subject: the *macaomh*. Traditionally the *macaomh* was a title given to Cúchulainn, a hero of Irish mythology, and carries a general sense of a courageous, physically fit, male fighter and leader. The word has a more specific dictionary definition of a youth or a boy, but Pearse's use of the term *macaomh* within St Enda's expresses the idea of a heroic, but scholarly, Irish-Ireland manliness created through the complementary discourses of Christian and pagan Celticism.

This newly emergent Irish masculinity, made up of the separate but intertwined models of the Celtic scholar and pagan warrior, was defined, promoted, exchanged and circulated within the school and its broader community. The cultural project of St Enda's was to fashion a generation of boys who would implement and articulate a distinct social and cultural order. The promotion of national identity as masculine identity and the production of a male revolutionary subject was made possible by an intricately structured system which 'taught' the boys masculinity and Irishness.

St Enda's had two homes during Pearse's tenure as headmaster and both locations held historical and geographical importance for nationalists. The first, at Cullenswood House in Ranelagh, was associated with the childhood of the historian William Lecky.[36] Lecky's birth in Cullenswood House gave the new schoolhouse a tradition of scholarship and devotion to Ireland. Lecky, hardly a nationalist hero, was nevertheless an outstanding scholar and was credited by Pearse with 'having a devotion to Ireland' even if his was not 'founded on [as] secure and right [a] basis as ours'. Lecky's academic achievements, 'which even the most brilliant of our pupils will hardly emulate', made him, in Pearse's eyes, a worthy role model.

Later, in 1912, the growth of school numbers necessitated the move to a larger premises at the Hermitage in Rathfarnham. In the meantime Cullenswood House became the site of a combined preparatory and girls' school, St Ita's, which Pearse had established in 1911.[37] The Hermitage in Rathfarnham provided the same heady mix of scholarship and history associated with Cullenswood House. Tradition linked the Hermitage with the United Irishmen, the Emmet Rising and with 1848. It was also the birthplace of William Eliot Hudson, Young Irelander, founder of the Celtic Society and friend of Gavan Duffy and Thomas Davis. The history surrounding the locations of Cullenswood House and the Hermitage contributed to the sense of St Enda's connection to a rich historical past and guaranteed for the school a lineage of impeccable nationalist genealogy.

Among the features of Pearse's educational scheme were the creation of an '*Irish* standpoint and atmosphere' conducted along Irish-Ireland lines by laymen. The creation of an Irish 'atmosphere' was achieved by wearing a specially designed uniform, teaching Irish music (harp, violin, uileann pipes and piano), Irish dancing and traditional singing, and an informal and 'clann' based tutorial system. 'Side by side with the language teaching', he said, 'the history and knowledge of everything relating to Ireland's past and present should be taught and expounded'.[38] Mindful of the paucity of popular literature for Irish boys in the all-important area of history, Pearse's answer was to propose 'a return to the sagas' of ancient Ireland. The ancient stories of valour and endeavour, preserved in the oral tradition, provided Irish boys with all they needed to know about Ireland in order to cultivate a sense of Irishness.

In St Enda's the curriculum favoured the models of masculinity offered by the heroic and Christian past. In Pearse's eyes the prevailing education system in Ireland had little to offer but a stagnation of the imaginative spirit and an internalized self-hatred. Pearse's radical vision for St Enda's is best appreciated when the conditions under which Irish students and teachers struggled for self-expression is understood.

2

Conquering Imperialism: The Educational Philosophy of St Enda's

'Take up the Irish problem at what point you may', insisted Pearse in 1903, 'you inevitably find yourself in the end back at the education question'.[1] Even the briefest study of the educational system in Ireland during the past two hundred years reveals the 'education question' to be tightly bound to 'the Irish question'. Historically, education systems, more than any other institutional organizations, represented the cultural and social agenda of British imperialism. The use of education as a socializing and 'civilizing' agent has been well documented, illustrating how children were taught formally as well as through complicated cultural, linguistic, moral and social networks.[2]

By sketching out the history of imperial education in Ireland I want to explain why St Enda's was so radical in relation to contemporary schooling and why Pearse was so committed to the establishment of a nationalist Irish-speaking school. This chapter situates the radical nature of St Enda's within the historically repressive imperial educational system of the nineteenth century. It also traces how Pearse's own enthusiasm for educational reform and his commitment to nationalism as a wide-reaching social and cultural project meant that the establishment of St Enda's in 1908 was inevitable.

The truly revolutionary aims and ideals of St Enda's can only be fully appreciated by an understanding of an often brutal colonial educational system which continually privileged the teaching of English history and geography and which promoted the cultural and moral superiority of Englishness over Irishness. No more was this in evidence than in the wholesale loss of the Irish language. This was achieved in part by emigration but, more insidiously, through the labelling of Irish literature and culture as impoverished and backward. Ironically it was the success of the so-called hedge schools in the early nineteenth century that first prompted the creation of a system of primary education for all children. Catering for those children who were denied formal education under the Penal Laws, the hedge schools were the source of much anti-English teaching. The educational historian John Coolahan notes that, in the political era after the 1800 Act of Union and Catholic Emancipation, the government felt that schools could serve certain goals by 'cultivating attitudes of political loyalty and cultural assimilation' and initiated a national educational system throughout Ireland.[3]

In the early nineteenth century the Commission of Irish Education Inquiry recommended the establishment of a national school system. Its recommendations were taken up by a philanthropic organization, the Society for Promoting the Education of the Poor in Ireland, which founded the Kildare Place Society in 1814. The Kildare Place Society favoured non-denominational elementary education for all children and was the prototype for what became known as the 'model schools'.[4] From 1831 there was a structured, state-supported national school system in place throughout Ireland which was separate from those schools operating under the management of the Kildare Place Society.[5] The establishment of a national school system resulted in the virtual elimination of illiteracy during the nineteenth century, but it also contributed to the near-eradication of the Irish language through its insistence on using English as the medium for instruction. The new educational system administered and organized architectural plans for schools, textbooks, educational publishing codes, inspectorates, commissions on education and examination regimes and practices, and formed a complex web of social and economic practices which continually privileged English over Irish.

The eradication of illiteracy marked the adoption of English as the literate language, which in turn led to a general perception of Irish as the language of ignorance. Establishment anxieties about seditious teaching exacted a close monitoring of teaching materials in the new school system and the British government swiftly brought the planning, development and writing of the school curriculum under its own supervision. Imperial ideals were institutionalized through a rigid curriculum with prescribed textbooks written especially for Irish schools.[6]

Textbooks in English especially for Irish children first appeared as early as 1813.[7] The publication and distribution of textbooks was part of a larger project on the moral and social education of Irish children. Joachim Goldstrom's analysis of school texts throughout the nineteenth century shows how texts promoted imperial expansionism and 'Englishness' as a touchstone for civilization.[8] Ireland was mostly absent as a subject to be studied and Goldstrom notes how the texts lacked any material focusing on Irish heritage or traditions.[9] The subsidizing of cheap texts meant that any other Irish-centred publications were beyond the financial means of schools.

For most children educated during the nineteenth century their sole learning materials were dull, uninspired texts. Apart from the Bible, Irish children's access to educational material in schools was severely restricted.[10] Later in the century the introduction of compulsory elementary education virtually guaranteed English-speaking students with basic numeracy skills who were essential to the bureaucratic running of the Empire.

Throughout the nineteenth century secondary school teaching remained an unattractive proposition for many men and women. The pay and conditions were poor and educational management was inadequately structured. Amateur teachers with no qualifications abounded, since there were no regulations with regard to qualifications and there was no formal training given or demanded of teachers. In general there was very little attention paid to educational reform for most of the nineteenth century. In 1870 the Powis Commission recommended a mandatory system of self-financing schools by what came to be known as the 'payment-by-results' system.[11] The implementation of a payment-by-results system can be credited with strangling any vitality or creativity within the classroom. Teachers were paid additional wages depending on the results of individual pupils: the better a school performed academically, and the more children who attended, the more the teachers earned. As no payment was made for any child who failed to pass in reading, spelling and writing, the results system was designed to accelerate the elimination of illiteracy and to make teachers more accountable in the classroom.

While initially designed to equip pupils with a rudimentary education, the results system ended up confining teachers to narrow curriculum demands. As a result of the payments system teachers were 'encouraged [to pursue] a narrow and mechanistic approach to teaching' and 'specific programmes were laid down in each subject for each grade in the school'.[12] Statistics suggest that the system did improve literacy and numeracy as well as increasing attendance figures. However, the emphasis on 'results' teaching meant that the concept of creative and enlightened teaching practice was effectively unworkable. Coolahan notes that at a time when European thinking on educational development was beginning to address the social and psychological needs of children, the Irish system was divorced from the realities of life and work outside the school.[13]

By 1897 the Belmore Commission on Education had recognized that the payment-by-results system was counter-productive. The Commission recommended serious reform in the areas of primary school teaching and was keen to promote schools as humane and challenging places of learning. However, this was not the case with secondary school teaching. Despite the recommendations of the 1899 Palles Commission for the abolition of the results system, successive Education Acts in 1900 and 1902 did little to inject creative teaching and learning into Irish schools. Instead the secondary education system remained mired in cumbersome bureaucratic networks of examination procedures, inspectorates and administrative reports.[14] So little had changed by 1905 that the Dale and Stephens Report was damning in its indictment of the Irish education system. The Dale and Stephens Report criticized the poor implementation of a broader curriculum, severe under-funding and lack of teacher training. The Report suggested that the Irish education system had regressed to the state it had been in during 1899, when the payment-by-results system was first abolished.[15]

The Irish educational historian Séamus Ó Buachalla considers the thirty-year period between 1890 and 1920 as being the most significant in the development of contemporary ideas on education in Ireland: a period roughly concurrent with Pearse's life. Noting that 'education dominated Pearse's life almost from the time when he graduated from school in 1896',[16] Ó Buachalla places Pearse firmly within what has come to be known as the New Education Movement – a loose cohesion of ideas advocating developments between sociology, psychology and pedagogy.[17] He identifies the New Educationalists' concerns as the rejection of instrumentary education 'whose narrow literary curriculum and prescribed methodology epitomised the education then available in most European countries'.[18] The New Educationalists were also critical of systems of funding based on the payment-by-results system and educational philosophies that discouraged the development or expansion of curricula according to the needs of the individual child.

It was self-evident to Pearse that a system which worked within an examination scheme of payment-by-results left little room for intellectual freedom, personal development, creativity, imaginative flair or child-centred welfare. Pearse came to recognize the social, material and economic advantages that the British government had by controlling access to learning. He identified the education system as primarily an exercise in social management, describing it as 'a convenient label for [a] system of administration' which sought to tame rather than to inspire.[19]

Pearse is at his best and most fluent when engaged in educational matters. His essays on education combine most effectively his role as myth-maker, poet and teacher, affording him the forum of orator and master. The administration of the Irish education system gave him a specific rather than a general grievance against the ills of Westminster and he entered an extant debate on education with force and passion. This focus of his energies and intellect means that Pearse's writings on education display a lucidity of thought that is often missing elsewhere in his work. From 1898, when he was elected to the *Coiste Gnótha* (Executive Committee) of the Gaelic League, Pearse was instrumental in formulating and implementing League policy on education. His work with the League Education Committee secured his commitment to guaranteeing the intellectual and cultural independence of future generations.

St Enda's could not have been established in 1908 without the unflagging enthusiasm of Pearse, but its very existence would have been inconceivable without the administrative and financial networks of the Gaelic League. The League had published its first weekly bilingual newspaper *Fáinne an Lae* in 1898, which later became subsumed into the more substantial *An Claidheamh Soluis* in 1899. The significance of the Gaelic League and *An Claidheamh Soluis* to the eventual emergence of St Enda's was its privileging of debates on education, the Irish language and cultural identity to an increasingly vocal and visible Irish middle class. The League's emphasis on educational debate and the importance of bilingualism provided a new forum for discussing what it meant to be Irish as well as making important contributions to wider cultural debates on the relationship between education and Irish society.

Pearse became the editor of *An Claidheamh Soluis* in March 1903 and in November of that year he published 'An Educational Programme' for the teaching of Irish in schools.[20] In his editorial he made it clear that his philosophy of education would be hammered out on the pages of *An Claidheamh Soluis*.[21] Among Pearse's many recommendations were the increase of written educational material in Irish, the teaching of Irish as a vernacular, the improvement of teaching methods, the increase of the number of Irish-speaking teachers and the extension of Irish classes outside school hours to facilitate adults and older children who were no longer in school. Later in 1903 Pearse's demands grew bolder as he insisted that the educational policy of the League ought to make 'Irish the home medium of instruction in every district in which it is the home language' and that 'Irish and Irish history be taught as specific subjects to every child in every class in every school in the country'.[22]

Desmond Ryan said that, in order to know Pearse at all, it was essential to have known him as a teacher and he indicates that Pearse's commitment to education allowed him to display his love of learning, flair for rhetoric, belief in the value of culture and tradition with his dedication to the Irish language.[23] Pearse shares a belief in education as social reform with Matthew Arnold; a relationship which has been explored by Seamus Deane.[24] Deeply anxious about the diminishing status of Irish as a vernacular, Pearse anticipated the eventual disappearance of oral and written Irish from the country altogether. Pearse's programme for educational excellence was aimed at reforming the teaching of the Irish language and he was indebted to modern language-teaching methods which were being advocated on the continent. Ruth Dudley Edwards points out that Pearse was not an original thinker but had the ability to map contemporary European thinking on education onto an Irish model.[25] He was especially interested in three innovations in continental schooling: bilingualism, the development of the Direct Method of teaching languages and the use of modern visual teaching aids.[26] In 1893 Father O'Growney, a scholar of the Irish language and literature at St Patrick's College, Maynooth, had published guidelines on modern methods for language teaching known as 'An Módh Díreach', a variation of the Berlitz method, which reflected contemporary European thinking on bilingual instruction. O'Growney's *Simple Lessons in Irish* grammar and textbooks proved enormously popular when they first appeared and had been serialized in *An Claidheamh Soluis* between 1897 and 1900.[27] Pearse published his own Módh Díreach lessons, 'An Sgoil', in *An Claidheamh Soluis* between 1907 and 1909. The lessons were based on a mixture of O'Growney's principles and modern bilingual teaching methodology and offered a comprehensive introduction for teaching Irish to beginners.

Articles on continental schooling and bilingual instruction had appeared in *An Claidheamh Soluis* before Pearse took up the editorship in 1903. However, Pearse approached the area of education with an eloquence which energized the debate in Gaelic League circles. The League had recognized the necessity for bilingual teaching as early as 1899. In that same year Pearse travelled to the Welsh Eisteddfod on behalf of the League's Education Committee. His visit informed his spoken and written contributions to the growing debate on language teaching and he later visited Germany, Belgium and Scotland on the League's behalf. Advancing the idea of summer schools in the west of Ireland for adults and children who wanted to learn Irish, the League opened the first Irish college in Ballingeary, County Cork, in 1904.[28] The League also spearheaded initiatives in training teachers both formally, through the college system, and informally, through grassroots organizations.

In 1905 Pearse likened the arrangement of the Irish teacher-training colleges to 'the bohemian university life of early Christian Ireland', praising the practice of having students live with families in the locality so that the pupils might experience their learning as an extension of a domestic arrangement.[29] As editor of *An Claidheamh Soluis* he reiterated the values and benefits of bilingualism and promoted curricular programmes in Irish by recommending certain textbooks and outlining possible syllabi. His enthusiasm met a generous response: the historian Eleanor Hull, the secretary and founder of the Irish Texts Society in London, wrote to Pearse in 1903 enquiring about the possibility of publishing inexpensive children's texts on Irish history for use in schools.[30] Pearse also encouraged the use of Irish outside the curriculum, for example in prayers, games, drills and school attendance rolls.[31]

The importance of the home as a place of learning and the promotion of Irish as the 'home' language meant that the Gaelic League initially focused its concerns about bilingualism on the needs of the Gaeltacht. Native speakers of Irish often had to attend

English-speaking schools, which meant that many children left school virtually illiterate in the English language (Irish was still not popularly understood to be a language that children could be taught to read and write). Pearse saw a broader dimension to bilingualism than ensuring that children were educated in their mother tongue. His visits to the continent and his observations of the multilingual skills of European children had convinced him that Irish and English could easily co-exist within a school system. Contrary to popular belief Pearse did not advocate the wholesale substitution of Irish for English; his was a more sophisticated philosophy. Every child, he maintained, has a right to learn his mother tongue and has the capacity for learning at least one other language. If a child is instructed in the medium of a language across a number of disciplines he will absorb it more naturally and more easily. If he is taught the literature and history of a language he will form an emotional and intellectual bond with that language, making learning a delight.[32]

From 1904 onwards Pearse used the forum of *An Claidheamh Soluis* with unflinching regularity to outline his methodology for bilingual teaching: one which took account of the dominance of English without neglecting the cultural value of Irish. On the pages of the League paper he nurtured the educational vision which would eventually be practised in his own school. While quick to map modern methodologies onto the Irish language, he was canny enough to recognize the commercial and technological importance of English. He suggested disposing of textbooks altogether and teaching from the blackboard viva voce and recommended the substitution of difficult texts with more up-to-date books commissioned by the League's Publication Committee.[33]

Pearse's personal educational philosophy begins to take on a coherent shape and form between 1904 and 1905. 'Real education', he states, 'is not the imparting of knowledge' but a preparation for complete living; 'the real education consists in the forming of the child's character, the drawing out of his faculties, the disciplining of his intellect . . . and the systemic inculcation of patriotism'.[34] By late

1905 Pearse's attention turned from primary school to secondary school education. His interest in schooling was quite firmly centred on the role of the teacher and his or her responsibility in the creation of a learning environment and was most probably influenced by the recommendations on teaching practice in the Dale Stephens Report of that year. There is a sense of urgency in his pleadings with teachers to direct their energies and enthusiasms 'towards the training up of a generation of patriotic and intelligent Irish boys and girls'.[35] Letters dating from early 1906 indicate that he was beginning to formulate ideas for establishing a school of his own.[36] Dudley Edwards notes that Pearse's idea of setting up an Irish-Ireland school was not original. For some time prominent Gaelic Leaguers had been aware that an independent bilingual school run along nationalist lines was a timely and necessary progression in restructuring the education system.[37]

It is easy to appreciate Pearse's radical vision for St Enda's when it is set against the backdrop of the stifling curricular constraints of the payment-by-results system, inadequate textbooks, insufficient teacher training, tedious and bureaucratic examination and inspectorate procedures, the apparently irretrievable erosion of the Irish language and squabbles over religious education at the expense and neglect of developing a challenging secular curriculum. Pearse's sister Margaret had founded a school for infants in 1907 that lent impetus to his personal desire to establish his own secondary school for boys. By 1908 his articles in *An Claidheamh Soluis* about the inadequate progress of Irish in the schools through poor teaching and low standards are pitched with a greater sense of desperation than before. He places emphasis on a school's duty and a teacher's responsibility not only to enrol children in Irish classes but to *educate* them as Irish speakers.

Later in 1908 Pearse began fundraising in earnest and wrote to prominent Leaguers seeking financial help for his 'educational adventure'. As Ó Buachalla points out, the rational response to his earlier grumblings on education was to make a practical commitment to an alternative system of education.[38] That year in a letter to Eoin

MacNeill, Pearse argued that there was 'no *Irish* High School in Ireland' and no 'High School for Catholic boys conducted by laymen in Ireland'; he also argued that many Gaelic Leaguers were anxious to secure 'a genuine *Irish* education' for their children which would also maintain educational standards and fulfil university entrance requirements. It must have been clear to many League members that the decline in educational standards could only be counteracted by founding a school true to League principles and ideas. Public reaction and support was overwhelmingly positive, as evidenced by the numbers of Gaelic Leaguers who were keen to enrol their sons for attendance.

Pearse's promotion of St Enda's as a genuinely *Irish* school highlights the inability of contemporary secondary schools to meet the educational needs of nationalist boys. Pearse had been educated by the Christian Brothers in Westland Row and it is puzzling that he did not rate the Christian Brothers' schooling, since they had a reputation for being nationalist in outlook.[39] It appears that Pearse felt that existing teaching structures were narrow-minded and harmful, including those of the Christian Brothers. Pearse had done well in school but his brother, Willie, had been bullied and in later years Pearse criticized the use of corporal punishment by the Brothers as well as their narrow teaching methods.[40] Barry Coldrey notes that the Christian Brothers produced and published their own textbooks.[41] However, while the subject matter of these books covered local history, Irish culture and literature it is clear from Coldrey's study that the texts formed part of a larger social programme of Catholic indoctrination and were less interested in nationalism than in highlighting grievances about the maltreatment of Catholics under imperial rule.[42] The Christian Brothers were expressly founded to attend to the educational needs of the poor, but many middle-class Catholic boys were sent to be educated by the Brothers with the promise of a secure position within the civil service, banks or insurance companies. Indeed Pearse's sister, Mary Brigid, notes that almost all her brother's school-fellows had entered the civil service after leaving Westland Row, a fact which Pearse despised.[43]

The emphasis on employment meant that, no matter how nationalist in tone their textbooks, the Brothers had an allegiance to the Intermediate Examinations and, by implication, the payment-by-results system. Desmond Ryan suggests that Pearse was not interested in perpetuating existing hierarchies in education and felt that a school should be a primary, secondary and university education rolled into one; he was especially critical of schools which operated as 'crammers' for civil service examinations and university matriculations.[44]

His clashes with the clergy belie the perception that Pearse was slavishly devoted to the Catholic church. In fact there are a number of incidents when Pearse was critical of the Catholic church where he saw unnecessary interference in educational matters or, indeed, failure to properly promote the broader social and cultural aims of nationalism. In 1909, for example, Pearse reprimanded the Christian Brothers for teaching the narrow, exam-based requirements of the Intermediate system at the expense of promoting a more child-centred and enlightened curriculum. Moreover, Pearse accused the Brothers of sacrificing the welfare of the Irish educational system on 'a cross of monetary interests'.[45] Pearse's dissatisfaction with the Brothers' teaching methods had as much to do with his dislike of clerical interference in educational matters as it had with their unquestioned devotion to the payment-by-results system. Throughout the nineteenth century ongoing stand-offs between clergy (both Catholic and Protestant) and government over the control of religious education had resulted in the sectarian segregation of education.[46] A few years earlier Pearse had been reprimanded for his criticism of the clergy on the pages of *An Claidheamh Soluis*, when he had denounced priests for carrying out parish duties in English in the Gaeltacht and for the failure of Maynooth College to promote Irish to its seminarians.[47] It was important to him that St Enda's should lie outside the administrative and intellectual control of the Catholic church whilst also being considered a Catholic school. Pearse was wary of how denominational interests had been established at the expense of the larger social and educational needs of children. In a 1908 letter,

Pearse states unequivocally that his school 'would be designed to meet ... the need for high-class education in and through Irish for a limited but important and growing section of the Youth of the country'.[48]

However, there are other factors, apart from clerical control, which fuelled Pearse's desire for a school. The emphasis on 'high-class' education suggests not only qualitative teaching but an appeal to an aspirational nationalist middle class. More telling perhaps is Pearse's vision of himself as Master or Scholar-Poet in charge of an educational community – a role that would have been denied him had he sought employment in a secondary school. Pearse had extensive teaching experience: since 1899 he had been involved in giving League-sponsored Irish classes to students at the then Jesuit University College (among his students was James Joyce, who was so bored by him that he chose to study Norwegian instead in order to enhance his reading of Ibsen). In 1904 he taught Irish in Alexandra College, a Protestant college for young women, and from 1906 he was running classes on language in University College in conjunction with Eoin MacNeill's classes on Irish history. Teaching standards were close to Pearse's heart and from November 1905 he had been regularly publishing articles in *An Claidheamh Soluis* on the responsibilities of teachers.[49]

Existing schools and colleges for Catholic middle-class and upper-middle-class boys operated as training grounds for service to the Empire or were seminaries or ecclesiastical colleges unreservedly loyal to the Crown. They were especially contemptuous of the importance of the Irish language. Pearse often referred to St Enda's as a 'college' as opposed to a 'school', revealing that he considered it to be an 'Irish-Ireland' version of eminent schools such as Clongowes Wood College, Blackrock College and Castleknock College – the three most prestigious boys' schools in the country.[50] Like the three colleges, St Enda's was also a boarding school on its own grounds (referred to by Pearse as equal to anything which Castleknock College could provide) and did not have an immediate catchment area but instead solicited attendances from boys at home and abroad. The boarding-school tradition in Ireland had become popularly established with the middle classes throughout the nineteenth century, due to the uneven geographical distribution of secondary schools. Pearse wanted to provide a boarding-school facility for native Irish speakers and for those boys whose parents wished them to be educated 'along bilingual lines', thus setting St Enda's in relief against 'the existing great ecclesiastical schools and colleges which, catering as they do for all Ireland and for the more anglicised classes in particular, must for many years to come remain predominantly English speaking'.[51]

The radically progressive nature of Pearse's educational vision was focused on a system where the child as child was paramount – not child as civil servant or examination result. According to Séamus Ó Buachalla, Pearse was influenced by the writings of Maria Montessori and discourses on social reform which saw education as an agent for social change.[52] Montessori advocated the use of the school as a space designed to cater for the physical, recreational, aesthetic, moral and cultural aspects of the child's development and encouraged a view of childhood as discrete and not merely a life-stage in the development of the adult. He was impressed by the Montessori method, whose 'main object in education is to help the child to be his own true and best self'.[53]

For Pearse the lack of freedom within the existing education system – freedom for the school, for the teacher and for the child – had led to the thwarting of 'knowledge' at the expense of 'information' and had resulted in a system which was 'a soulless thing', 'without pity and without passion'.[54] In 'The Murder Machine' Pearse argued forcefully against educational systems which treat children 'like raw material', sending them to 'grinds' and 'crammers' to accumulate education and be 'finished' before being churned out to the pattern of Civil Service Commissioners, devoid of any imagination, creativity or inspiration.[55]

In a 'true' education system, Pearse maintained, 'love of beauty . . . love of books . . . love of knowledge' and love of 'heroic inspiration' would exist alongside lessons on grammar and mathematics.[56] Any such system did not exist in Ireland, he argued, and therefore it was impossible to speak of educational reform or even of the reconstruction of existing schooling. Since contemporary schooling was founded on the fundamental negation of Irish culture, Irish language and the Irish nation, Pearse argued that there was no existing educational system which was worth overhauling but only an overwhelming responsibility to return to the pre-colonial models of the monastic and bardic communities. The fosterage system, favoured by both monks and druids, provided both the inspiration and freedom that Pearse craved. He envisaged that St Enda's would be a school where a child could discover creativity and imagination and that to nurture a child into manhood was the most powerful and humbling role an adult could undertake.

Given his ideological and imaginative attachment to the west of Ireland, Pearse would have liked to have established St Enda's in the Aran Islands. The school's patron saint was after all St Enda, the holy man of Aran.[57] Practical considerations made it impossible to situate the school away from the urban networks of the Gaelic League and the social, literary and administrative connections which made St Enda's a financially viable project. Ruth Dudley Edwards' biography of Pearse details the extent to which St Enda's was financially indebted to the nationalist community.[58] Nationalists at home and abroad were generous in their financial endowment of the school and showed their support by sending their children to be educated by Pearse. However, Pearse did manage, some years later in 1912, to establish a summer retreat in Rosmuc in Íar Connacht, for the use of St Enda's boys.

As already mentioned St Enda's had two homes, the first in Cullenswood House from 1908 to 1912 and the second at the Hermitage in Rathfarnham from 1912 onwards. The high urban profile of the school and the nationalist importance of the sites of Cullenswood House and the Hermitage went some way towards appeasing Pearse's initial desire to locate St Enda's in the west of Ireland. The 1908–9 prospectus of Cullenswood House outlines how the 'modernity' of the school, set against the ancient Irish models of education, was reinforced by special attention to the sciences and to what Pearse called 'modern education generally'. Even by today's standards, perhaps especially by today's standards, the curriculum seems modern, liberal and engaging. The school offered European languages (French, German, Italian and Spanish), botany, zoology and geology, as well as more vocational subjects such as typewriting, book-keeping and shorthand.

The boys were encouraged to organize, administer and promote from within, their own corps and branches of Éire Óg (a juvenile branch of the Gaelic League), established in the school from the outset. 'Manly self-reliance' was encouraged through self-discipline in the classroom and at play. In the sports field he nurtured a love of Gaelic games, which he considered contributed 'to the systematic inculcation of patriotism and training in the duties of citizenship'. Drill was taught along with hurling, Gaelic football, handball and gymnastic exercises, with a view to prizing 'bodily vigour, grace and cleanliness'. The boys were encouraged to work outdoors, both in the garden, on the playing field and 'in the summer months as much as possible of the school work is [to be] done in the open air' in order to instil in the boys 'a love of comely surroundings'. Above all, the school promoted 'the formation of a sense of civic and social duty', an allegiance to Irish-Ireland and represented 'earnest efforts towards the awakening of a spirit of patriotism'.[59]

The school at Cullenswood House was certainly impressive in size and structure. Apart from well-equipped and colourful classrooms and well laid-out gardens it boasted a science laboratory, a playroom, three dormitories, an infirmary and fully certified 'sanitation'. The gardens covered five acres and included flower and vegetable gardens, fruit grounds, conservatories, greenhouses, vine and peach houses and 'all the other conveniences of a well-equipped country mansion'.[60] Apart from the agricultural gardens, the grounds included an orchard, playing fields, a handball court and an open-air gymnasium.

By the end of the first year St Enda's reputation for scholarly excellence and cultural and educational innovation was well secured. The first weeks of the year had seen visits by Edward Martyn,

Douglas Hyde and Maud Gonne MacBride, three significant cultural figures in the Celtic revivalist movement. There was also a party of visiting Egyptians who were brought to the school by a Mrs Dryhurst, suggesting perhaps that St Enda's had a certain amount of novelty value for guests seeking some form of nationalist authenticity.[61]

Certainly the high profile and academic qualifications of full-time and visiting lecturers was very impressive. On the teaching staff proper there was also an impressive range of talents. During the first year Thomas MacDonagh, lecturer in French literature, had his play *When the Dawn is Come* produced at the Abbey Theatre, which left the St Enda's boys 'yearning for rifles'.[62] William Pearse, the art teacher, had been trained at the Metropolitan School of Art and had studied under Oliver Sheppard. Many of the teachers had previously taught at those middle-class secondary schools, such as Rockwell College and Blackrock College, which Pearse tried to emulate. Other masters had taught at seminaries and universities: Thomas MacDonnell had been a Professor of Irish in the Connacht College of Irish and the Leinster College of Irish, while T. P. O'Nolan had previously lectured in classics at University College Dublin and St Patrick's College, Maynooth. Harp, violin and Irish dancing were also on offer. Even the full-time gardener and horticulturist had flawless nationalist credentials. Micheál Mac Ruaidhrí was a well-known author of standard works of Irish literature, which were prescribed texts for the National University and Intermediate examinations.[63]

Pearse had instituted a series of 'Half Holiday Lectures', whereby visiting scholars and university lecturers would come to St Enda's and talk to the boys informally on different topics. Taking stock at the end of the first year shows how removed St Enda's was from the suffocating curriculum of most Irish schools. In the first year alone the boys heard talks on Irish, French and German literature, phonetics, philosophy, physics, botany, archaeology, Egyptology, topography and medieval history – erudite subjects for a secondary school. Visitors for the first year include most of the luminaries of nationalist intellectual and cultural life. The translator of *An Táin,*

Margaret Hutton, addressed the school, as did Standish O'Grady, Seumas MacManus and Ethna Carberry, the Honourable William Gibson, Edward Martyn and others. Later that year D. P. Moran, W. P. Ryan, the Count and Countess Markievicz and W. B. Yeats were among those who came to pay their respects. Later visitors to the school included the illustrator Ella Young, Dora Sigerson and her husband the journalist Clement K. Shorter, and Roger Casement.

The combination of curricular innovation, child-centred learning and an active, imaginative input from writers, artists, linguists and dramatists involved in the Celtic revivalist movement meant that the quality and vibrancy of the education offered by St Enda's was far in excess of the standards offered by the average Irish classroom. The cultural and social engagement at St Enda's with nationality, language, history and ideas of public service disguised a more fundamental, but more abstract, deliberation on the nature of masculinity: how is an Irish boy made? At St Enda's the search for 'authentic' yet historical models of masculinity copperfastened Pearse's aim to create and sustain a blueprint for Irish boyhood.

3

Saints and Scholars: Models of Celtic Manliness

On 3 April 1911 a notice appeared in the *Irish Times* announcing a Passion Play to be performed in the Abbey Theatre on Good Friday and Holy Saturday of Easter Week. The newspaper reported that the boys of St Enda's, aided by students from their sister school St Ita's, were to perform a three-act play in Irish, *An Páis,* which was to be arranged, written and directed by their headmaster Patrick Pearse.[1] The *Passion Play* was performed on Good Friday and Holy Saturday, 7 and 8 of April. Pearse addressed the audience beforehand in Irish and in English explaining the biblical origins of the piece and how he hoped the audience might receive it in the spirit of reverence in which it was conceived.

The cast was enormous, befitting a school production where parental expectations were high, but the main parts were played by staff and not students. Given the time of year and the larger drama that was to unfold at Easter five years later, the cast list was infused with significance. Three of the teachers appearing on the stage that night were to be executed in 1916: William Pearse the art master played Pontius Pilate, Pearse himself played, with considerable relish, the unrepentant thief, and Thomas MacDonagh, dramatist, poet and teacher of French literature, played the repentant thief. Other known participants included Mary Maguire (an author and critic who later married Padraic Colum), a teacher at St Ita's. She played Mary Magdalene with her long red hair wound three times around her neck while Micheál Mac Ruadhrí, the school gardener, made a memorable Barrabas clad in leopard skin and villainy. Other cast members included Thomas MacDonnell, the music teacher and composer of the original score for the play, who played Christ. Most who saw the play agreed that the outstanding performance of the evening came from Mary Bulfin (a senior student at St Ita's and future wife of Sean MacBride), who played the Virgin Mary. The names of those who played other character parts are unknown, but there were almost fifty child actors involved in the usual crowd scenes and as guards, scribes, ancients and general rabble-rousers. For a stage that must have at times seemed crammed with bodies the play's simplicity was singled out for praise.

As a straightforward adaptation from the Gospels its three acts were set in the Garden of Gethsemane, outside Pilate's house and on the hillside of Calvary. The piece was not published, at the express wishes of Pearse, its author, so there is no script of the play in existence. However, Desmond Ryan has left a detailed description of the event documenting the fusion of Celtic tradition and biblical form which so excited the audience.[2] Theatre-goers took their seats to the sound of Rossini's *Stabat Mater*, a lament of the Virgin Mary. The theatre was packed, the stalls, balcony and pit full to the brim, as the curtain rose. In the Garden a sequence of tableaux took place: a group of pure-voiced boys singing the *Laudate Pueri Dominum* from the Psalms at twilight; Christ praying for the burden of his sins to be taken from him while flanked by his sleeping apostles; and Judas, surrounded by torches of fire, betraying his master with a kiss. The third act, on the hill of Calvary, introduced a Celtic influence, signalling a shift away from Judaism towards Christianity. A procession of women singing a *caoineadh* wound their way upstage. Words, off-stage, floated out to the assembled gathering, amongst them the gentle tones of Christ, the mocking of the crowd and the unrepentant thief, and the beseeching voice of the repentant thief. At the moment of Christ's death the theatre was plunged into darkness and lit by dramatic lightning flashes. Shuddering peals of thunder harmonized with 'the loud, poignant, agonised keening of the women' in Irish traditional form and the curtains fell.[3] Requested beforehand by Pearse not to applaud at the play's close, the audience's silence was read not merely as acquiescent but as reverential and humble. Desmond Ryan noted that the audience stumbled out onto the street quietly and slowly with 'much to think of',[4] while Joseph Holloway recorded in his diaries that 'all who followed the incidents were deeply and wonderfully moved'.[5]

Of the many public events and plays staged by St Enda's school the *Passion Play* seems to have been a defining moment for the school and its audience. While later political events lent the evening a retrospective significance that its contemporary audience could not foresee, the sense of witnessing an historic 'moment' in Irish culture is nevertheless communicated by those who recorded their impressions. Mary Colum commented that, while 'every happening' in nationalist Dublin at that time inevitably 'aroused an interest . . . out of proportion to its significance', the *Passion Play* captured the imagination on a number of different levels. She recalled how the play created a minor dramatic sensation which was reported in the London and continental papers.[6] Ryan recorded that the play 'roused Dublin' and was hailed as a magnificent success.[7] Padraic Colum praised it as 'the first serious theatre piece in Irish' and complimented it on its 'root power' in the drama of the miracle and morality play. Asserting that 'this Passion Play gives the emotion out of which a Gaelic drama may arise', he declared that the school's production might provide the much-needed cornerstone for a modern movement in Irish-language drama.[8] It has not been recorded who attended that night, but the audience that settled down to watch the show was almost certainly illustrious. St Enda's was at the zenith of its fame and reputation and many of the children on stage came from well-known nationalist families. Literary revivalism keenly promoted theatre as a vehicle for the expression of national culture and so the sense of a national collectivity was almost to be expected.

Desmond Ryan saw the play as representing 'our national and individual struggle', which in some ways 'was a faint reflection of the great one just enacted . . . the man is crucified as the Nation, and the Soul moves slowly, falteringly, towards the Redemption'.[9] Others, perhaps unable to understand Irish, merely saw it as a strikingly visual representation of the Passion. However, Ryan felt that, far from obscuring the narrative, 'the Irish medium, strange to most [of the audience], had not veiled but intensified the meanings and pathos of the story'.[10] The 'celticizing' of the piece was achieved most obviously through the use of the Irish language, but it also drew heavily on Irish folk traditions in the telling of the Passion and the careful mix of liturgical and traditional music.

The Irish tradition of vocal and instrumental lament was worked into the piece through the keening of the women and the use of uileann pipes. In Irish traditional lament the *caoineadh* is one of the oldest forms of music to have survived and is the most meaningful of the many different poetic laments for the dead in Irish culture. Within traditional culture the *caoineadh* is performed in the presence of the corpse, usually by women, and mounts to a crescendo in three discrete stages. The first stage is the murmuring, quietly but distinctly, of the loved one's name, usually by the chief female mourner – the mother or wife. The second stage involves a partly extempore, partly delivered, verse or eulogy on the dead person's character and goodness, again by a single mourner or close group of mourners. The third part marks the communal mourning of the corpse in a collective choral cry accompanied by the *cumha* of the harpers and pipes.[11] Pearse and Douglas Hyde had collected a number of versions of traditional *caoineadh* from west Connacht. Pearse's translation of a traditional lament was published in *An Claidheamh Soluis* in 1904 and in a piece for the *Irish Review* in March 1911 he outlined the history of 'The Keening of Mary'.[12] This *caoineadh* also appeared as one of the laments in Hyde's translation of 'The Keening of the Three Marys', which he published in *The Religious Songs of Connacht*.[13] The dramatic ritualistic quality of the *caoineadh* sung in Irish over Christ's body (and accompanied by the knowledge that the tradition was known in rural mourning rites) was undoubtedly beautiful and moving.

The iconography of the piece drew special attention. Holloway's diary speaks of beautifully composed tableaux, perhaps heightened by the unfamiliar idiom, effective lighting and a dramatic colour scheme which created and recreated 'undying', beautiful and perfect pictures.[14] The dramatic tradition of ecclesiastic performance and pageantry was familiar to the Pearse brothers and the *Passion Play* drew on the rich influence of the morality plays as well as the more contemporary visual styling of the tableaux vivants tradition. Admitting that he had not been prepared 'for so touching a performance', the *Irish Times* reviewer praised the 'beautiful, yet simple, scenery', 'well-managed lighting effects' and graceful and splendid costuming of the figures arranged in a series of 'pictures of solemn beauty'.[15] Scenes constructed within the play seemed poised between the dramatic tradition of the tableaux vivants, which had been in vogue in nationalist circles since the late 1890s, and the more contemporary static image of the photograph.[16] Padraic Colum describes the form of the tableaux as presenting 'statuesque groups introduced by some familiar piece of music, and holding their pose for some minutes – an elementary show in which costume, music, and striking appearance were ingredients'.[17] When the fashion for staging temporal historic events found a more permanent and solid way of being communicated through the medium of the photograph, these images still tended to reproduce standard fine art conventions of composition, lighting and staging. The painterly quality of the *Passion Play* scenes is remarked upon by Mary Colum, who described Mary Bulfin as a 'Murillo Virgin', and a subsequently published picture postcard of Bulfin as the Virgin Mary is composed in the tradition of a Renaissance portrait (Plate 1). Other photographs of the production were composed and circulated as postcards; one shows a detail from a larger photograph which shows Willie Pearse dressed as a contemplative Pontius Pilate (Plate 2). A further full-length studio portrait shows Willie/Pilate in a stiff but beseeching pose (Plate 3). The publication of, and public demand for, the picture postcards after the event signal more than anything an acknowledgement of the *Passion Play*'s significance in the popular cultural imagination of nationalism. Photographs of the *Passion Play* not only present the Passion of Christ as an event in history but they legitimize and authenticate St Enda's role in the storytelling or historicizing process.

Pearse's desire not to have the play published, coupled with the significance of its performance dates on the holiest days in Easter Week, contributed not only to a sense of Christian reverence but also to a more secular sense of theatrical occasion. The announcement by the school that it intended to make the play a triennial event further reinforced a popular impression that something important had taken place that night on the Abbey stage.[18] How did it happen that a small school, barely two years old, staged an amateur production in the Abbey Theatre which Pearse later described as one of the high points of the entire literary revival?[19] What was it about this rather simplistic staging, in Irish, of Christ's Passion that captured the public imagination and led those who were there to speculate so extensively about the occasion's significance?

First of all, the reputation of St Enda's in the larger nationalist community must be considered. At that time the school was at the height of its popularity and success, both as an academic project and as a nationalist educational experiment. The school annals of 1910–11 show that many of the older boys had gained entrance to the universities; Denis Gwynn was awarded the first Classical Entrance Scholarship at University College Dublin in October 1910; the school also won the 1910–11 Dublin Juvenile Hurling League; while the school had already, prior to the *Passion Play,* successfully produced and staged dramas on the Abbey stage and in the grounds of St Enda's. Pearse's editorial comments in *An Macaomh,* the school yearbook, display a pride and quiet confidence in the work and achievements of St Enda's. The success of the *Passion Play* seemed merely to confirm St Enda's special place in the nationalist imagination by annexing the Irish language to a highly-charged collective spiritual and theatrical moment.

Secondly, the play was seen as an example of a newly emergent Celtic modernity, highlighting how the creation of new forms could be based on old styles. Padraic Colum's rapturous response to the *Passion Play,* describing it as springing 'from the origins of modern European drama',[20] highlights one of the levels on which the piece was received. To appreciate the power of the theatrical occasion one needs an understanding of the heady mixture of Christian pageantry, the Irish language, child actors and native drama for a contemporary audience made up of intellectuals, philologists, writers, socialites, painters and others interested in the concept of Celtic revivalism. The cast of the *Passion Play* crystallized a moment by bringing together the traditional and contemporary and by so doing managed to articulate, or appear to articulate, a number of different concerns within its audience. There were those already mentioned, like Desmond Ryan, who saw it as an allegory of nation. Padraic Colum's reading of the play as a 'celticized' symbolist morality tale can be understood as part of a broader European interest in the revival of folk and morality tales in vernacular forms.[21] What marked this staging from its European counterparts was its use of the Irish language as the vernacular form at a time when in some circles the status of Irish was considered to be little more than a pidgin language. For this reason Gaelic Leaguers were particularly pleased with the lyrical quality of the spoken Irish as well as the simplicity and beauty of its child actors.[22] As a social occasion the event bespoke a cultural moment in which strands of ancient Christian and contemporary Celtic culture were effectively woven together.

Thirdly, and most importantly for an understanding of the ongoing formation of the cult of boyhood within St Enda's, the *Passion Play* functioned as part of a larger narrative on Celtic maleness. One of the pedagogical functions of the story of the Passion is to illustrate the humanity of Christ and, through its exploration of Christ's human relationships, the *Passion Play* conveys the life and death of Christ as a man as well as a god. The traditional laments of the women keening the loss of their friend, the grief of Mary for her son and the loneliness and vulnerability of the Son of Man placed the

Passion Play firmly within an Irish social context. Within Celtic revivalism it was not unusual for the rural Irish-speaking family to be juxtaposed with the Holy Family. For Pearse, as for any Christian teacher, the figure of Christ offered an inspiring model of manliness for young men: Christ is modest yet passionate, humble yet enraged by injustice; born into a close family yet determined to follow his own path. The representation of Christ as male, heroic and Irish speaking was daring and inspired. It placed the Christian model of intelligence, sacrifice and holiness into an Irish context. Further it suggested that the so-called 'feminized' emotions, such as compassion, tenderness and humility, could be expressed, through the experience of Christ, as Celtic masculine virtues. The 'celticizing' of Christ's Passion also fulfilled certain nationalist needs by annexing the Irish language to the most sacred moment in the Christian tradition.

However, the recuperation of Christ into a Celtic context was nevertheless troubled. Christ could never comfortably be claimed as Irish, no matter how fluent his *gaeilge*, and, despite the enthusiasm of nationalists, there was something a little indecorous about hijacking the Passion for revivalist ends. The Lord Chamberlain had outlawed the depiction of biblical scenes on stage in England and a letter to this effect had already appeared in the *Irish Times* calling for a boycott of the St Enda's production.[23] In Pearse's *Passion Play* the celticizing of Christ was an attempt to illustrate the innate spirituality of Irish-speaking people and the sacredness of the Irish language, as well as providing a Christian male role model for St Enda's boys. However, and although it may seem outlandish, for Pearse there were more attractive Christian male role models closer to home. For the audience in the Abbey Theatre, what was apparent was that in the histories of the Irish saints Christ-like men were already to be found in the imaginative landscapes of rural Ireland, thus bringing the concept of an Irish-speaking Christ to a natural close.

The sensitive, yet Christian, model of manliness employed at St Enda's was found in the lives of the Irish monastic saints. For Pearse, St Colmcille offered an infinitely more suitable home-grown role model for Christian Celtic manliness than the figure of Christ. For all the success of the *Passion Play* in 1911, the Christian Celtic monk offered a model of manliness which also incorporated the notion of artistic endeavour and labour. For Pearse the figure of the medieval Irish monk offered the school a masculine role model who was both artist and male, both scholar and saint, both Christian and Celt. The artistic ability of the saint was praised not only in terms of creativity but as *work*. Throughout the nineteenth century there was a suspicion that art and artistic production somehow 'unmanned' men. In the early twentieth century, as women became increasingly involved in art (and literature), the role of the artist was perceived as being quite feminized.[24] Pearse's reconfiguration of the Christian Celtic artist as worker was influenced by contemporary debates about Christianity, manhood and labour. The lives of missionaries (whether contemporary or medieval) lent themselves to heroic treatment and missionaries were seen as Christian adventurers and explorers. Throughout the nineteenth century medieval monasticism, as an imaginative and moral model for masculine behaviour, was very popular, even before the late-century revival of interest in early Christian artistic culture.[25]

The monk as a man of autonomy, intellectual excellence, moral integrity and possessed of a work ethic was also a man of community and the monastic settlement was often likened to the domestic arrangements of family life. For St Enda's, which organized itself around the principles of the domestic home, the monastic unit provided a scholastic model which was both home and school. The French philosopher, Michel Foucault, has observed that the architectural and religious structure of the cloister was often mapped onto nineteenth-century boarding schools as a means of reinforcing a closely monitored educational and disciplinary regime.[26] The monastic model allowed for the distribution of pupils within particular spaces (dormitories, classrooms), which balanced the concept of confinement with community. Foucault's argument that such cellular arrangements facilitated the regulation of behaviour (particularly sexual behaviour) suggests that narratives of masculinity promoted by the school were upheld by the juxtaposition of surveillance with self-discipline evident within the monastic model.

St Colmcille was an important figure at St Enda's and one of the dormitories at the school was named after him. The liberal and wide-ranging curriculum of Colmcille's monastic communities at Iona and Aran informed the school's inter-disciplinary curricular structure and his life provided Pearse with the exemplar prototype of the Celt as artist, scholar, worker and man. St Colmcille was an inspirational figure within linguistic and artistic revivalism. As a respected poet and scholar as well as a teacher he was considered something of a renegade, who failed to defer to the central authority of Rome. He was dedicated in his pursuit of self-knowledge through abnegation and meditation. Perhaps most importantly for language revivalists, although from Donegal, he was associated with the Aran Islands and with a personal and abiding love of Ireland. As a revivalist icon his historicity was unquestioned (unlike Cúchulainn's) and his poems were concise, imagistic and easily translated. Colmcille was born in 521 in Donegal and educated at the monastic schools in Clonard and Glasnevin before settling on an island off the coast of Derry. He also founded a celebrated school at Durrow, but owing to a series of political manoeuvrings he was exiled from Ireland, much to his great personal sorrow, and founded the famous settlement at Iona in Scotland.[27] It was Colmcille who declared that if I die it shall be from an excess of love for the Gael' – a catch-phrase which appealed to Pearse's romantic imagination.[28]

Pearse was not the only Gael who was inspired by Colmcille. There was substantial interest in him throughout the nineteenth century. Interest in Colmcille's life and works traces the move from philological and antiquarian enquiry to a less academic interest in artistic representations of Celtic form.[29] There was also interest in the poems of Colmcille, whose reputation as a lyricist was considerable. John O'Donovan had published fragments of the poems as early as 1846. However, Whitley Stokes and other eminent scholars and literary historians from the 1870s onwards seemed occupied in reproducing early medieval editions of the *amhradh* or elegies written to the saint, rather than collecting the saint's poetic works.[30]

Celtic revivalism in the arts, and in particular the demand for ecclesiastical art, maintained Colmcille's high profile throughout the 1890s and early 1900s. A popular figure amongst revivalists, he was often depicted with a dove, his symbol, or with books and scholarly material on banners, stained-glass windows and tapestries epitomizing the artistic excellence associated with early Christian Ireland.[31] However, Colmcille's high profile in the arts was almost certainly due to the commemoration of his death in 1897, which did more than any antiquarian enquiry to bring the life of the saint into the public domain. To a certain extent it was this event which secured Colmcille as a model for the aspirations of St Enda's some ten years later. The publicity surrounding the centennial elevated Colmcille as an Irish patriot and poet who had suffered personal sacrifices for his love of Ireland. Douglas Hyde remarked that Colmcille 'is the first example . . . of the exiled Gael grieving for his native land . . . and as such he has become the very type and embodiment of Irish fate and Irish character'.[32] The Bishop of Raphoe's address at the commemorative rally in Gartan, County Donegal, referred to the saint as 'the patron of the exile, of the patriot, of the total abstainer [and] above all . . . the patron of schools'.[33]

Gaelic League attention regarding the centennial events in Donegal was firmly focused on exploiting the benefits of the occasion for the Irish language. One of the ongoing problems facing the League in its promotion of Irish as a vernacular was a general perception – especially amongst those who spoke it – that Irish was a form of patois. A primary reason for the perceived devaluation of Irish was its association with illiteracy. Not only was it considered the language of the ill-educated, but it was impossible for parents to pass on in a literate form owing to their own illiteracy.[34] The problem was compounded by the lack of realization by native speakers that Irish was a written as well as a spoken language; many of them considered literacy only to be possible in English.[35] While the League celebrated the Irish language's historical and poetic riches, the language was dwindling in the Gaeltacht, not merely because of emigration but also because it was considered a vernacular which was not quite respectable.[36] A record of the events at Gartan claims that it did 'much for the revival of the Irish language' and that it was responsible for impressing 'the popular imagination with the true ideals of life [as] found in Columba'.[37] The Catholic Church in Ireland also made much of Colmcille's allegiances to Ireland and to religious piety, suggesting that the Church's educators were the saint's natural pedagogic successors.[38] The Gartan Festival was reported extensively in the national and English newspapers.[39] Douglas Hyde noted that thousands of people travelled to Donegal to celebrate the life of 'a great Irish patriot, prince, and poet'.[40] Much was made also of Colmcille's life of service, sacrifice and denial; Cardinal Logue, Professor of Irish and Theology at Maynooth, maintained that, 'whenever a thought forced itself upon his mind in contemplation over and above the thoughts which bore him towards Heaven, it was a thought for Ireland'.[41]

The combined talents of Colmcille as scholar, poet, mentor, patriot and pedagogue made him a heady mix for any Celtic revivalist and for Pearse his credentials as a role model for St Enda's were above reproach. As an exemplar of Irish manhood the figure of Colmcille fits easily into prevailing discourses of masculinity and the monastic. The ideal of the monastic offered a model of self-discipline and self-denial, the belief that male communities were natural, ahistorical and necessary, and a model of artistic masculinity that was godly rather than effeminate. The model of manliness offered by Colmcille, despite its appeal, was none the less a model of adulthood and to this extent it carried the more complex readings that adult masculinity carries. While the monastic, sexually chaste model of the cloister was endorsed by Catholicism, and to a lesser extent by Irish revivalism, Colmcille remained more of a personal ideal for Pearse than a role model with whom teenage boys could identify. The social isolation and personal choices of adult, celibate life were not really very easily mapped onto the lives of the St Enda's boys, although they were taught to revere and admire Colmcille as an indefatigable worker for Ireland, the Irish language and Christianity.

Within late nineteenth-century discourses of the monastic as a way of life, the cloistered lives of monks became subject to unspoken anxieties about the social and sexual isolation of men from the larger community. There is a noticeable shift of emphasis within cultural and religious writing, throughout the latter half of the century, from praise for the monastic cloister as a space which conserves male energy to a suspicion of the cloister as a homoeroticized all-male community. As early as the 1840s Thomas Carlyle had praised the cloistered life in *Past and Present*, proposing that celibacy was a means of conserving male vitality and creativity and that sexual abstinence ensured the proper regulation of male energy.[42] The Pre-Raphaelite Brotherhood was also engaged by the model of artistic fraternity and male society which the monastery offered, although their work also explored the sexual isolation and frustration of the cloister within the social and moral codes of chivalry. Towards the end of the century the figure of the male ascetic living with other men and creating artistic works became open to the censure of effeminacy; indeed much of Walter Pater's aestheticism (often considered suspect) was informed by the homoerotics of the medieval male community.[43] The preoccupation with chastity in much of these writings may perhaps be seen as a displaced anxiety about unregulated sexuality.

The charge of effeminacy levelled at the monastic community came, in part, from a suspicion and fear of Catholicism, since inevitably pre-Reformation monastic life was associated with Catholicism. Studies suggest that late nineteenth-century Catholicism's (and particularly Anglo-Catholicism's) dedication to ritual, symbolism, liturgy and mystery left it open to the accusation of 'unmanliness'.[44] Towards the end of the century, narratives of chaste male love and friendship promoted by early Victorian literature were subject to charges of 'unmanliness' as the interest in medievalism valorized cloisters, guilds and brotherhoods, leaving the boundaries between homosocial and homosexual relationships open to contest.

The Irish medieval saint was doubly open to being inscribed within the fears of monastic unmanliness *and* the feminizing discourses of Celticism. By the early part of the twentieth century, when Pearse was advocating the Irish monk as a model of Celtic masculinity, the figure of the monk was accordingly an unstable, and ambiguous, cultural role model. Pearse's search for role models had led him to the early Celtic Church. Accordingly his quest for Christian purity became transferred onto children as embodiments of the divine rather than the more complex histories and psychology of adult men. Victorian sentimentalization of childhood throughout the nineteenth century meant that the figure of the child was almost inevitably seen through a veil of innocence and spiritual purity. It has been argued that Victorian culture's idealization of the child and its nostalgia for childhood was symptomatic of a more deeply felt anxiety about progress, technology and industrialization.[45] Indeed, since the eighteenth-century 'cult of feeling', the importance of representing childhood to symbolize something apart or 'other' from adult existence has been an important theme within Romanticism and Romantic literature. Within Victorian visual culture there also emerged a sub-genre of painting on religious themes which dealt with the childhood of Christ.[46] The representation of Christ as a child meant that the tricky subject of how to paint Christ as a *man* – loincloth or no loincloth – were avoided. Representations of the child Jesus placed him within the life of the bourgeois family and firmly within sentimental narratives of childhood and thereby avoided any troubling sexual thoughts about Christ as a man.[47] As a parallel, these same concerns, no matter how subtly expressed, meant that the child offered a less troubled model of innocence and Christian virtue.

Consequently a spiritual orthodoxy which saw the child as pure and innocent became mapped onto the bodies of all children, so that by the late nineteenth and early twentieth century the innate spirituality of children was almost a given.[48] Within nineteenth-century Catholicism in Europe there were a number of societies dedicated to the childhood of Christ. One of these was 'The Association of the Holy Childhood', of which only children could become members. The Association was founded in France in the 1840s and a branch appeared in Ireland during the 1880s. The function of the Association was to encourage the devotion of children to the Christ child and had the effect of securing a popular perception of a child as a vessel of religious purity. It is not difficult to see how Pearse's estimation of children falls into popular cultural and religious discourses of the century's idealization of childhood. For Pearse, the child offered a purer, simpler vision of Celtic Christianity than the adult monk. The Christian child was *expected* to have the 'feminine' virtues of sensitivity and compassion. Therefore the monk as a role model for Celtic manliness was jettisoned for the less problematic and, arguably, pre-sexual body of the child. The figure of the divine boy, the embryonic Christ-child, was more easily accommodated into revivalist fantasies of the relationship between the Irish language and spiritual purity and fitted seamlessly into contemporary narratives of the moral and spiritual excellence of childhood. For Pearse, political and spiritual salvation comes in the form of golden-haired ethereal boys, a preoccupation made clear by his writings in which Irish-speaking boys offer redemption, often in opposition to the spiritual uncertainties expressed by adult Irish monks and saints.

Plate 1 Mary Bulfin as the Virgin Mary, *Passion Play* (1911)

Plate 2 Detail, William Pearse as Pontius Pilate, *Passion Play* (1911)

Plate 3 William Pearse as Pontius Pilate, *Passion Play* (1911)

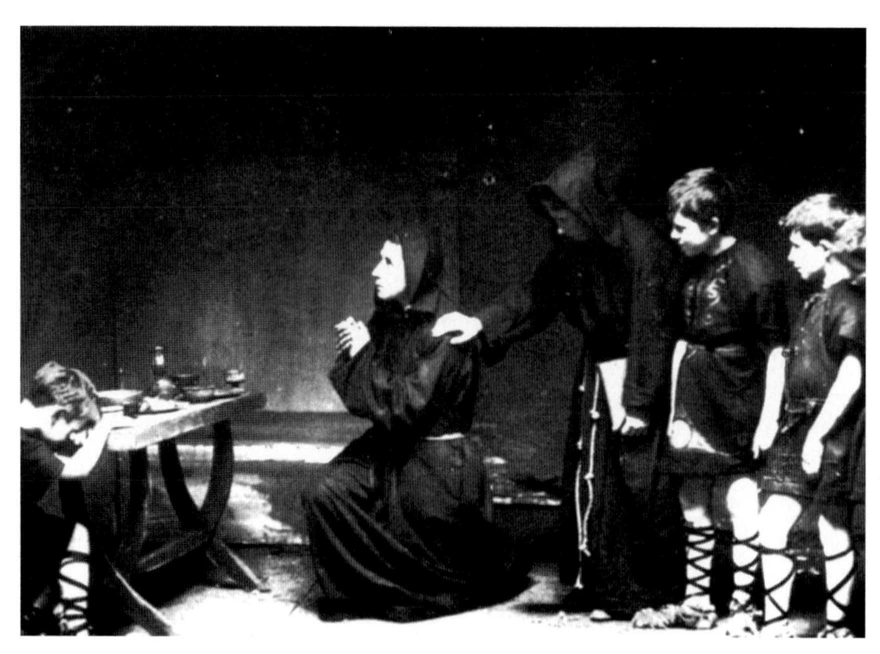

Plate 4 Production photograph of Douglas Hyde's *The Lost Saint* (1909)

teaċ ḟeaḋa ċuilinn, ráṫ ó máine,
baile áṫa cliaṫ.

Féile Éanna, 1909

Léirneoċaiḋ mic léiġinn na sgoile

"An naoṁ ar iarraiḋ"

(An Craoiḃín Aoiḃinn do sgríoḃ).
agus

"The Coming of Fionn"

(Sgaimirléir ó Gráḋaiġ do sgríoḃ).

20, 21 (Lá Féile Éanna), agus 22 Márta, 1909.
Ar a 6 a ċlog tráṫnóna.

Plate 5 *Féile Éanna* Programme illustrated by Patrick Tuohy (1909)

Plate 6 Illustration, front cover of *Íosagán*, by Beatrice Elvery (1907)

Iosagán.

Plate 7 Illustration, 'Íosagán' by Beatrice Elvery, in *Íosagán* (1907)

Plate 8 Illustration, 'Íosagán' by 'Gear', in *Íosagán* (1950)

Plate 9 Oil Painting by Beatrice Elvery, *Éire Óg* (1907)

Plate 13 Irish Language Teaching Chart (*c*.1908)

Plate 14 Pen and ink drawing by Joseph Campbell in Margaret Hutton, *An Táin* (1907)

Plate 15 Studio photograph of
Frank Dowling as 'Cúchulainn' (1909)

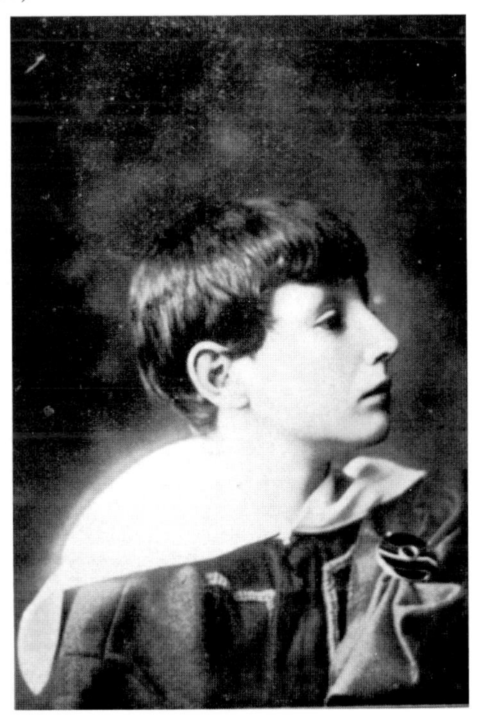

Plate 16 Photograph, three-quarter profile of
Frank Dowling as 'Cúchulainn' (1909)

Plate 17 St Enda's school crest and motto (1909)

Plate 18 Photograph, Desmond Carney as 'Giolla na Naomh' (1912)

Plate 19 Illustration, 'Finn Mac Cumhal' by Stephen Reid (1909)

Plate 20 Illustration 'Setanta' by Stephen Reid (1909)

Plate 21 Photograph of pageant, *The Coming of Fionn* (*c*.1909)

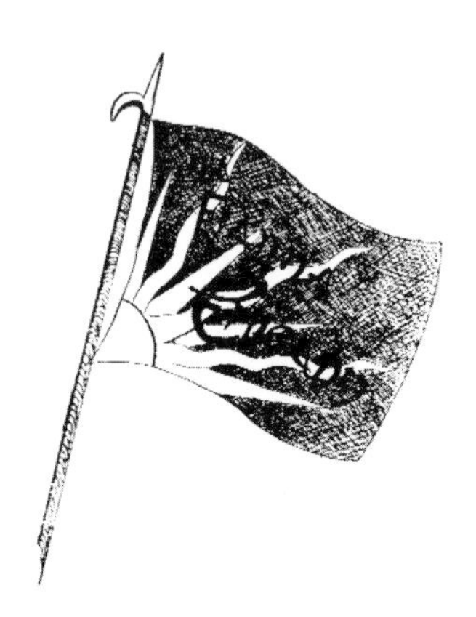

Plate 22 Illustration of the Fianna Flag in *Fianna Handbook* (1914)

Plate 23 Illustration of the Fianna Badge in *Fianna Handbook* (1914)

Plate 24 Frontispiece by Constance Markievicz, *Fianna Handbook* (1914)

FIANNA HANDBOOK

Issued by the Central Council
of Na Fianna Eireann for
the Boy Scouts of Ireland

PUBLISHED BY
THE CENTRAL COUNCIL OF NA FIANNA EIREANN,
12 D'OLIER STREET, DUBLIN.

Plate 25 Imprint page of *Fianna Handbook* (1914)

Plate 26 Illustration of 'Rifle Exercises', *Fianna Handbook* (1914)

Plate 27 Photograph of Con Colbert drilling the St Enda's boys (*c.*1910)

Plate 28 Photograph of St Enda's Gaelic football team as holders of the Dublin Schools Cup (1911)

Plate 29 Photograph of boys bathing at St Enda's (*c*.1909)

Plate 30 Photograph of Desmond Carney as 'Owen' in *Fianna* magazine (1915)

4

Divine Boys:
Primitivism and Celtic Landscapes

Within romantic nationalism the literary and visual image of the child is often used to recall a common past: the collective childhood of the nation. However, a child may also represent the promise of the future. Child figures, and the idea of childhood, may be used as a way of ordering the past and of tracing a way of thinking that is linked to the contemporary.[1] In his book *Inventing Ireland* Declan Kiberd notes that romantic nationalist writing's preoccupation with the psychic spaces of childhood may be read as combining a yearning for escape with a selective nostalgia for the past.[2] However, within Pearse's brand of nostalgic literature the boy does not represent *escape* but spiritual and moral certainty. Kiberd argues that the presence of strange 'redemptive' children in nationalist narratives are double-edged. Although they might function as metaphors for the past within nationalist readings, he also argues that they feed into pre-existing imperialist ideas of the 'infantile' nature of native cultures.[3] By shaping the Irish collective experience in terms of childhood, Kiberd argues that at times romantic nationalists merely internalized, and therefore reinforced, the imperial strategy of seeing all colonized cultures as childlike.[4]

Narratives about childhood are not always nostalgic longings for the past and indeed may function as deeply ambiguous and contradictory statements about the present.[5] The figure of the child may be a symbol of loss and disintegration as well as of progress and civilization. This is, in part, why sentimental narratives on the family often focus on the death of a child. The association of the child figure with death as well as with the promise of a future suggests that the redemptive child is a more problematic and intricate figure than Kiberd's reading might allow.

This chapter looks at the complex figure of the 'redemptive' boy within Pearse's Christian dramas and stories. This boy is usually very young, in contrast to the early adolescents of Pearse's bardic and pagan dramas, thereby emphasizing his purity and innocence. The redemptive boy of Pearse's imaginings is easily read within narratives on the sentimentalization and idealization of childhood, which were common currency both in popular and religious literature of the time. However, within Pearse's stories and dramas the spiritual purity of the boy is linked to the Irish language and to the west of Ireland as a site of romantic transcendence. This is most evident in Pearse's morality tale, *Íosagán* (Little Jesus), where Christ appears as an Irish-speaking boy in west Connacht. The boy/Christ-child appears in a number of dramas and productions staged by St Enda's between 1909 and 1915. This chapter looks at the importance of the Gaeltacht in underlining Pearse's admiration for the spiritual purity of boys, making connections as he did between the Irish language, the Garden of Eden and the romanticized geography of the western seaboard. Indeed, for other Celtic revivalists the combination of the 'natural religion' of childhood with the Irish language was also to prove inspirational.

In all, St Enda's produced five Christian plays between 1908 and 1915 which focused on themes of boyhood and Christianity. The Christian Celtic plays, as they will be called here, are *Íosagán* (performed in 1909, 1910 and 1915), the *Passion Play* (1911), *The Lost Saint* (1909, 1910), *An Rí* (The King) (1912, 1913) and *The Master* (1915). The *Passion Play* is the only production which featured Christ and which places Christ as a man in an Irish setting. All of the other plays are centred around the figure of a young, intensely spiritual, boy. In many of the plays the child's spirituality and faith is set against that of an older man (often a monk or a saint) who is struggling to rediscover a simplicity of belief. Within these narratives it is the boy and not the saint who represents the most powerful combination of Irishness and spiritual integrity. The early plays, *The Lost Saint* and *Íosagán*, feature young, childish boys while the boys in the later plays, *The King* and *The Master*, are slightly older, but all of the plays reflect how the figure of the boy, rather than the man, was used to promote a model of Celtic masculinity.

The first dramatic production at St Enda's, *The Lost Saint,* was written by Douglas Hyde as a one-act Christian morality tale set in a monastic community. An Irish-language play, it was performed with an English-language adaptation of Standish O'Grady's *The Coming of Fionn* for the first time in March 1909.[6] Pearse made reference to the thematic connections between the pieces, suggesting that they were symbolic of the 'twin standard that was raised so finely by such Gaels as Colmcille . . . in the day when Ireland was a more religious and a more heroic land'.[7] Reviews praised *The Lost Saint* as 'a delicate and tender little drama' based on an episode in the life of St Aengus Céile Dé.[8] *The Lost Saint* had been published in *Samhain* in 1902 with a translation by Lady Gregory. It represents Hyde's attempt to draw on his research into early Christian monastic life and was praised by Yeats for its purity and simplicity.[9] A miracle play, Hyde's piece is a reworking of an incident recorded in an early hagiography of the saint's life. Set in a monastery in Tallaght in the ninth century it features the saint, called Cormacín, who is employed as a caretaker in a school. Cormacín takes pity on a young boy, Conall, who is unable to recite a verse from the saint's calendar. Kept at his desk as a punishment, Conall is discouraged and, exhausted, he falls asleep. Cormacín prays over the child and asks God 'to put wisdom in his head, cleanse his heart, scatter the mist that is upon his mind, and let him learn his lesson like the other boys'. On waking, Conall is able to recite his lessons perfectly and both the teacher and the children realize that Cormacín is not what he seems. The teacher and children kneel in front of 'the lost saint' and ask for his blessing.

The 'lost' saint may be read as a metaphor for Ireland's rich oral, cultural tradition, which, significantly, is entrusted to the memory and imagination of a young boy who represents a physical and emotional link to the future. More importantly, however, the play shifts the importance from the role of the saint to the role of the boy, suggesting that the innocent body of the boy replaces the saint as a more fitting metaphor for spiritual and cultural 'truth'. A simple play, it is perfectly suited for children since the action is carried by only two adults (or older boys) and as many children as can fit on a stage. There were fourteen boys in the 1909 production at St Enda's, with Eoin MacNeill's son Niall playing the part of Conall. A photograph (which was subsequently published as a postcard) shows the moment when Cormacín is discovered as a saint (Plate 4). Joseph Holloway singled Padraic Ó Conaire out for praise. Ó Conaire was from the Connemara Gaeltacht and Holloway thought he possessed 'the stage gift' and 'the knowledge and sympathy necessary for the proper interpretation of the Gaelic character'.[10] The photograph shows the boys dressed in tunics, with handmade shoes and leather leg-bindings, giving the production a medieval air, while the saint and the teacher are garbed in monastic robes. The play was performed again in 1910 with *Íosagán, The Coming of Fionn* and Colum's *Destruction of the Hostel.* The programme for the 1909 production was designed and drawn by Patrick Tuohy, a student at the school and, later, an accomplished painter and a member of the Royal Hibernian Academy. The programme's illustration demonstrates the pan-Celtic feel of the evening with a depiction of Fionn facing the Lost Saint across an interlocking Celtic design and is evidence of the school's early interest in the figure of the boy (Plate 5).

It is, however, the figure of Íosagán that was the central visual and literary image of Christian Celtic masculinity at St Enda's. The boy child Íosagán brings together Pearse's precoccupations with the nature of childhood, the importance of Irish Christian medievalism, the concept of a Celtic manliness organized around the virtues of art as work, scholarship, piety and humility and the spiritual purity of Irish as the language of the west of Ireland. *Íosagán,* a morality tale of the Christ-child in Connacht, had already appeared in a number of guises. It was originally published as a short story which appeared in *An Claidheamh Soluis* in 1906; then it became the title of a series of short stories set in Connacht, also published as a series in *An Claidheamh Soluis* during 1906 and 1907, and was finally published in book form in 1907. Pearse adapted the tale for stage in 1910, and it was performed by the St Enda's players twice in that year, once at Cullenswood House and once at the Abbey Theatre, and finally in 1915 at the Irish Theatre in Hardwicke Street. *Íosagán agus Sgéalta Eile*, the 1907 collection of short stories, was illustrated by Beatrice Elvery (Plates 6 and 7). The stories were republished in two editions in 1911 and 1918; the 1911 edition was a reprint of the Elvery edition, the other a new translation by Joseph Campbell. The Elvery edition was reprinted again in 1920; a new edition with illustrations by 'Gear' appeared in 1950[11] (Plate 8) and, more recently, in 1990 an edition appeared on cassette tape. Its early reprints were due to the book's popularity as a school text and in the 1920s the book was sanctioned and prescribed as a textbook for the Intermediate Board of Education.

Íosagán falls somewhere between a child's story book and a set of simple morality tales for adults learning Irish. At its first publication in *An Claidheamh Soluis*, short glossaries were attached to each story, which were retained with each subsequent Irish-language publication. The collection, *Íosagán and Other Stories*, contains four of the ten short stories which Pearse wrote in Irish; the other six appear in his collection *The Mother*, which was published in January 1916. *Íosagán* and the other stories in the collection are all set in the fictional town of Rosneeragh in west Connacht. *Íosagán* remains the only one of Pearse's short stories that was dramatized for the stage.

Pearse describes *Íosagán* as being about 'the beauty of childhood', and particularly 'the beauty of boyhood'.[12] Written in Irish, the story focuses on an old man who has become isolated from the adult villagers because he refuses to attend mass. Instead he spends his time talking to the young local boys and telling them stories about the past. The boys love Matthias because of his gentleness, his knowledge and love of nature and his fine repository of tales and stories. The villagers reassure themselves about Matthias's apparent godlessness by observing his kindness to the boys and his respect 'for the cleanest and most beautiful thing that God created – the shining soul of the child'. One morning a strange, barefooted, golden-haired child appears, wearing an unusual white garment. His face is radiant and there is a peculiar light surrounding him. Playing with the other children the strange child seems to disappear when the villagers come out of mass. Matthias learns the child's name is Íosagán and that his father is a 'High-King'. Making himself known to 'the Holy Child', Matthias asks him questions about his life. Íosagán relates how he has been 'travelling the roads, and walking the hills, and ploughing the waves' and confirms the 'natural' spirituality of children by saying that 'there isn't any time or place that children do be amusing themselves that I am not along with them'. That evening the priest is visited by a boy with 'rays of light shining from his countenance and about his head' who tells him to visit the ailing Matthias. On his deathbed Matthias is able to make restitution before he dies 'with a smile on his mouth' and 'his two arms stretched out', with the word 'Íosagán' on his lips.

It is easy to scoff at *Íosagán:* it is sentimentally naïve, clumsy and painfully idiomatic, yet it has a simplicity of form and language that is curiously pleasing. *Íosagán,* the play, draws out the connections between the special insight of children, the spirituality of Connacht and Pearse's reverence for boyhood that are evident in the short story. The dramatic version, also written and performed in Irish, is slightly longer and is more focused than the story on the character of Íosagán and his playful interaction with the other boys. *Íosagán* was first performed as a double bill with Padraic Colum's adaptation of the saga of Da Dearga, *The Destruction of the Hostel,* in February 1910. Padraic Ó Conaire played Old Matthias and Íosagán was played by Eunan McGinley, who later died in the War of Independence. Addressing the audience in the small school theatre, Pearse 'explained that the two plays symbolised the gospel of patriotism'. *Íosagán* 'stood for the spirituality of Ireland' and *The Destruction of the*

Hostel stood 'for her heroism'.[13] Pearse wrote that it was not a play 'for ordinary theatres or for ordinary players'[14] and it is difficult to imagine it staged effectively without indulging the sentimentality of the piece.

Presumably the fact that it was performed in Irish bypassed much of the 'staginess' of the language, since the performance at the Abbey in 1910 delighted the audience with 'the childlike innocence' of the piece. With more characters, lots of singing and banter between the boys the drama is obviously designed to facilitate as many students as possible. Unlike the *Passion Play* all the parts were taken by boy actors, a point which drew admiration from the play's reviewers. At last, it seemed, there was a native children's drama in Irish, performed by children for adults and children alike. Pearse felt that whatever beauty *Íosagán* had was owed to the beauty 'of interpretation' and to the young actors who brought 'something of the beauty of their own fresh lives' to the play. The boys, according to *An Claidheamh Soluis*, had 'the knowledge and sympathy necessary for the proper interpretation of the Gaelic character' and were commended for the sophistication of their 'stage gift'.[15] The paper singled out the acting of the Gaeltacht boys remarking that their ability was greater than 'adult actors in Irish plays in Dublin'.[16] It is fair to assume that, because the actors were from the Gaeltacht, they were considered to be able somehow to communicate an unmediated, essentialized, purity to the audience. Joseph Holloway was charmed by the child actors and noted how the audience was delighted 'by the childlike innocence of their playing'.[17] The first, 1910, production in St Enda's was attended by several hundred people. The second production, in the Abbey Theatre a few months later, attracted many people who had heard of, or already seen, the boy players. *Íosagán* drew particular praise for its depiction of rural life as a fusion of simple lifestyle and moral goodness. *An Claidheamh Soluis* reported that 'everything on the stage tended to command respect for the simple life of the poor, but noble, Gaeltacht', suggesting that rural life 'save when it served to amuse the thoughtless', had not been deemed worthy of considerate representation.[18]

The Pearse brothers were keenly interested in art, were exposed to movements within Celtic revivalism and determined that art and aesthetic appreciation should form an important part of the school curriculum.[19] Willie had trained at the Dublin Metropolitan School of Art under Oliver Sheppard and had spent time in London and Paris in the 1890s. There was a real interest in art at the school and a number of artists working within Celtic revivalist traditions contributed works to the school, among them George Russell, Jack B. Yeats and Sarah Purser.[20] Artworks which complemented the school's promotion of boyhood as a special place included two symbolist paintings of Celtic masculinity by Beatrice Elvery (later Lady Glenavy): *Éire Óg* and *Íosagán*.[21] The first of these paintings, *Éire Óg* (Young Ireland), was given as a gift to the school by Maud Gonne (Plate 9). *Éire Óg* is an allegorical painting of Cathleen Ní Houlihan with a young child on her knees shadowed by 'a ghostly crowd of martyrs, patriots, saints and scholars'.[22] This was the picture that apparently inspired a pupil to take up arms to fight for Mother Ireland – a confession which horrified Elvery.[23] The second painting, *Íosagán*, was donated by Elvery to Cullenswood House (Plate 10).

Elvery's painting of *Íosagán* was reproduced in *An Macaomh*, the school magazine, and is now in the Pearse Museum (Plate 10). The inscription, in Gaelic script, reads in translation: 'And the Child grew and waxed strong; full of wisdom and the Grace of God was in him'. The painting is a pastoral setting of the Christ-child. Set against two sturdy apple trees, Íosagán stands with arms spread out, as if anticipating crucifixion, while a rabbit and a bird go undisturbed at his feet and lambs feed idly in the background. The quotation at the base of Elvery's painting of Íosagán has a slightly different meaning in Irish than in English. The inscription is adapted from St Luke's account of the childhood of Christ,[24] but in the Irish 'the child' is translated as *an macaomh*.

The use of *macaomh* here is revealing. Pearse had adapted this word, originally meaning a young warrior scholar, from bardic literature but extended its reading within the context of St Enda's to refer to youthful ideals of Christian service. The use of *an macaomh* to refer to the figure of Christ as a boy suggests the conflation of pagan and Christian Celticism to produce an image of a Christian warrior.[25] While the figure of the boy warrior (such as Cúchulainn) continued to have particular currency within St Enda's, the depiction of Íosagán as a Christian *macaomh* suggests that the boy is a fighter for the Celtic Christian virtues of truth and spiritual purity. The mapping of the pagan onto the Christian, which is visualized most effectively in Elvery's painting of Íosagán, offers the boy as a symbol of a new Celtic culture which is informed by the pagan world of courage and war and the Christian world of humility and self-sacrifice.

Placing the boy in the rural rather than the urban landscape situates *Íosagán* (whether as story, play or painting) within a discourse of romantic nationalism which privileges rural life as spiritually 'authentic'. Íosagán is not merely placed in the world of nature but in the particular terrain of the west of Ireland Gaeltacht. Pearse's investment in the 'authenticity' of the rural was in keeping with a larger European-wide interest in folk culture as an aspect of the modernist concern with primitivism. Indeed, Pearse's Irish staging of the *Passion Play* is illustrative of this trend. The nationalist demand for 'authenticity' expressed through a primitivist search for 'origins' was firmly focused on the west of Ireland as a nationalist 'other', but it also threw an essentializing eye over the figure of the boy. Pearse was of the belief, like other Irish-Irelanders, that the west of Ireland had a spiritual quality which was lacking in other more anglicized parts of the country. Irish-Ireland's interest in the Irish language and its accompanying literature, rural regeneration and the simplicity of peasant life, meant that a shift of emphasis towards the west of Ireland as a spiritual terrain, far removed from the influence of anglicization and urbanization, was understandable.

Pearse had first visited Connacht in 1898. His experience had been exhilarating, starting a love-affair with the place and its people that was to continue throughout his lifetime. The combined vulnerability of young children and the fragility of the language were enough to pierce him to the heart and make him feel that Connacht was *the* touchstone of Irish-Ireland. In a letter from Connacht during this time he admits that 'in the kindly Irish west I feel that I am in Ireland'.[26] For Pearse, the special beauty and morality of all children was embodied most completely in the Irish-speaking child. The Irish-speaking child was not merely closer to nature, he was an extension of nature. By 1907, the same year that *Íosagán* was first published, he was passionate enough on the subject of Connacht and childhood to declare that 'the Irish speaking child is the most important living thing in Ireland today'.[27] The child is capable of revealing to the rest of Ireland 'the real Ireland which has hitherto been concealed . . . as though by a drawn veil'. The children 'whose lips have never known any speech than Ireland's' have not been educated out of their instinctual and elemental relationship to landscape and language, are untainted by anglicization and remain 'the fairest thing which springs up [in] Ireland'. The child is the repository of 'the voice of Éire . . . and generations of soldiers and poets' whose culture is tied up with local oral narrative and folklore.

In a separate article on the Connemara Gaeltacht, Pearse fancies himself within the frame of a Renaissance painting, since the local faces are so 'beautiful and spiritual' that they could provide a study for a portrait of 'St John, St Peter or a Mater Dolorosa'. In fact, he argues, there might not be 'so many gross and merely earthly conceptions of the Madonna' if 'some of the Old Masters had known rural Ireland'.[28] Representations of the Holy Family in rural Ireland, or of families who appeared to have qualities of the divine, were not unusual within Celtic revivalism. The title story of Pearse's *The Mother and Other Stories* is originally from a local source and places Pearse in the familiar territory of the natural spirituality of Connacht. A gentle and pleasing illustration by Mícheál Mac Liammoir of a mother and child in his personal copy of *The Mother* demonstrates more than anything the overlapping of the rural family with the divine family found within 'folk' revivalism (Plate 11). In this simple and precise story a young woman prays to the Virgin Mary for a child. Pearse, in his comments on the story, says that a belief in the appearance of the Virgin on Christmas Eve was quite commonplace in the west of Ireland and many households left their doors open and food on the table for her. The woman, who sings the ancient lullaby 'Crónán na Banaltra', beats herself as a penance for being childless. Late on Christmas Eve Mary comes to the door with the child Jesus, who stretches out his hands and lays them on the woman's cheeks. Blessed by Íosagán, the woman conceives and has a child. The divine family is 'made flesh' in the rural family unit.

A Christmas card designed by Jack Yeats for St Enda's further plays on the sacralized landscape of rural Ireland. Printed by the Cuala Press, the card features an Irish lullaby collected by Pearse in his *Songs of Sleep and Sorrow*, which he published in 1914 (Plate 12). The poem 'Cronán Mná Sléibhe' or 'Lullaby of a Woman of the Mountain' is a love-song from a mother to her child. The child's 'little gold head' is the 'house's candle' that guides wayfarers home. Mary, the Baby Jesus and Christ all kiss the child and lay hands on him as they pass through the countryside.[29]

The juxtaposition of the divine family with the Irish-speaking rural family further secured Pearse's belief in the natural spirituality of children. However, Pearse's fictional treatment of women and girls is very different to that of his treatment of boys. While females are configured within Catholic orthodox teaching on the domestic and nurturing roles of women, Pearse's fictional boys are presented as having only temporal relationships to the family. Unlike his sisters, the boy is not expected, in adult life, to reproduce another family unit. If girls are constructed within the social world, then boys are framed beyond the limits of the social and belong to the broader terrain of the natural world. *The Roads* tells the tale of a young girl, Nora, who leaves home tired with her lot as a female, echoing perhaps another Nora, that of Ibsen's *A Doll House.* Nora cuts off her hair, dresses as a boy and heads off on the open road. On the way she stops in a forest for a nap and has a vision of Christ in the Garden of Gethsemane. Christ's agony pierces her to the heart and she feels she has grievously wronged the order of things. Collapsing in the woods she is found by her father, returns home and is restored to the family. In Pearse's, rather than Ibsen's story, Nora embraces her role as female and is described clasping her baby brother (as a portent of the 'natural' procession of her life as a woman). The baby, infused with a holy glow, puts his arms around her neck and curls into the shelter of her body, bringing the circle of the family to a close.

In all of Pearse's stories women are situated within narratives of home, confirming the centrality of the *idea* of family for a nationalist continuum. The women are important as re-producers (of children and of tradition) and function to facilitate the more significant figures of the boy-children. While men may live together in surrogate families (like monasteries) and reproduce knowledge, women literally and figuratively die when removed from the family unit. The woman that has no family unit in which to re-produce tradition withers away, as in the story *Brigid of the Songs*, or she becomes 'de-feminized' and therefore cursed, as in *The Dearg Daol. Brigid of the Songs* (originally called *Brigid of the Winds* but hastily amended after some covert sniggering by Gaelic Leaguers) tells the story of an old woman who travels by foot for days in order to sing her ancient Connacht lullabies at the Dublin *Oireachtas*. After a rapturous reception and the award of the gold medal she dies from exhaustion and hunger. The story was designed to be read as a metaphor for the dying traditions of the Gaeltacht and the need to preserve and cherish them. In the same year as this story appeared in *An Claidheamh Soluis*, in 1906, Pearse urged the collection of as many stories as possible, since 'many precious scraps of lore have been lost because . . . on returning to look for them the seanchaidhe was dead'.[30] The personification of tradition has particular potency when mapped onto the body of an old woman and suggests barrenness, infertility and lack of reproductive capability. A childless old woman also features in the tale of *The Dearg Daol.* Attributed to a local source, it is a ghost story narrated by a travelling man who tells the tale of the Dearg Daol (literally, 'the devil's coach horse'), a cursed woman with no family or children, who befriended his child.[31] The child trusted the woman and spent time with her but sickened and died; misfortune fell on the man's family and he was forced to wander the roads until the day he died. These stories imply that women with no children have no maternal role to play and are therefore deemed to be at best unfulfilled and at worst cursed.

Pearse's short stories and plays carve out a different social reality for boy-children, suggesting that, unlike girls, boys have more important responsibilities than family life. Íosagán's family is literally 'unearthly' and when on earth he belongs, not within a social unit, but with a community of boys. In *The Priest,* which is allegedly an autobiographical tale, little Pádraig sneaks away from the family to say mass in an upstairs bedroom and looks forward to a time when he can belong to a community of men.[32] In Pearse's stories, boys, like Jesus, do not belong to the family but occupy the same space for a while until called on to a higher spiritual vocation in priesthood or in death. In *Eoineen of the Birds,* a short story in the *Íosagán* collection, another strange golden-haired boy communes with nature and intuits his impending death. Eoineen is a frail child and waits by his bedroom window for the return of the swallows from 'the Southern World'. An ethereal, quiet boy, even his mother thinks he is full of 'queer talk'. Eoineen is a child in the same vein as Íosagán, slightly puzzling to the adult world but at ease with the natural world. It is only a matter of time before Eoineen heads off to the 'Country of Light', which he imagines to be almost as beautiful and peaceful as Ireland.

It is perhaps easy to read stories like *Íosagán* and *Eoineen of the Birds* as simple Christian allegories for children, on the one hand because the sentimentality of such tales was not uncommon in children's moralistic literature and, on the other hand, because the juxtaposition of the divine and the rural was a feature of Celtic revivalism. The tales suggest that Íosagán and Eoineen are incarnations of the Christ-child and that the world is no place for a child of moral and spiritual integrity. However, this reading is troubled by the presentation of *Ireland* as Eden, and specifically Irish-speaking Ireland, a concept which differs greatly from the orthodox Christian idea of heaven. In *Eoineen of the Birds* the landscape of Ireland is preferable to that of the 'Southern World', to where the birds are travelling. In *Íosagán* the Christ-child finds himself at home, spiritually and geographically, in Íar Connacht.

As Celtic masculinity within Pearse's narratives becomes framed within the body of the Irish-speaking boy, his idea of Celtic maleness becomes removed from the social and domestic world of adult masculinity (the family, the cloister) and situated instead in the natural world and aligned to an animistic natural religion. Pearse's opinion that the Irish-speaking child was not merely closer to nature but *was* nature has already been discussed earlier in this chapter.[33] The Irish-speaking boy, he opined, 'is more beautiful than any flower, more graceful than any wild creature of the fields or the woods', suggesting that not only was the boy a part of nature but that he represented the epitome of perfection in the natural world.[34] This Irish-speaking Edenic paradise is also, like the original Eden, devoid of sexual knowledge, since the boy, morally and sexually, is 'purer than any monk'. Here Celtic masculinity exists in splendid perfection, at one with the natural world, removed from the social obligations of family and work and free, unlike the monk, from the taint of effeminacy, since there is no sexuality.

The theme of boys in nature, informed and educated by the natural world, runs throughout Pearse's fictional narratives. His understanding that boys carry an 'innate knowledge' about the natural world places his boys in an animistic and sacramentalized universe.[35] By suggesting that the sacramental and mystical qualities of the natural world also inform Celtic masculinity he constructs Celtic maleness within the frame of mystical medievalism. This philosophy is still recognizably Catholic but remains outside the boundaries of Catholic institutional orthodoxy, suggesting that masculinity, unlike femininity, is not confined by social and religious law.

Despite Pearse's unothodox sacramental and poetic vision of the universe St Enda's adhered strictly to Catholic doctrine and ritual. The allegiance to Catholicism is demonstrated by the unusual instance of a lay school forming a Guild of the Apostleship of Prayer and an Arch-confraternity of the Sacred Heart.[36] However, there were others who taught at the school who shared Pearse's mystical Catholic vision, and Joseph Campbell's poetic construction of Celtic masculinity, in particular, intersected with Pearse's own. Campbell, a friend of Thomas MacDonagh's, taught history at St Enda's for a time in 1913. Pearse, Plunkett, MacDonagh and Campbell shared a deeply religious Catholic faith, a creditable knowledge of the Irish language, a fervent belief in national culture and the practice of poetry. As poets they were especially drawn to the imagistic quality of much devotional poetry in Irish, particularly that of Colmcille. Katherine Tynan is often considered the only poet of the revival movement who wrote religious verse, but Campbell was the first poet to attempt to write devotional English poetry in the Gaelic manner. Campbell, Pearse, Plunkett and MacDonagh all used religious themes in their work to articulate their feelings about Ireland.

In 1907, the same year that *Íosagán* was published, Campbell produced *The Man-Child*, a collection of twenty-six poems. In his preface he identified the 'Man-Child', 'as a symbol of the virile and regenerate Ireland which is now springing into being'.[37] Campbell's treatment of Christ, 'born in hardship, betrayed in manhood, mocked and crucified', was related to his conception of the Irish 'as a people who have known suffering' and in this he complements Pearse's blend of faith and fatherland.[38] His 'masculinization' of Ireland anticipates Pearse's own blend of hero-worship and martyrdom.[39] The poems display a late-Victorian preoccupation with childhood coupled with a romantic call for individuality, freedom and elementalism, but the Man-Child is placed in a Gaelic landscape. Like Íosagán the Man-Child is 'perfect in form'; his is the land of Oisín who 'strayed upon the mountain-top' with his 'holy head, crowned by a flight of birds'. Campbell names him 'the Singer of the Dawn' which may have given Pearse the name for his 1915 play *The Singer*, in which the character MacDara is a mixture of messiah and nationalist hero.

Later that year, 1907, Campbell published a second volume, *The Gilly of Christ*, which again is close to Pearse's contemporary preoccupations with Christian Irish settings. The 'gilly' or *giolla* of Christ is a servant, guide or follower and Campbell's poem is based on an Irish legend that when Christ visited Ireland a local boy showed him around.[40] Pearse's play *The King* features a young servant boy who is a gilly to an abbot. The play, written in 1911, is subtitled

'A Morality' and is one of two Irish-language plays performed by St Enda's which juxtapose a Christian and pagan setting. The other play, *The Master,* was not written until 1915 and was performed at the Irish Theatre in Hardwicke Street with (the ever-popular) *Íosagán* that year. The Irish Theatre had been founded in 1914 by Thomas MacDonagh with the assistance of Joseph Plunkett and the financial help of Edward Martyn.[41] *The King* is interesting for a number of reasons. It was first performed as a pageant by pupils of the school on the banks of the river at the Hermitage on 15 June 1912. It was later reworked and performed by the pupils on the Abbey Theatre stage as a double bill with Rabindranath Tagore's *The Post Office* on 17 May 1913 and later that year at the St Enda's Fête at Jones's Road. It had a further incarnation in India when it was performed in Bengali dress at Tagore's school, 'the Indian St Enda's', in 1915.[42]

The King manages to fuse many of Pearse's personal and professional interests. As a dramatic work it straddles the divide between the outdoor spectacles and formal dramas produced by the school since it had an incarnation as both pageant and play. It was published and performed in Irish and in English and enjoyed brief international attention in India. The play suggests a dynamic fusion between pagan and Christian culture incarnated in the body of a young man. Moreover, it marks a shift within the dramatic output of St Enda's from the world of the Celt as Christian artist to that of the Celt as warrior. Where the artistic Celt is associated with the Christian values of service and humility, the Celt as warrior becomes aligned with the masculinized Gael of Moran's Irish-Ireland rhetoric. *The King* may be seen as a piece of writing or a dramatic event, where the boy Celt enters into adolescence through a masculine rite of passage. The boy Celt does not lose his Christian faith but maps it onto the masculine models offered by pagan culture.

The King opens in the grounds of a cloister. A group of boys discuss the rumour that the pagan King is going to battle. As they talk, the sound of the King and his men on horseback passes by. The boys, mesmerized, fantasize about being a king or a warrior. One young boy, Giolla na Naomh (the servant of the saint), says he would rather be a monk than a warrior. Suddenly a beautiful bloodstained young man stumbles out of the woods and begs the Abbot to curse him. It is the defeated King who claims that God has forsaken him because of his evil ways. He begs the Abbot to take his divine right away and bestow it on somebody pure. The monks and boys agree that the crown belongs to Giolla na Naomh, who is 'the noblest jewel in the house'. The boy humbly and obediently takes on the duties of the crown. Clothed in royal raiment, Giolla na Naomh's 'golden head' goes into battle 'like a torrent through a mountain gap' and the enemy retreats. Killed in the fray, his body is lifted up and borne back to the monastery on a bier. Keening women, opportunely close by, flank his body to the green outside the monastery. The King kisses the dead boy and pays homage to his 'white body, since it is [his] purity that hath redeemed my people'. The Abbot gently assures the King that 'this child . . . hath purchased freedom for his people'.

The King suggests that the King and the Abbot are cast adrift from the certainties of childhood. The Abbot is a man of thought and not of action, whereas the King is denied the divine blessing of victory because of his 'polluted hands'. Giolla na Naomh, the familiar golden-haired, self-effacing boy of Pearse's imagination, is neither bold nor fearful. He represents the correct mix of youthful idealism, Christian humility and manly courage that produces the *macaomh.* Leaving the cloisters of childhood he moves upwards, on horseback, into the dangerous male territory of the forest where the reality of battle is taking place. As a symbol of purity and justice he leads the troupe of men into battle and is sacrificed at the crucial moment of victory. Having achieved and lost manhood (through death), Giolla na Naomh manages to combine promise and loss, Christian and pagan, past and future, and boyhood and manhood. The body of the man-child lies not in the closed community of the scholar saints nor in the warrior battlefield but in a pastoral space linking one site to the other.

Ruth Dudley Edwards comments that *The King* embodied three important aspects of Pearse's thought during this period: his 'growing preoccupation with Calvary', his 'reaffirmation of . . . the essential purity of childhood' and the necessity of sacrifice 'to save a decadent nation'.[43] The Christian imagery of the play, the monastery, the liturgical lament and the sacrifical lamb situate it in the tradition of the *Passion Play*, but *The King* suggests that the Irish Christian community exists alongside an older, equally inspirational, culture. Louis Le Roux, Pearse's hagiographer, declared that *The King* illustrated Pearse's 'favourite thesis', that 'authority' retreats when the spirit of the people is aroused.[44] The Christian themes of the play are overshadowed by the pagan iconography of the school's productions. The 1912 outdoor production, in the grounds of St Enda's, took place 'with much pageantry of horses and marchings', which suggests that the battle scenes were more important than the monastery boys at play.[45] The grounds of the Hermitage contained 'Emmet's Fort', apochryphally the site of Robert Emmet's hide-out. This, and a castellated bridge which served as the entrance to the monastery, were put to great visual and dramatic use. The presence of newspaper reviewers at the St Enda's event demonstrates the high profile that the school had in Dublin circles. The *Evening Herald* described it as 'highly creditable' in 'intelligent interpretation' and 'spectacular effect'.[46] The *Irish Times* was generous in its praise for St Enda's contribution to the language movement and was particularly effusive about the location. The reviewer commented that the grounds provided 'a perfect background to a natural stage' and the 'little performers in their traditional Gaelic dress' seemed as if they had always lived in that natural habitat.[47]

The piece was performed again, with some modification for the stage (presumably without horses), in May 1913. This Abbey Theatre production was a fundraiser for the school, which was then in financial difficulties. W. B. Yeats offered the use of the Abbey to Pearse as a particular favour and to show his support for the work of St Enda's. *The King* was performed as a double bill with Tagore's *The Post Office* (1913), which has much in common with the allegorical child-centred narratives of Pearse's dramas. Tagore's play centres around Amal, a seriously ill boy with a sunny disposition and an inquisitive enthusiasm for life. Bedridden, he makes friends with those who pass by – the flowerseller, the watchman, the postman and the dairyman. Like Pearse's redemptive boy-children, Amal, who is an adopted child of unknown parentage, is considered to be mysterious. However, Tagore's Amal is less sentimentalized than Pearse's ethereal boys; Amal is mischievous and good humoured rather than otherworldly. While Pearse's children long to be reconciled to nature, Amal is also drawn to the social world of community and work. He is captivated by the lives of those who pass by his door and offers them an understanding of the value and beauty of their work. From his window Amal can see the King's Post Office and resolutely believes that he will receive a letter from the King, a symbol of God or benevolent death. Eventually he hears word that the King is due to visit the village. As Amal waits, his pain leaves him and he determines to ask the King if he can be one of his postmen, 'delivering his message from door to door'. The play ends as Amal falls into a deep sleep and his little friend the flowerseller places some flowers in his quiet hands.

In this religious symbolist play he reflects Pearse's belief in the redemptive quality of children. They share a simplicity and directness when they write about rural life and both writers use nature as a literary device for human emotion and perception. However, Tagore is a more sophisticated writer than Pearse. His characterization of Amal is less static than Pearse's more one-dimensional children. He avoids the temptation of making Amal, like Íosagán, a manifestation of the Christ-child and consequently his play has greater depth and is more emotionally affective. Although *The Post Office* venerates childhood it is a more descriptive and literary piece of writing than any of Pearse's dramas. Pearse's plays suffer from a moralistic didacticism and sacrifice humour and depth of characterization for homilies on the beauty of childhood. Amal is told that he may ask for anything he wants from the King and when he determines to ask if he can be a postman the bemused frustration of his impoverished uncle is understandable. It is almost impossible to imagine a scene in Pearse's dramas where the parents of visionary children would wish for bread rather than salvation. In this respect *The Post Office* possesses a gentleness and poignancy that is missing from the more pious works of Pearse.

Due to their similar structure and theme it might have been expected that Tagore would favour *Íosagán,* but it was *The King* which he requested permission to perform in India. Pearse felt that *The King* and *The Post Office* were antiphonal pieces and that both writers had 'in our minds the same image of a humble boy and of the pomp of death'.[48] In 1915 a letter to Pearse on behalf of Tagore praises *The King* and quotes Tagore's description of the play 'as the very thing I have been longing for in my school for boys'.[49] Tagore had been sent a copy of the play – probably by Yeats – and the letter describes the Indian production of *The King* at the school's dramatic festival. The play was performed as a double bill with Tagore's *The Spring Festival,* described in the letter as the story of 'a company that lost its way and became conventional and old' but finds 'the springtime of its own youth' in the figure of a blind singer. The Indian performance of *The King* must have been particularly impressive played in native Bengali dress in the Indian moonlight on an open-air stage.[50] Tagore's letter requests permission to re-perform *The King* the following year and also for publishing rights to include the text in a reader he was preparing, which suggests a similar dearth of nationalist educational material for Indian boys.

Pearse wrote one other play that combines Christian and pagan culture. *The Master,* written in 1915, was first performed at Whitsun at the Irish Theatre in Hardwicke Street that year. That occasion also saw the final production of *Íosagán* performed with *The Master* as a double bill. It is an interesting pairing, since *Íosagán* dates from 1907 and is wholly constructed within a discourse of Celtic Christianity. *The Master* on the other hand is a more ambitious play and demonstrates Pearse's increasing militarism. Pearse had joined the Irish Republican Brotherhood in December 1913 at the exhortation of Bulmer Hobson and 1914 marked his deepening involvement and commitment to physical force. During 1914 Pearse published *Songs of the Irish Rebels* (a number of which had already been printed in *The Irish Review*), but *The Master* is the first drama written after he joined the IRB. As a result *The Master* is a convoluted piece of writing which is torn between the passive values of Christian service and a tortured personal belief in the necessity of military action.

The Master was written during a period when Pearse was orchestrating the mystical marriage of nationalism with religion and, as such, the play is deeply conflicted and problematic. Set in an all-male community the action takes place in Ireland at the historical point when the new religion of Christianity co-exists uneasily with an older druidic culture. The play is centred on two characters: Ciarán (played by Willie Pearse), the master of a Christian school, and Daire (played by Eamon Bulfin), a king. Daire has come to Ciarán to ask him to prove the superiority of the new religion. Set in a cloister, the set demands the presence of two arches: one that leads to a forest and sunshine on a far hill and the other which leads to a chapel or cell. Like *The King* the play suggests two psychological landscapes: the interior, private and domestic space of the cloister and the public world of outside. There are also the same two models of masculinity offered in the figures of the scholarly Celt and the military Celt. Young Iollann Beag is the, by now familiar, young boy who is the master's favourite pupil. Iollann Beag is an innocent who praises God by climbing trees and watching birds. He is a child who is understood by the other boys to be special. Ciarán begins to teach the boys the story of Christ and his Apostles, emphasizing the importance of 'friendship and kindly fellowship' between men. Iollann Beag sings a ditty he has composed about Jesus as a boy. Pearse had already published this poem, 'The Rann of the Little Playmate', in the *Irish Review*. The poem is a childish rhyme about Íosa (Jesus) playing 'tig and pooken and hide-in-the-hay' with Iollann Beag. The chorus, 'with an óró and an iaró', is in a gibberish baby Irish and highlights the *naïveté* and simplicity of Iollann Beag. His song is interrupted by the arrival of the King's messenger, who invites Ciarán and the boys to join Daire, the King, for a forest picnic.

Staying behind together Ciarán tells Iollann how he and Daire were once boyhood friends. Ciarán recounts how he travelled abroad to be educated and returned home a Christian and discovered that Daire was King. Ciarán's new Christian beliefs set him against his old friend. Isolated and lonely, Ciarán's faith has begun to waver and he is tortured with self-doubt. Daire arrives at the cloister and the two men discuss the paths they have chosen. Daire pities Ciarán for spending his life 'pursuing shadows' and for squandering his 'noble manhood' in a life of celibate contemplation. Ciarán accuses Daire of leading a life of public aggrandisement and fame, and of being content with 'the little, foolish, mean, discordant things of a man's life'. The dialogue between the two men plays out personal conflicts in Pearse's psyche: the tension between public service and private belief and the integrity of intellectual thought versus the 'manliness' of action. Angered by Ciarán's Christianity, Daire asks for a sign that his religion is true. Fixing on 'the daintily fashioned' figure of Iollann Beag, Daire calls on Ciarán to ask 'God to send down an angel' to save the boy from being slain. Unwavering, Iollann Beag kneels before Daire and calls on the Archangel Michael to save him. The angel, appearing as 'the figure of a mighty Warrior', descends 'winged and clothed in light' and stands before the child. The angel describes himself as 'the Captain of the Host of God' and his words are fierce and vengeful as opposed to the familiar language of Christian service and humility. Daire submits to the angel's superior power, while Ciarán, with his 'faith restored', dies to the sound of 'the thunder of the coming' of the seraphim and the cherubim ringing in his ears.

Ruth Dudley Edwards argues that Ciarán *is* Pearse, uncertain about his choice to reject the obvious temptations of the world, but it could be argued that Pearse is also Daire the King, who fights social injustice and enjoys the loyalty of his community.[51] What Dudley Edwards neglects to address is that the body of the young boy is the conduit for *both* sets of ideologies. The figure of Giolla na Naomh in *The King* dies at the moment of battle victory and the two communities, pagan and Christian, come together over the death of the boy. However, in *The Master* it is Ciarán who dies and Iollann Beag who is left to fuse the pagan virtues of loyalty and manliness with an unswerving faith in a Christian orthodoxy.

Both *The King* and *The Master* leave the boy-child on the brink of attaining full manhood and both plays illustrate the development of Pearse's construction of Celtic masculinity. The figure of the boy is poised between the values of the Celtic Christian tradition and the physical and emotional demands of adolescent manhood. Celtic masculinity cannot be fully achieved in the domesticated space of the cloister and is only partially formed within the crucible of Christian orthodoxy. In *The Master,* Iollann Beag is offered a vision of his future role when the awe-inspiring and physically imposing figure of the Archangel Michael appears to him as a Christian warrior. In *The King,* Giolla na Naomh achieves his finest moment (sealed by death) when he leaves the cloister to become a soldier.

In these dramas Christianity as a rite of passage equips the boy with the language of martyrdom and of mystical faith, but in order for the boy to grow up and move out into the world of political action, he must leave childhood behind. In Pearse's later dramas and political philosophy there is no room for a spritely barefooted *Íosagán,* who signifies redemption and salvation. Instead Pearse draws on the harsher, more elemental, connections between the Irish landscape and the Irish language than the one offered by the pious and sentimentalized boy Christ-child. While Christ may have appeared in Íar Connacht in recent folk culture, there was, as D. P. Moran had always insisted, an older Irish-language tradition rooted in the bardic and pagan past. It was Cúchulainn, the warrior boy of bardic culture who offered Pearse the deliverance of a more robust masculinity than the ghostly redemption of a golden-haired boy-child.

5

Imperial Romanticism: Cúchulainn, Wagner and Heroism

It is difficult to trace the awakening of Pearse's interest in Cúchulainn, since his autobiographical writings suggest that he learned the stories of Irish mythology and history as a young boy from his mother's aunt. Pearse's recollections of his childhood show him to have been an imaginative, highly suggestible boy with a love of high drama. Writing of his childhood home he tells how his playroom was transformed into a landscape of the imagination, where ordinary objects became suffused with meaning and stories from history were re-enacted in its nooks and crannies.[1] According to their own accounts the Pearse children had a happy childhood full of play, storytelling and amateur drama, reinforcing as adults their romantic investment in childhood as a mystical and magical place and their love of theatre as a storytelling device.[2] Pearse writes wistfully of the completion and closure of the childhood imagination, where the 'half-real, half-imagined adventures' of a child are 'fully rounded, perfect, beautiful', unlike the 'real adventures of a man', which often end unsatisfactorily or even ingloriously.[3]

Born in the same year, 1879, that Standish O'Grady published his first volume of the *History of Ireland*, Pearse's childhood and adolescence were concurrent with a popular imaginative awakening to the riches of Irish bardic culture. Pearse was not a native speaker of Irish and did not start to learn the language until he joined the Gaelic League in 1893, so he was dependent, for the most part, on translations of the Ulster and Fenian cycles into English. By 1898, and still only nineteen, he published a series of three lectures on Gaelic culture illustrating his ongoing fascination with Cúchulainn. His lecture on Cúchulainn and the Red Branch cycle, originally read to the New Ireland Literary Society, extolled the excellence of the figure of Cúchulainn as a role model for masculinity and for the Gaelic ideal. Reports of the meeting show that Pearse urged the assembled listeners to recognize 'that the noble personality of a Cúchulainn forms a true type of Gaelic nationality, full as it is of a youthful life and vigour and hope'.[4]

Cúchulainn was a central figure at St Enda's from the very beginning. The end of the first, triumphal, 1908–9 school year at St Enda's was marked by a prize day and open-air pageant. The dramatic spectacle was arranged by Pearse and told the story of how the boy hero Setanta took arms for the first time and became known as Cúchulainn. The pageant made public the relationship between Cúchulainn and St Enda's, a relationship which had already been sealed within the everyday life of the school. Cúchulainn's presence at St Enda's throughout that first year had been made palpable by the visualization of Cúchulainn in a number of different forms. In Cullenswood House the Morrow Brothers' fresco of the boy hero taking arms dominated the front hall, for Pearse thought 'it would be a noble thing to set somewhere where every boy that entered the school might see it'.[5] Around the mural was an inscription encircled in old Irish lettering of Cúchulainn's famous choice between life and fame: 'I care not though I live but one day and one night if only my name and deeds live after me'. The panel, delicately detailed, showed the youth with an uplifted shield and spear poised for imminent battle.[6] The school's exercise books and Módh Díreach lesson charts were also illustrated with the figure of Cúchulainn. The Dundalgan Press in Dundalk published a series of three 'Cúchulainn Charts' (for nouns, adjectives and verbs) as well as a 'Cúchulainn Módh Díreach Reader' and a Cúchulainn primer for teaching the Irish language, all of which were in use at the school (Plate 13).

The symbolic value of a pageant based on the rite of passage of Cúchulainn from boy to man, or at least adolescent youth, was not lost on the pupils of the school. Pádraic Ó Conaire recalls that it was not long before 'we understood that it was Pearse's goal to make every student a Cúchulainn for Cúchulainn was his exemplar'.[7] It was clear from the outset that Cúchulainn was to be a central figure in the school and, each day after religious devotions, Pearse told a tale from the Cúchulainn saga to the assembled school.[8] It is arguable that the daily inculcation of the devotional and the heroic was crucial to the school's investment in mapping Christian themes onto bardic heroic deeds. Stephen McKenna, the sometime editor of *An Claidheamh Soluis*, suggested to Desmond Ryan that Pearse's ideal Irishman would have been Cúchulainn baptised.[9] Ryan himself recalls how the boys joked that the pervasive presence of the Hound of Ulster made him an 'important if invisible member' of staff.[10]

Pearse's overriding desire was that the end-of-year pageant, *The Boy-Deeds of Cúchulainn*, would consolidate the boys' devotion to Cúchulainn and 'crown our first year's work with something worthy and symbolic'.[11] His wish was that his students would 'leave St Enda's under the spell of their most beloved hero, the *Macaomh*', who was, he argued, not only 'the greatest figure' in Irish epic but 'in the epic of the world'.[12] It is noteworthy that the pageant was based on an early event in Cúchulainn's life that emphasized the exuberance and promise of the youth as opposed to a tableau featuring Cúchulainn as a doomed warrior facing overwhelming odds. As a performative spectacle (for participants and audience alike) the effect of the pageant was to visualize Cúchulainn's boyhood and to capture the vigour and vitality of youthfulness. Not only was Pearse anxious to promote 'the knightly words' of Cúchulainn to his boys, but he wished also to inscribe 'the knightly image' of the hero 'in their hearts'. Pearse's presentation of Cúchulainn as the ideal Gael owed much to contemporary ideas of the gentleman as well as of heroic manhood. In one of his earliest lectures on bardic literature Pearse argued that 'true . . . Gaelic nationality' promoted a 'chivalrous love of what was great and noble' and that Cúchulainn and his contemporaries were 'men of noble impulse and elevated inspirations . . . in short, what would be now called a thorough gentleman'.[13]

Pearse's interest in the *macaomh* owes much to his own increasing militarism and his preoccupations with history and heroic masculinity, but his concerns obliquely mirror many of the anxieties expressed by men throughout the nineteenth century. Eamhain Macha, Pearse's fantasy playground, where the boys of the ancient Fianna Éireann lived and were educated together, is a version of the homosocial world of larger society; his desire to recreate the historical community of the Fianna Éireann owes much to the contemporary privileging of male power. As well as seeking inspiration in mythological manhood, Pearse's struggle for the intensification of Irish manliness borrows from the contemporary rhetoric of imperial heroism and the medieval idea of male chivalry.

Towards the end of the nineteenth century, as religious authority declined in England, definitions of manly behaviour became less influenced by Christian guidelines of humility and humankindness than by paternalistic imperialism's chivalric codes of *noblesse oblige.*[14] The English construction of chivalric masculinity owes much to the enduring popularity of Arthurian legend throughout the Victorian and Edwardian period.[15] The figure of the chivalric knight had little to do with historical reality but 'was a reflection of contemporary virtues and values, cloaked in chivalric raiment'.[16] The knightly hero was easily recognized by contemporary Englishmen since the historical figure was considered to embody those ahistorical, atemporal qualities possessed by all Englishmen. As Debra Mancoff notes, 'the hero of revivalist chivalry was not an accurate reconstruction of a past ideal but an icon of modern aspiration'.[17] Joseph Kestner's study of visual iconography and masculinity suggests that the imaging of men as knightly warriors, and the equation of maleness with knighthood, lasted until well after the First World War.[18]

The chivalric code was therefore reformulated to provide a meaningful code of behaviour to 'gentlemen', who were seen 'as the embodiment of bravery, loyalty, courtesy, modesty, purity and honour'.[19] As a model of masculinity it provided an alternative to the Christian/monastic ideal, which privileged asexuality, self-denial and passivity. The chivalric model eroticized men as heroic warriors in its focus on male physical strength, beauty and vigour. Indeed, although the concept of chivalry invokes images of devotion and respect towards women, the chivalric code actually reinscribes male dominance rather than male service. The position of female figures within the visual and literary tradition of chivalry suggests that codes of honour were not played out between men and women but were directed towards other men.

While, for the most part, Irishmen were subject to the same prevailing ideologies of Edwardian manhood that were being circulated in England, there was an argument in place amongst nationalists that the English tradition of medieval knightly chivalry had been corrupted by imperialism. In a 1909 essay on chivalry Roger Casement suggested that the idea of English fair play and justice had been negated by that nation's 'unchivalrous' behaviour towards other nations.[20] 'True' chivalry was to be found in the Irish bardic tradition of the Fianna Éireann, which, after all, was alive in Ireland long before the appearance of English knights. Redefining the notion of chivalry in an Irish context, Casement's essay suggests that Irish boys are the natural inheritors of the male chivalric tradition. 'The purpose of chivalry', he states, 'is to fit the boy to be the man . . . the heart of the boy must find it: the strong arm of the man deliver it'. Casement's shaky historical observation that the ancient Fianna Éireann defended Ireland from the expansionism of the Roman Empire not only suggested that the role of the newly formed youth movement, the Fianna Éireann, was to protect Ireland from British imperialism but fed into contemporary anxieties that the British Empire, like the Roman, was in imminent danger of decline and fall.[21]

Irish nationalists seeking hypermasculine histories of masculinity found in the *Táin* both a literary epic equivalent in content and pedigree to the Arthurian cycle as well as deeds of male prowess of a highly exaggerated quality. The *Táin* provided Pearse with an 'authentic' Irish source upon which to base his school's code of honour. The advantage of the *Táin* was that it predated the Arthurian cycle and therefore any similarity between the chivalric code of the knights and the ethics of the Fianna was easily explained by the pre-existence of the latter. Such narratives from the pagan, rather than the Christian, past inspired the creation of a contemporary boy warrior and helped to form a consensual agreement of what it meant to be both Irish and manly.

The changing accent on bardic, rather than Christian, codes of masculinity was quite literally played out in the dramatic representations of Irish pagan manhood produced by St Enda's. Between 1909 and 1915 four open-air pageants adapted from Irish bardic tales were produced by the school, as well as seven theatrical productions of contemporary plays based on Irish mythology. In 1909 and again in 1910 the school performed an adaptation of Standish O'Grady's *The Coming of Fionn.* Twice in 1910 the boys staged Padraic Colum's *The Destruction of the Hostel,* a play adapted from the legend of Da Dearga's Hostel and the death of Conaire, the High King of Ireland. A pageant on the boyhood of Cúchulainn was performed, as already mentioned, in the school grounds in 1909 and once again later that summer. A few years later a pageant on the incident in the *Táin* which recounts the slaying of Ferdia by Cúchulainn was performed a number of times in the public grounds at Jones's Road (now Croke Park) in Dublin during 1913. An accompanying pageant on the Fianna of Fionn was also performed during the summer of 1913 and again in September 1915 at various military displays, or *aeriðheachtaí,* to raise funds for the Fianna Éireann and for St Enda's respectively.

The popularity of public pageants and dramas on historical themes can be situated within a late nineteenth- and early twentieth-century pan-European preoccupation with heroic masculinity. The content and styling of these productions illustrates how the reconstruction of Irish heroic manhood, organized around the bardic tales of the Ulster cycle and the Fianna Éireann, was indebted to contemporary imperial visual and literary discourses of heroism and masculinity. Karl Beckson has commented on the nineteenth-century fondness for representations of, and treatises on, heroic men. He argues that fears about mob rule surfaced after the enfranchisement of the 'lower' social classes in the middle of the century, consequently giving rise to treatises on the need for strong individuals, leadership and the necessity for heroic male role models.[22] Thomas Carlyle's hugely influential *On Heroes, Hero-Worship, and the Heroic in History* (1840) introduced the concept of the 'man-of-action' as a catalyst in the making of history. In Carlyle's rhetoric, history is not destiny but is willed and shaped into being by visionary men. Carlyle's understanding of history is less dependent on events than on the recording of masculine will. Carlyle's role models included men with social, religious, political, as well as military vision; men like Frederick the Great, Cromwell, Napoleon, and also Rousseau and Goethe.

The influence of Carlyle's writings on the pedagogical importance of history and of heroic role models is evident in the work of Standish O'Grady.[23] O'Grady's work was central to the popularization of Irish mythology in the late nineteenth century. Æ called him the 'Father of the Irish Literary Revival' and credited him with unleashing Irish folklore into the popular imagination.[24] F. S. L. Lyons argues that it was O'Grady's 1879 *History of Ireland* which influenced Yeats and Æ to borrow from Celtic mythology over the appeal of Madame Blavatsky's brand of eastern mysticism.[25] O'Grady is to be credited with popularizing, in novel form, ancient mythologies that were previously the provenance of antiquarians, but he cannot really be said to have 'discovered' Cúchulainn as has been asserted elsewhere.[26] In his introduction to the first volume of the *History of Ireland* O'Grady states his interest in moving towards a more popularly written version of the *Táin*.

If the health of English national culture was a cause for concern in the 1840s, when Carlyle was writing his treatises on history and heroism, then Irish cultural morale in the decades after the Famine and the demise of the Young Ireland movement was in danger of expiring altogether. Although there was European-wide antiquarian interest in Irish culture, there was little public appreciation or knowledge of Irish literary history. O'Grady had stumbled across Irish mythological literature practically by accident and he was quick to recognize, as well as its literary merit, its value in fostering a pride in Irish national culture. O'Grady astutely realized that Irish historical tales and legends would have a far more popular readership than academic manuscripts. The successful 'rescue' of literary history is indebted to O'Grady's reworking and representing of bardic tales in popular and readable forms. His *History of Ireland* was written between 1878 and 1880, when he introduced stories of Cúchulainn to a popular audience for the first time.[27]

Like Carlyle, O'Grady believed in the importance of a national epic which was moulded from the past of a country and of the importance of a central hero driving on the narrative of history. Carlyle's belief in the ability of a hero to transform his age provided O'Grady with a framework for his heroic treatment of Cúchulainn. O'Grady was keen to emphasize the continuity of history and by whittling down the bardic epics he was able to present shortened synopses which accentuated connections between the contemporary and the historical.

O'Grady's sense of the importance of history and historical tradition remained his most abiding legacy within St Enda's. He was a regular visitor to the school and attended the productions of his *The Coming of Fionn* in 1909 and 1910. Pearse's recognition of the potential of mythological and historical narratives for teaching self-control, greatness and patriotism was directly influenced by his reading of O'Grady. The 'loss of manhood' is a recognizable theme in Pearse's writings; a loss caused by alienation from Ireland's heroic past. The physical and intellectual dominance of England over Ireland created an emasculation of Irishmen, who remained in ignorance of the manly role models to be found in Irish literature and history. Whilst drawing inspiration from Ireland's religious past Pearse asserted that the bardic tradition must also form part of a child's spiritual education. The cultural impotence that occurs under imperialism may be subverted if children are taught that 'spiritual religion' may be found in a variety of sources. Defining 'spiritual religion' as 'a preparation for complete life', Pearse argues for the inspirational value of 'the hero-stories . . . of our own people' whilst at the same time revealing the influence of contemporary thinking on the formation of masculine identity.[28] The remasculinization of Ireland, he argues, could only come about through 'a new birth of the heroic spirit' and 'the fostering of knightly courage and strength and truth'.[29] The purpose of St Enda's was not merely 'to restore a national culture' but 'to restore manhood to a race that has been deprived of it'.[30] If Ireland returned 'to her sagas' then the necessary 'hardening' of Irish manhood would be assured.

Pearse's hopes for an enlightened education system are couched, not merely in the language of physical prowess, but in the rhetoric of hypermasculinity. It is not sufficient for Irish boys to grow up with a knowledge of Irish culture, they must also take 'their manful part' against imperialism and with 'lusty strokes' 'hew away' the 'rotten and worm-eaten boards' of the English education system.[31] The 'virile fighting faith' of ancient generations of men must prove to be the inspirational touchstone of the modern education system.[32] 'The Irishising of the hearts and minds' of boys at school and 'the kindling in their souls of the quenchless fire of patriotism' are as important as 'setting before them . . . a great and glowing ideal of *Duty*' and all this can be achieved by returning to the sagas of Irish literature.[33]

Yet for Pearse it was not sufficient that the boys become familiar with the sagas as they were written down but in the actual way of moral and physical life that they espoused. That is to say that the boys not only imbibed and digested the stories of the Fianna and the Ulster Cycle in the classroom but acted them out as pageants and dramas, thereby indirectly internalizing the forms of masculinity promoted within the tales.

While Pearse was keen to resurrect the ancient Irish models of heroic manhood he was enormously impressed by the highly theatricalized models of masculinity on display in the operatic works of Richard Wagner. At the turn of the century the popularity of theatrical pageantry, and particularly of epic musical drama, owed much to the influence of Wagner, whose mystical, highly visual, operatic dramas were phenomenally successful across Europe in the late nineteenth century. Some of the popular success of Wagner's work in England during the latter half of the nineteenth century can be attributed, in part, to the status of Germanic culture amongst artists and intellectuals and an admiration for the heroic models of Teutonic masculinity.[34] Saxon, Teutonic and Nordic culture offered male, semi-mythical, role models considered as endangered within English cultural life. The scholar Walter Houghton explains the interest in medieval legend and Greek, Norse and Celtic mythology as crucial to the century's preoccupation with heroic masculinity as symbols of power and beauty. Houghton notes that, in a period of increasing secularization, it was heroic legend, associated with nature and great men, which was 'welcomed as another manifestation of the divine spirit working in the world'.[35]

Wagner's work drew European-wide attention to the Germanic and pagan roots of Celticism. As a student of medieval literature Wagner had become familiar with Celtic sources drawn from Cornwall, Wales, Brittany, Ireland and Northern Germany. For example, the sources for his opera *Tristan and Isolde,* first performed in Munich in 1865, may be traced to his interest in Celtic medieval literature.[36] William Morris's trips to Iceland in the 1880s and his translations of the Icelandic epics, *Volunga Saga,* and the Germanic *Das Nibelungenlied* did much to popularize Nordic myth and literature in England and Ireland during the 1880s and 1890s and capitalized on Wagner's growing European reputation.

Wagner had already produced a version of the Germanic myth of Nibelung's Ring, mixed in with some legends from the Scandinavian *Edda* and mythological stories of the Norse gods and heroes. The resulting series of operas, *Der Ring des Nibelungen,* were first performed as a complete cycle in Bayreuth, Germany, in 1876.[37] The late-nineteenth-century interest in Celticism has already been discussed in relation to the influence of Celtic Christianity on art forms and indigenous design. However, Wagner's pan-Celtic musical dramas created a forum for the public expression of national identity in the highly visual form of dramatic pageantry. Heroic narratives or national sagas came to be understood as containing essential truths about indigenous culture and proved useful teaching tools within nationalist education. They also offered a moral and chivalric code of male behaviour and naturalized the relationship between masculinity and history.

Pearse had long been an admirer of German culture. Louis Le Roux's biography suggests that Pearse was familiar with, and considerably influenced by, the writings of Lessing, Goethe, Nietzsche, Heine and Hegel.[38] Bypassing the model of neighbouring English society, Pearse looked to Germany for pointers on how best to teach patriotism and manhood. In German schools the fact that 'the first duty' of the teacher was 'to foster an ardent spirit of true patriotism in the young' was particularly inspiring to him.[39] Pearse had been involved with the Pan-Celtic movement when it briefly emerged as a force within the Gaelic League in 1900.[40] He was in favour of pan-Celtic exchange and had travelled many times to cultural and educational meetings in Wales, Brittany, Scotland and Belgium while serving on the Educational Committee of the Gaelic League. However, the appeal of northern European culture was not merely in the efficiency of its educational models. Pan-Celticism, and in particular Germanic culture, offered models of romantic manhood which were less prevalent within English cultural formations of masculinity.

The tremendous intellectual and popular appeal of Wagner had circulated a model of national culture that was influential over many Irish nationalists, like Edward Martyn, who is generally considered, along with George Moore, to be the major proponent of Wagnerian culture in Ireland. Some years after leaving St Enda's Denis Gwynn wrote an appreciation of Martyn's place in the Irish revival movement.[41] Gwynn suggested that Martyn had been one of the first to recognize the possibilities of national support for a revival of theatrical art. The founding of the Irish Literary Theatre in 1899 was, in part, inspired by Wagner's success in producing passionate dramas out of Celtic and Nordic myth. Martyn first visited Bayreuth in the

1890s, but the Wagnerian operas *The Flying Dutchman* and *Lohengrin* had been produced in Dublin as early as 1877.[42] Stoddard Martin notes that the cult of Wagner was 'as much inspired by the reputation of the man as by performances of his works'.[43] Excerpts from other Wagnerian works were performed in Dublin during the 1880s and 1890s[44] and Stoddard Martin claims that 'the mystical, pagan and vaguely Catholic' dramas seemed purpose-built for 'the culturally and nationally deprived Irish'.[45] The Pearse brothers both loved opera and operatic drama. Willie 'went to operatic performances as often as opportunity afforded'.[46] Pearse's sister, Mary Brigid, attests to Pearse's admiration for Wagner and recounts how Pearse visited Germany to see the complete *Ring* operas.[47]

Edward Martyn was a much-loved benefactor of St Enda's and it is probable that he regarded the school as an exemplar of how national culture could be produced and proliferated. Martyn had known Pearse since the early days of the Gaelic League and they became good friends when Pearse took on the editorship of *An Claidheamh Soluis* in 1903.[48] Gywnn makes the point that, as Pearse's friends married, he became increasingly close to Martyn and that they shared many romantic and cultural ideas about the importance of boyhood. Martyn is described by Gwynn as having 'an intense love of boyhood' and of 'hating all women with an instinctive, almost perverted antipathy'.[49] Martyn's love of ecclesiastical music and art (he founded the Palestrina Choir in the pro-Cathedral), his appreciation of the high aesthetic of liturgy and Catholic ritual, his commitment to the revival of indigenous Irish musical forms, his desire to produce plays in Irish and his admiration of masculinized heroic narratives undoubtedly influenced the aesthetics of Pearse's romantic nationalism. If there was a possibility for the creation of an Irish 'Wagnerian' aesthetic then St Enda's was the place where it might be conjured into existence.

The *Ring* operas offered a model of the Nordic Viking which, even though very similar to the Anglo-Saxon paradigm of masculinity, was easily incorporated into narratives of Celticism. The Nordic world of testosterone, heroism and death had much in common with the warrior culture of pagan Ireland and similarities between the cultures offered the possibility that the Viking warrior and the Celtic warrior were of the same genealogical mould.

Apart from the pan-Celtic links between northern European and Scandinavian literature and Irish folklore there were other reasons why Nordic culture might have been so attractive to Irish nationalists. There was a dynamic cultural revival in Scandinavia under way by the beginning of the century, especially in Norway, which gained its independence from Sweden in 1905. There is evidence of much cross-fertilization of ideas and influences between Finland and Scotland in the 1890s and early 1900s.[50] William Morris's popularization of Nordic legends are certainly known to have influenced the young W. B. Yeats.[51] In Finland the success of the language movement (switching the vernacular from Swedish to Finnish) impacted on a general revival of Viking culture known as the Dragon Style. At the Paris Exposition in 1900 Finland made a huge impact on design culture and had lasting cultural influence in European art circles for demonstrating how modernity could be combined with a sense of national character. An article in *An Claidheamh Soluis* in 1909 makes reference to the enormous impact of Scandinavian culture on Irish revivalism.[52] The close contacts between the Vikings and the Celts are illustrated by the similarity of artefacts and designs produced by the two cultures; the development of the Nordic Dragon Style formed part of the same late-romantic interest in cultural history which inspired a rise in nationalist consciousness in Ireland.[53]

It is perhaps significant for an understanding of the ideological currency of pagan/Nordic/Celtic iconography at St Enda's that, while both the Viking and the Celt were constructed within the pagan/heroic model of masculinity, it was also possible to assimilate the figure of the Viking/Celtic warrior into a Christian paradigm. For example, the reported meeting of Oisín, son of Fionn, with St Patrick and the co-existence of Viking and monastic culture allowed for a construction of the 'tamed' warrior within Christian discourse. The use and adaptation of Nordic imagery and iconography was most apparent for its 'non-Englishness', yet the Viking, like the Celtic, suggested the possibility of being incorporated into narratives of Christianity (martyrdom and sacrifice). This is especially evident in Pearse's plays *The Master* and *The King,* discussed in the previous chapter, where the primary adult figures are a pagan king and a Christian monk, neither of whom is able to represent, create or articulate a desperately needed new form of society. That task falls to a young boy (the *macaomh)* who embodies the principles of religious martyrdom and pagan warriorship and who is a catalyst for change.

The theatrical and visual spectacle of Wagnerian opera undoubtedly precipitated Pearse's interest in pageantry. Indeed, Stephen McKenna, in a short article for the *Freeman's Journal* in 1909, noted that the medieval form of the pageant was undergoing something of a revival in Europe.[54] Pearse asked for permission to republish McKenna's article and it reappeared in *An Macaomh* in the Christmas 1909 edition. McKenna praised the form of the pageant for its ability to combine great intensity of emotion with 'varied and blended colour costume', 'lyric poetry' and 'the ornate prose of solemn discourses'. McKenna's observation that the pageant as a cultural form could 'gather together the broken threads of our own national history' was directly related to his attendance at the Cúchulainn pageant at St Enda's a few days previously in June 1909. 'The new order' of the pageant, he wrote, was made amply apparent by 'the inspiring presentation of the Youthful Exploits of Cúchulainn' by the schoolboys. Remarking that he had been visibly moved by the 'new generation Gaelic', he suggested that the pageant signalled 'a prophecy of hope' for the scores of spectators present. Complimenting the pedagogical, as well as the inspirational, value of the event, he suggested that similar pageants be staged 'in every town in Ireland' in order to educate a disaffected generation of young men.

The June 1909 production of *The Boy Deeds of Cúchulainn* was performed in Irish but it was primarily a visual, and not a textual, piece. Pearse had extracted the story and modified the dialogue from the event recorded in the *Book of Leinster Táin* as translated and published by Ernst Windisch in 1905. Philip O'Leary notes that the available text of Pearse's pageant differs very little from Windisch's edition and that Pearse's proficiency in German would not have precluded him from understanding Windisch's notes and comments on the text.[55] However, despite the availability of contemporary editions of the saga Pearse was equipped with a broad scholarly knowledge of Irish literature.[56] O'Leary notes that opinion on Pearse's literary knowledge is divided, but those who knew him personally were impressed by his scholarship. Stephen McKenna claimed that Pearse knew his sagas as well as other men knew their arithmetic[57] and, more recently, David Greene has commented favourably on the extent of Pearse's reading in Irish literature.[58]

At the time of the 1909 St Enda's pageant, the story of Cúchulainn had moved from its place as a myth of erudite interest to occupy a central importance within the nationalist popular cultural imagination. After the publication of the second volume of O'Grady's *History of Ireland* in 1880, subtitled 'Cúchulainn and his contemporaries', a number of popular editions of stories from the Ulster cycle appeared on the market. From his study of Pearse's adaptations of bardic tales O'Leary concludes that Pearse undoubtedly had a copy of Kuno Meyer's translation of *The Wooing of Emer*, because he quoted from it more than once.[59] However, Pearse was more likely to have owned Eleanor Hull's edited collection, *The Cúchulainn Saga in Irish Literature* (1898), in which Meyer's translation was republished. Hull was a friend of Pearse and had founded the Irish Texts Society in London in 1899 (an organization devoted to the translation and publication of early Irish manuscripts).[60] Hull, like Pearse, believed in the pedagogical value of having children's versions of Irish myths and legends available and had written to Pearse from London suggesting the possibility of publishing an inexpensive school text on Irish history for distribution through the publishing and educational networks of the Gaelic League.[61] She was also responsible for the editing and publication of a number of children's texts, notably an edition of *Cúchulainn the Hound of Ulster* published in Dublin in 1909 and exquisitely illustrated by Stephen Reid. Lady Gregory had of course published her first popular edition of tales of Cúchulainn as early as 1902 and translations of other sagas and legends in *Gods and Fighting Men* in 1904.[62]

Mary Hutton published a juvenile verse translation of the *Táin* in 1907.[63] Hutton visited St Enda's for the first time in April 1909 and her edition of the *Táin* was enormously popular in the school. One twelve-year-old pupil told her that he was about to read it for the third time.[64] Hutton's book was handsomely illustrated by Joseph Campbell, author of *The Man-Child,* and the bold and forceful pen-and-ink images undoubtedly influenced the styling and costuming of the St Enda's pageants (Plate 14). The popularization of the Cúchulainn stories involved incorporating the 'ancient' into the realm of a national popular culture. The 'cult' of Cúchulainn may be placed within a contemporary European-wide enthusiasm to make an ideological statement about national identity through visual or literary material. The reproduction of the stories and image of Cúchulainn within nationalist popular culture is indicative of the way in which 'the ancient' is recreated or reworked into public forms such as badges, statues, medals, postcards and pageants.[65]

As a consequence of their popularization the bardic tales became somewhat sanitized. This was an inevitable side-effect of the larger modernizing project of nationalism that sought to promote a unified or cohesive 'national culture'.[66] The 1909 Cúchulainn pageant is a case in point, since it was not only an abridged version of the literary event but it was conceived as an instructional public spectacle of the work of the school. The programme that accompanied the performance of *The Boy Deeds of Cúchulainn* summarized the story for those members of the audience who were unfamiliar with either the legend or the Irish language (or both). It carries quite an extensive description, running to three closely printed pages, written in English by Pearse. Given the acoustically challenging circumstances of producing a play out-of-doors, the programme may be considered as the text to a type of moving tableau vivant. Each act in the three-act piece was introduced by a chorus who, after the style of Greek drama, recounted the incidents that were to follow. The combination of the chorus and the explanatory programme notes further contributes to the importance of the visuality of the piece. *An Claidheamh Soluis* reports a picturesque 'procession of chieftains, warriors, druids, monks, musicians, boys and noble women' moving through the grounds.[67] The six women had been borrowed from St Ita's School for the day.

The first act of the pageant tells the story of the arrival of the boy Setanta at the royal enclosure, Eamhain Macha, in Ulster. The boys invite Setanta to join their game of hurling and he plays magnificently. After the game an argument breaks out between the boys drawing the attention of the King, Conchubhar Mac Neasa, to the playing field. The King asks the boys to look after Setanta and he requests the boy 'to place himself under their protection'. Setanta refuses and asks the boys to come under *his* protection. The boys agree and Setanta then reveals his royal lineage: he is the King's nephew. Welcomed warmly, he is carried into the King's house.

The second act tells the story of how Setanta came to be called Cúchulainn. On a visit to his friend Culann's house, the King arranges for Setanta to join him but on the evening of his expected arrival forgets that he is due. Hearing a sound outside, and fearing intruders, Culann's dogs are let loose. Suddenly remembering Setanta, the household fears that he has been killed by the dogs. However, Setanta appears, unhurt and unafraid, having killed the dogs with his bare hands. Setanta earns the name Cúchulainn (Hound of Culann) because he offers to train new dogs and to act as Culann's hound until the dogs are ready.

The third act records the day on which Cúchulainn took up arms for the first time. Cúchulainn overhears the druid prophesying that 'the youth that taketh arms today will be famous above all the heroes of Éire but his life will be short and fleeting'. Cúchulainn requests arms from the King but all of the weapons splinter and break until the King offers him his own. Cúchulainn is sworn in as a warrior, takes the King's chariot and drives a victory circuit around the royal green saluted by the entire Boy Corps of Eamhain Macha. Leaving the royal household Cúchulainn sets out for battle to prove himself a man. Two days pass and Cúchulainn returns, 'a solitary chariot hero' drawing close 'terrifically'. The pace of his chariot 'is as the pace of the pure cold wind' and the chariot is full with 'the swords and spears and shields of warriors'. Despite having achieved manhood, he is described as 'a small, dark, sad boy, comeliest of the boys of Eire'. The company come out to greet Cúchulainn and welcome him home as a hero and a warrior.

There are some important differences between Pearse's *Boy Deeds* and versions in Irish manuscripts. Most obvious is the fact that Pearse's version omits certain incidents which are unflattering to Cúchulainn. On his arrival at Eamhain Macha Cúchulainn is said to have killed fifty members of the Boy Corps and to have murdered a servant who woke him up too early. O'Leary notes that Pearse's modifications of the *Book of Leinster Táin* involve a rejection of 'episodes which present Cúchulainn in a negative, especially an excessively violent light or which are marked by the crude exaggeration or an unnecessary venture into the supernatural'.[68] For ease of performance and for stage management purposes many of the incidents central to the tale of Cúchulainn happen off-stage: for example, the fight with Culann's hounds and the rite-of-passage fighting with the enemies of Ulster wherein Cúchulainn proves his manhood. O'Leary wryly notes that Cúchulainn was supposedly greeted by a troupe of naked women on his return to Eamhain Macha and that Pearse's unwillingness to be true to the text was understandable in the presence of an excitable adolescent cast.[69] However, there are other changes in the pageant which are less obviously necessary. On Cúchulainn's arrival at Eamhain Macha, Pearse has the boys invite him to join their hurling. In the *Book of Leinster Táin* Cúchulainn interferes without being asked and shows considerable arrogance to the boys. In the pageant Cúchulainn accidentally overhears the druid Cathbadh's prophecy, whereas in the original texts he obtains this information by lies and trickery.

For a school which placed such a premium on chivalry and honesty it is hardly surprising that the less savoury aspects of Cúchulainn's life story were expunged from Pearse's version of events. Despite the plethora of English juvenile fiction and pedagogical literature for boys which promoted the concept of national fidelity and honour,[70] Pearse insisted that St Enda's was influenced, not by contemporary society, but by the ancient code of the Fianna Éireann, also known as the Boy Corps of Eamhain Macha. The boys of St Enda's, he proclaimed, were inspired by 'the noble tradition of the Fianna' and their oath that 'we, the Fianna, never told a lie, [and that] falsehood was never imputed to us'.[71] It was therefore not merely desirable, but essential, that the figure of Cúchulainn was beyond reproach.

The *Boy Deeds of Cúchulainn* was performed again in 1909, when Sir Henry Bellingham invited the school to perform at a summer *feis* in Castlebellingham in County Louth. It was a moving occasion for Pearse, since the pageant took place within the landscape 'that Cúchulainn once knew as a boy'.[72] Recalling it as 'the most spacious day' at St Enda's he had yet experienced, Pearse recorded his memories almost eighteen months after the event. The pageant was evidently still fresh in his mind, since his description is vivid and colourful. He recalled 'the march of the boys around the field in their heroic gear' and 'the sun shining on comely fair heads and straight sturdy bare limbs' all infused with 'the buoyant sense of youth and life and strength that were there'.[73]

Photographs of the 1909 production of *The Boy Deeds of Cúchulainn* show the *macaomh* played as a very young boy. It is unclear whether this was to illustrate the vulnerability and slightness of Cúchulainn and the enormity of his task or that an aesthetic decision was made to cast a particularly beautiful child. Cúchulainn was played by Frank Dowling, one of Pearse's favourite pupils, and whom he describes as embodying 'in face and figure and manner' his personal ideal of the boy hero. The boy who was chosen to play Cúchulainn had to be able to communicate Pearse's vision of the *macaomh* as a 'small, dark, sad boy' who was the 'comeliest of the boys of Éire'.[74] However, Dowling was called upon to play more than the part of the boy hero, since, in Pearse's vision, Cúchulainn represented the very essence of masculine boyhood. Distilled in the figure of Cúchulainn was 'a boy's aloofness and a boy's mystery', 'a boy's earnestness . . .

and a boy's irresponsible gaiety'.[75] Although it is evident that, for Pearse, Cúchulainn was not merely a mythological figure, he was not merely a boy either. Cloaked in the exquisite form of a boy, Cúchulainn, like Íosagán, was 'unsuspected for a hero' by those who encountered him daily. It was only 'in his strange moments of exaltation' when 'the hero-light shone above his head' like the Christ-child's halo, that his peers recognized him as an heroic 'radiant figure'.[76]

Pearse's investment in Cúchulainn, and particularly Frank Dowling's representation of the hero, is made explicit in the production and circulation of photographs of Dowling as the boy hero. Unlike other photographs of the outdoor pageants in circulation the pictures of Dowling are studio shots. Originally printed in *An Macaomh* the photographs were made into postcards and contributed to the popularity of St Enda's within nationalist circles. There are two shots of Frank Dowling. Both show him posed as Cúchulainn but the first is a full-length portrait of the boy against a tree (Plate 16). Holding a hurley he looks out of the frame with composure but with an air of vulnerability and youth. He is dressed in a short dark tunic with white sleeves and a hood that suggests the aristocratic birth of the child. However, the densely wooded backdrop suggests that the child is placed in an atemporal and ahistorical space: the timeless landscape of ancient Ireland. Placing his foot at the bottom of a huge tree the child is illuminated by a shaft of light in an otherwise dimly lit wooded area. The photograph is more than an image of Frank Dowling posing as Cúchulainn; he is presented as a visual link between contemporary and ancient Ireland. The second photograph is a head-and-shoulders, three-quarter profile of Dowling looking off camera (Plate 15). He seems to be dressed in the same costume, with a *brat* securing a white-hooded cloak.

The second photograph, perhaps because of the close-up, makes Dowling look much older than the isolated and rather lonely figure he appears to be in the first photograph. The second image shows Dowling more clearly to be a dark 'comely boy' but, situated quite low within the frame of the picture, his figure appears weighed down by the blackness of the backdrop. This is undoubtedly an intentional framing designed to illustrate the gravity of the life mapped out for Cúchulainn. Photographs of Frank Dowling as Cúchulainn are not merely images of a boy actor posing as a mythical hero, nor are they representative images of the importance of Cúchulainn for a generation of schoolboys, they are images which suggest that Frank Dowling (as a representative St Enda's boy) and Cúchulainn, the legendary *macaomh,* are one and the same thing.

Yet history has determined that it is the body of Pearse, and not that of a St Enda's boy, that has become interchangeable with the body of Cúchulainn. Pearse's death in 1916 was linked in public memory to Cúchulainn through Oliver Sheppard's famous bronze statue of the dying warrior-hero. Sheppard's work, modelled between 1911 and 1912, now occupies a central position in the window of the GPO as a memorial to the 1916 Rising. By 1935, when the statue was installed, the figures of Pearse and Cúchulainn were undeniably linked within the public imagination, to the extent that Cúchulainn's bravery in the face of death was mapped onto Pearse's 'finest moment'. At St Enda's, tales of Cúchulainn tended to focus on his life as a boy-hero, a sportsman and as a daredevil soldier, rather than on his martyrdom and death. While the image of Cúchulainn remained popular, after 1916 it lost its association with imagination and energy, *joie de vivre* and a certain boyish mischieviousness. The potency of Cúchulainn's image as adult heroic martyr (rather than as boy hero) is absolutely linked to the death of Pearse. Arguably the legend of Cúchulainn was mixed into popular narratives on the modern heroes of the Rising, which erased other, more childish, representations of his life.[77] The boyish, life-affirming figure of the adolescent *macaomh,* so familiar to St Enda's boys, gave way, after Pearse's death, to more adult representations of sacrifice and martyrdom.

6

Literary Revivals: Dramatic Histories for Boys

Part of the urgency which drove Pearse back to the sagas of ancient Ireland for inspirational tales of boyhood was a concern, expressed within the larger nationalist community, about the effects of English culture and publications on young adults. Although juvenile and popular editions of the legends and deeds of Cúchulainn and the Fianna were in circulation, there was an awareness that the imaginative interests of large numbers of boys were being met by English stories and comics.[1] It was not the popular content of these Boy's Own adventure stories that worried vigiliant nationalists but the fact that they tended to promote allegiances to Empire.

Between 1900 and 1916, a period which covers the germination of the imagining of St Enda's as well as its coming into being, there were quite literally hundreds of references within the popular nationalist press on the infecting taint of English culture.[2] While most of these anxieties were directly related to the diminishing status of the Irish language, many were linked to the lack of any indigenous, contemporary popular literature for children. The sagas and legends of Ireland provided rich historical material but lacked the attractions of modern tales which reflected boys' lives back to them in small and imaginative ways. The lack of an Irish-based literature for boys (not even especially nationalist) was highlighted by Father Stephen

Brown, who published lists of suitable reading material for children in 1916.[3] Home-produced Irish stories for boys were transparently borrowed from the existing models of English literary culture. Studies have shown how concepts of Englishness and ideals of imperial behaviour were well established within children's literature.[4] In nationalist Ireland there was no such corresponding literature to appeal to the sentiments and spirit of Irish boys. The Gaelic League did have a commitment to the publication of children's literature of a specifically Irish nature, but, as already argued, the need for a nationalist canon was only partially fulfilled by the publication of sanitized and expurgated versions of bardic tales. The domination of the junior market by English historical fiction and English school stories necessitated the wholesale importation of English story lines and plots by Irish writers, illustrating, once again, nationalism's cultural appropriation of imperial forms.

Father Brown's main criticism of Irish literature for children was its lack of excitement and storytelling. He pointed to the number of English books containing spy stories, detective fiction and school tales. The lack of 'boy-scout literature', 'tales of the war', 'thrilling German spy stories' or tales of the 'army and navy and the merchant service and of the sea in general' meant that Irish boys were excluded 'from whole realms . . . into which the imagination of our young folk would gladly adventure'.[5] Irish magazines and periodicals for boys such as *Young Ireland* and *Our Boys*, and others which appeared in adult publications like *The Shamrock, The Irish Packet, Ireland's Own* and *The Catholic Bulletin*, were no match for English comics. The illustrations and adventure tales in weekly magazines such as *Boys of the Empire* (which ran from 1900 to 1903), *Boy's Friend* (1907–1909), the *Boy's Own Annual* (1880–1906); as well as *Chums* (1890–1913), the *Magnet* (1908–1914) and *Marvel* (1900–1922) made them infinitely more interesting publications than their Irish counterparts.[6] To what extent they were available in Ireland is unclear, but they were certainly in circulation.[7] Pearse attempted to bridge the gap between the popular, but imperialist, form of the adventure tale for boys and the perceived need for Irish-Ireland subject matter. While there were a number of beautifully written and illustrated books on Irish mythology in circulation, there remained a shortage of modern stories for children.[8]

In 1905 Pearse published an adventure story, *Poll an Píobaire* (The Piper's Cave), in serial form over three issues of *An Claidheamh Soluis*. The story was written under the pseudonym of Colm Ó Conaire, since at that time Pearse was also the editor of the newspaper. It was later republished as *An Uaimh* (The Cave), since some mischievious native speakers had drawn attention to the fact that the original title was open to the more crude translation of 'The Piper's Hole'. The tale follows the adventures of two boys who spend two days and nights exploring a cave off the west coast of Ireland. Pearse's story is similar in style and content to those adventure stories for children written by Standish O'Grady. O'Grady had already published two contemporary novels for boys: *Lost On Du Carrig: Or 'Twixt Earth and Ocean* (1894) and *The Chain of Gold: A Boy's Tale of Adventure* (1895), as well as three historical novels, *The Coming of Cuculain* (1894), *Finn and His Companions* (1892) and *The Flight of the Eagle* (1892), which was based on the adventures and boyhood of Red Hugh O'Donnell.[9]

Pearse's prolific output for children has been praised for fostering a contemporary awareness of the importance of national identity in children's literature.[10] Certainly Padraic Colum's book for children, *A Boy in Eirinn* (1913), echoes the simplicity of Pearse's narrative and the use of Ireland as an emotional, as well as a geographical, terrain.[11] Complemented by Jack Yeats' illustrations, the book acknowledges Colum's debt to Pearse in its dedication 'To a Teacher of Irish Youth, P. H. Pearse'. The boy hero of Colum's story is named after Finn McCoul (*sic*) and legends of the ancient warrior are interspersed throughout the tale as successive characters in the narrative tell stories from the past. Aimed at a readership of between seven and eleven years of age, *A Boy in Eirinn* is an action-packed narrative which continually switches from past to present and from adventure story to historical fiction, and for the discerning reader it includes a visit to a school suspiciously like St Enda's.

In 1915 Pearse tried his hand at writing an adventure of school life based in Ireland. His tale, *The Wandering Hawk,* was published in a monthly newspaper, the *Fianna,* between February 1915 and January 1916. A broadsheet newspaper, the *Fianna* was sold as 'a journal for men and boys' and was plainly a nationalist version of the popular papers for children that were available in England. In an early edition the paper proclaimed that it had been specifically established in opposition to English juvenile monthlies and weeklies.[12] The paper carried spy stories, fictional tales of boyhood heroism, tales of boy heroes in Irish history such as 'The Boys of Wexford' as well as tales of boyhood ingenuity in the French and American revolutions. The content of the *Fianna* promotes life as an uncomplicated masculine adventure for young men.[13]

The Wandering Hawk is set in a school, St Fintan's, which is recognizably St Enda's. Pearse used the names and nicknames of many of the school's teachers and pupils for the leading characters of the story.[14] He appears himself, somewhat ingenuously, as 'Old Snuffy', the rather doddery but well-meaning headmaster. *The Wandering Hawk* quite obviously tries to map a nationalist setting onto a standard format. The eponymous 'Wandering Hawk' is a Fenian teacher who inspires the students with his tales of Irish history and nationalism. Historically the 'wandering hawk' or *seabhac,* was the name given to the nineteenth-century Fenian revolutionary, James Stephens. The 'hawk' of the story is called John Kilgallon, named for an actual teacher at St Enda's during the school year 1915–16. Kilgallon, an American, later gained some notoriety in the GPO in 1916 when he appeared dressed as Queen Elizabeth I after raiding the waxworks in Henry Street.[15] *The Wandering Hawk* remains unfinished, but its lively, if rambling, narrative follows the adventures of four boys who conspire to protect their Fenian schoolmaster from the police. With considerable ingenuity, bravado and the tacit approval of Old Snuffy, the boys outwit the police on a number of occasions and secure the escape of John Kilgallon. *The Wandering Hawk* is engaging and energetic, perhaps because it was modelled on the daily life of St Enda's; it certainly lacks the stiffness and piety which mark so much of Pearse's earlier writings for children.

Pearse's writing provided the nationalist literary canon with a number of unlikely boy heroes and revolutionary schoolboys. However, despite the best efforts of the writers of popular childrens' books, it was clear to Pearse, and O'Grady, that it should be Irish history, and not pseudo-imperial adventure stories, that proved inspirational for young men. However, part of the problem of using the ancient legends was their very historicity and their form of expression. Despite the reissuing of updated and richly illustrated versions of the Ulster and Fenian cycles, the stories remained school-bookish and text bound when compared to the thrilling spy stories of *Boy's Own.* Pearse's talent for reinventing the past, as already discussed in the case of Cúchulainn, coupled with his knowledge and familiarity with boys' literary culture, made possible the re-presentation of history in the form of an adventure story. Pearse's imaginative coup was to rewrite the stories and tales of the Fianna and Cúchulainn into living pageants performed by the boys of St Enda's. The stories of the Fianna Éireann had particular currency for contemporary boys' culture, not only because of the reissuing of the tales, but also because of the newly formed youth movement, the Fianna Éireann, in 1909. Therefore the St Enda's pageants on the stories and legends of the Fianna were more than historical retellings; they were a reminder of the authenticity of the ancient Fianna Éireann at the same time as being acceptable within the contemporary popular themes of boys' heroic stories. More importantly, however, for Pearse the open-air Fianna pageants provided a public profile for St Enda's through which he was able to display the visual and historical continuity between ancient and modern Ireland. The boys at St Enda's provided a form of nationalist spectacle by which the heroic became, quite literally, played out and performed and where the boys were collectively understood to represent a living link, not only to the past, but also to the future. To this end the St Enda's pageants created a consensus of understanding of what it might mean not only to *be* Irish, but to *become* Irish.

Pearse had long identified the histories of the ancient Fianna as worthwhile material for lessons on Irish identity and as exciting boyhood tales. In the newly launched *Fianna Éireann Handbook*, first published in 1909, Pearse wrote an historical essay on the moral excellence and physical bravery of the ancient Fianna under the captainship of Fionn, the warrior poet.[16] The Fianna motto, taken from the Irish, reads in translation: 'Strength in our hands, Truth in our tongues, and Purity in our hearts'. For Pearse the motto represented 'the starkness of the ancient world', where every man was 'an efficient soldier' for spiritual and earthly justice.[17] Accordingly every child must learn what it means 'to fight . . . his own, his people's, and the world's battles'.[18]

The Fianna motto seemed, to Pearse, to encapsulate the essentials of manly behaviour and he adopted it as the St Enda's motto. The motto, with its emphasis on strength, truth and purity, offered not only a moral code but a guiding principle on how St Enda's should be run. The moral virtues and ethics of the ancient Fianna were wholeheartedly adapted by St Enda's, although Pearse failed to acknowledge that the principles of sportsmanship, self-discipline, fair play and chivalry were prevalent within imperial public-school systems. Whilst the 'strength of hand' of the boys was best illustrated by the school's reputation for sportsmanship, Pearse understood the phrase 'to cover much, in many places and by divers ways' of being men.[19] For a man who had always placed a high premium on truthfulness the Fianna's dedication to 'truth on our tongues' was particularly important to Pearse. His instinct, perhaps naïvely for a headmaster, was to believe that a boy was essentially a truthful being and he celebrated the fact that he had only ever chastised one pupil for dishonesty in his entire career at St Enda's.[20] Willie Pearse 'often remarked that his brother was never deceived in trusting to [boys'] honour'.[21] To illustrate the rigorous honesty of the boys Pearse told a story of asking a pupil why a St Enda's boy should never tell a lie. The prompt answer pleased him: 'because the Fianna never told a lie'.[22] A past pupil, Kenneth Reddin, recounts that 'the discipline at St Enda's was good' and functioned by 'enshrining the Triple Vow of the ancient Fianna'. 'You were not watched, or kept under constant observation' at the school, he recalls, but instead 'were put on your honour', so that as schoolboys they, in effect, monitored their own behaviour.[23] Pearse was proud of the fact that many times his boys came to him 'spontaneously [and] confessed faults and asked to be punished'.[24] Desmond Ryan's recollections of his schooldays suggest that the boys upheld a rigorous moral code amongst themselves in a type of suzerainty which had control over internal affairs but which was overseen by an adult authority.[25] 'Pearse's very presence . . . was a discipline in itself', writes Ryan and recalled that the headmaster rarely had to resort to corporal punishment, as the authority of his figure was enough to silence a room.

The concept of a self-regulating 'child-republic' was an echo of a similar order of self-rule within the Boy Corps of Eamhain Macha (also evident within the monastic model), whereby the central authority (the headmaster) and his aides (prefects, monitors, class captains) were allocated roles within the community. Consulted as to curricular change, internal organization and work schedules, the pupils were invited to elect their own leaders at the beginning of the school year. The offices of School Captain, Vice-Captain, Secretary, Librarian, Keeper of the Museum, Captains of Hurling and Football and a House Committee were open to senior pupils for election. Ryan recalls that they were allowed to shape 'the internal government of the school' and that the annual elections were a significant and exciting point in the school calendar conducted with great decorum and operating 'as an Ireland in miniature'.[26] The motto's third promise, 'purity in our hearts', may be read as a reflection of contemporary Edwardian discourses of masculinity and the influence (and adaptation) of the chivalric model mentioned in the previous chapter.

A very specific example of the way in which the lessons of the Fianna were quite literally mapped on to the structure of St Enda's can be found in two images. The first is of the St Enda's school motto, the wording taken directly from the Fianna (Plate 17), and the second is an image of Desmond Carney playing the part of Giolla na Naomh in Pearse's *The King* (Plate 18). As previously discussed, *The King* is one of Pearse's plays which manages to combine Christian martyrdom with pagan heroism. However, the image of Carney bears few Christian iconographic references and suggests a pan-Celtic influence. The winged helmet and the shield is a recognizable feature of the La Tène Celts who originated in Northern Germany in the sixth century BC. The image also owes much to the visual influences of Wagnerian romanticism. Carrying a sword by his side, the image of Carney is intended to represent that moment in the play where the young adolescent takes on the mantle of the defeated King and valiantly faces battle, his coming to manhood and his own death. The photograph, in style, costume and position, is almost identical to the school crest and motto, which shows a Fianna warrior in full battledress. The overlapping images suggest that Carney quite literally embodies the historical, and perhaps mythological, reality of the Fianna Éireann and produces a contemporary reading of the Irish warrior body.

The highly moral and principled nature of the pagan Fianna oath, and its adapation as the school's Christian motto, informed the choice of tales from the Fenian cycle to be performed as pageants and plays. They had to be morally edifying yet physically thrilling, indeed as thrilling and exciting as any *Boys' Own* adventure story. There was, as ever, an attempt to create a continuum between the ancient and the modern and the Christian and the pagan. For example, Standish O'Grady's *The Coming of Fionn* was presented in March 1909 as a double bill with Douglas Hyde's Christian morality drama, *The Lost Saint.* A newspaper review of the evening commented on the clash between the contemporary and the ancient and observed that the purpose of the evening was to bring 'the native Irish thinking mind' 'into contact with modern culture'.[27]

The staging of the *The Coming of Fionn* was a big event at St Enda's. Standish O'Grady was a good friend to the school and a man of high standing within the nationalist community. *The Coming of Fionn* was initially written as the first episode in O'Grady's *Masque of Fionn.* It had been performed previously, probably in Kilkenny, between 1898 and 1901, when O'Grady was editor of the *Kilkenny Moderator*, and it had certainly been performed in Kilkenny in 1907, before featuring at St Enda's. At the time of the school's production the play had never been published, although there were a few copies in private circulation that might have been printed for the Kilkenny performance. Pearse's programme notes summarize the background to the masque. The Fianna Éireann had been divided by a blood feud between rival factions from Connacht and Leinster. Cumhall, a son of the chief of the Clann Baoisgne, had been murdered by a man from the enemy Clann Morna. In retaliation the chief of the Clann Morna started a war of annihilation against the Clann Baoisgne. Cumhall's brother, Crimall, determined to fight the excesses of the Clann Morna and before Cumhall's death he had prophesied that 'in seventeen years an avenger would arise'. Fionn, the youngest brother of Cumhall and Crimall, had been smuggled out of his father's house at the height of the bloodshed until seventeen years later he emerged as the saviour of the battle.

Addressing the audience before the play, O'Grady himself spoke 'in a ringing, racy speech counselling a return to the manliness of the antique world and life of the Fianna'.[28] He was not merely speaking to the assembled staff and students of St Enda's; the school records show that W. B. Yeats, Edward Martyn, D. P. Moran, Eoin MacNeill and the Count and Countess of Markievicz, amongst others, were in the audience that night. Judging by the reports of the evening, the audience were captivated by *The Coming of Fionn* as a visual spectacle. Padraic Colum noted the lack of 'dramatic speech', which suggests that the play was not especially text-driven, and Joseph Holloway, W. P. Ryan and the reporters for *An Claidheamh Soluis* and *The Irish Nation (and Peasant)* commented favourably on the visuality of the piece. Denis Gwynn, whose father Stephen was in the audience, played Fionn and Eamonn Bulfin, son of William Bulfin, played Cairbre. The popularity of T. W. Rolleston's *The High Deeds of Finn* is visually echoed in the styling of *The Coming of Fionn*, which borrows Stephen Reid's beautiful illustrations of the boy Finn and Setanta in Rolleston's *Myths of the Celtic Race* (Plates 19 and 20). W. P. Ryan felt the tableau to be so convincing that the audience suspended their disbelief and imagined themselves to be part of 'heroic antiquity'.

'Intense and interested as [the boys] were', it was easy, 'without much straining of the imagination', to picture them in Tara or Eamhain Macha.[29] In the production's programme notes Pearse revealed that, for the younger boys at the school, 'Cúchulainn and Ferdia, Fionn and Oscar, are already closer and dearer than any other personages . . . of fiction . . . or history'.[30] Ryan felt that 'the heroic spirit had entered into [the boys'] hearts and minds' as they re-enacted the stories of bardic culture so convincingly. However, when the actors appeared in 'ordinary garb' after the performance, he realized that 'the evening's life and spirit were not something isolated' and that whatever spirit the boys displayed was part 'of a natural continuation' of school life.

Ryan was not the only observer to feel that 'Fionn and Cúchulainn and their high heroic kin had become part of the mental life of the teachers and the taught'.[31] The vividness of the ancient stories was not merely considered to be re-presented, or even re-enacted, by the boy actors but to be reconstituted in a modern form. *An Claidheamh Soluis* reported that Irish civilization 'may be seen in living and natural actuality any day of the week' at the school.[32] The feeling that St Enda's was upholding the very heart of Irish civilization is evident in Thomas MacDonagh's poem *For Victory*, which formed part of the production's programme notes. The seven verses are a thanksgiving to God for his unchanging providence and love for Ireland, but the poem maintains that 'We hold the flag/That our sires held always/And we make new dreams for Erin'. The 'we' of MacDonagh's poem might legitimately be read as the male community of St Enda's (both teachers and pupils), but the last verse suggests that only a child may secure victory for Ireland: 'Sweet little child/To thee the victory/Thou shalt be now as the Fianna'.

The boys at St Enda's, costumed in the garb of ancient Ireland, were considered by the contemporary audience to have successfully blended ancient and contemporary Ireland. One particular photograph, taken in the grounds of St Enda's, illustrates the synthesis which occurs between photography, tradition and the male body to produce a record of the self-constructed *imaged community* of

St Enda's (Plate 21). By a process of elimination, the photograph almost certainly relates to the production of O'Grady's *The Coming of Fionn* in 1909, although I have not been able to prove this. The boys are dressed as the Fianna Éireann, complete with winged helmets, swords and shields. In this they echo the costuming of Denis Gwynn and Eamonn Cairbre in *The Coming of Fionn.* They also mirror the costuming of Desmond Carney in the 1912 production of *The King,* as well as embodying the school's Fianna crest.

The photograph of the grouping in St Enda's is more than a record of a theatrical event: it is an image which abbreviates the complexity of history to a single reading. As is evident from contemporary commentators, the St Enda's boys were not seen to be merely acting out historical stories but were part of the *ongoing* construction of historical narrative. What such images achieve is to condense a particular moment, caught in space and time, and represent it as ahistorical and timeless. What is absent (but implied) from the photograph are the many other 'real' male bodies involved in the nationalist project throughout history. The very presence of the boys in the photograph suggests the existence of an invisible family: ancestors, forefathers, grandparents and so on. However, the photograph also evokes an ideological genealogy placing the boys within an uninterrupted historical continuum of both Irish identity and masculinity. The invisible nation-family of male heroes, warriors, poets and scholars throughout the ages resonates throughout the image.

Studies of popular entertainment during this period have recorded the existence of 'tribal shows' and ethnic tableaux vivants that travelled around England in order to demonstrate the strangeness of racial difference and, by default, the cultural superiority of white imperialism.[33] Such extravaganzas were particularly prevalent after Britain's defeat in the Boer War and may be attributed to a psychological need to uphold imperial morale and reinforce cultural and social confidence. It is unclear whether any such shows came to Ireland, but sensationalist press coverage, commercial sponsorship and popular interest secured enormous public fascination with such ethnic spectacles.[34] The grouping of the Fianna warriors in the grounds of St Enda's visually echoes images of these ethnic displays and suggests the legitimacy of the Irish 'tribe' and of a culture which predated imperialism by centuries. Indeed, in later years, one past pupil described the boys in the photograph as being dressed like 'Boer Warriors', suggesting perhaps that the styling was more influenced by contemporary events in South Africa than by Irish pre-history.[35] The 'native' costuming is discernible in the use of sheepskin, the plain tunics and cloaks of the foot soldier and the leather leg-bindings. The spears and shields are in keeping with artefacts associated with early medieval Ireland. In the centre of the photograph stands Willie Pearse, looking slightly overweight for a manly warrior, dressed in the aristocratic clothing of the day. Overall the impression is of a tribal community of men dressed and armed for war – reinforced by the 'slain' figure in the foreground and the hunched, ready-for-action, soldier in the middle background. The visual styling of the photograph is drawn, not from any ethnic warriors, but from northern European pan-Celticism.

The number of pageants and parades increased the profile of St Enda's throughout the country, although public pageantry within other schools was not uncommon at this time. The St Enda's boys attracted attention even when they were not performing just by virtue of what they, and the school, represented. In 1913, after the Castlebellingham *feis* in County Louth at which the boys enacted *The Boy Deeds of Cúchulainn*, they marched home from the train station. A past pupil described the experience of being part of a contemporary pageant with pipers heading a procession 'behind our school banner of blue poplin, adorned with the gold sun disc of the Fianna'.[36] Some of the students were still in costume and carried battleaxes and 'tall gilded spears which glinted like polished bronze in the lamp-lit streets'. A number of people gathered, curious at the sight of such a throng of boys, and soon the rapidly swelling crowd began to sing a popular ballad about the 1798 Rising as they followed the parade along the road. Thomas MacDonagh was 'delighted at the commotion we had raised' as 'the crowd swelled to the dimensions of a riot'. 'Perhaps they expect us to lead them against the Castle', he proclaimed.[37] The public reading of the costumed boys inspired a collective, and spontaneous, expression of nationalist sentiment, so that the boys came to represent a historical event (the 1798 Rising) as much as a contemporary one. It did not matter that the costuming and staging of nationalist dramas were not historically accurate, since to this select and random audience alike they were understood to be accurate.

In general, even cynical Gaels were moved by the spectacle of the St Enda's pupils in costume. In Sean O'Casey's *Drums Under the Windows* he recalls the St Enda's fête, which took place in Jones's Road in June 1913. The week-long fête was a fundraiser for St Enda's, which at that time was in serious financial difficulties. Each evening the students produced a pageant, alternating between *The Fianna of Fionn,* the tale of 'The Defence of the Ford' from the *Táin* and Pearse's own *The King. The Fianna of Fionn* was not so much a drama as a tableau vivant. Pearse described it as 'a rhythmical march symbolising the activities of the ancient Fianna'.[38] It featured harpers, hunters and singing warriors. There was a more militaristic feel to the occasion than previous theatrical outings in the St Enda's grounds. The pageants were the culmination of evenings which featured the usual Irish-Ireland entertainments, such as pipe bands and troupes of dancers; there is an impressive array of musical talent – including seven choirs – listed in the programme. However, there were also drilling and signalling displays by the Fianna Éireann.

O'Casey admired Pearse's work at St Enda's and had enlisted Jim Larkin's help to print and distribute, five thousand handbills advertising the Jones's Road fête. He remembers torrential rain on the opening night and that the crowds who gathered in the grandstand were 'saturated, gloomy, and low in heart'.[39] Pearse, 'the nadir of dejection', cursed the bad weather for betraying the Gael, while Douglas Hyde, who opened the fête, 'boomed out windy joy' in an effort to raise the spirits of the crowd. A series of disasters plagued the first night: apart from the wind and water there was also fire, when some Fianna boys inadvertently set light to the tented dressing-rooms.

O'Casey's wryly irreverent tone is a welcome antidote to the breathlessly romantic versions of events penned by loyal Gaels. His description of Pearse's encounter with the brazen owner of a 'Tara-ra-boom-de-ay roundabout organ' satirizes the self-righteous indignation of Irish-Irelanders. Carousel music from the organ was interrupting the Cúchulainn pageant, much to the 'agony of the Gaels', and Pearse's request for the organ to be silenced was met with an utter lack of respect for 'Ireland's greatest hero who had the ninety-and-nine gifts'.[40] The impudent organ-grinder, on discovering that Cúchulainn was long dead and had not even known Daniel O'Connell, refused to dim 'the boisterous blare'.[41] However, despite the organ-grinder, the fire and the weather, O'Casey was impressed by the St Enda's pageants and the troupe of boy soldiers parading around the grounds of Jones's Road. Successfully suspending disbelief, 'Sean thought he saw the Men of Eireann, clad in all the colours of the rainbow, marching, their chiefs dashing about in chariots of brass, bronze, and buckskin, shaking spears that entangled the clouds'. Again, as was expressed by so many commentators, there was the feeling that the boys of St Enda's were not merely re-enacting the past but were bringing their audience back in time. Watching the spectacle O'Casey was moved by 'the caoining skirl of the pipes, and the sad rolling of the drum' as the boys marched around the field in their costumes: 'hues of red, brown, green and purple kilts and shawls'. The evening ended in 'a scene of song' that for O'Casey was, 'in colour, form, dignity of movement, and vigour of speech', the 'loveliest thing that had ever patterned the green sward of the playing-field of Jones' Road'.[42]

The visual pageantry of the St Enda's displays was not only consumed as a temporal tableau or performance but somehow managed to become fixed within the nationalist imagination long after the events had passed. O'Casey's vivid memories of evenings spent in Jones's Road highlights the way in which the theatrical efforts of the St Enda's boys achieved an iconic status which isolated and framed the moment like a colourful snapshot or a sepia-tinted photograph of a long past happy event. The St Enda's productions were praised not only for promoting 'a delectable blend of the old Gaelic Ireland and the new' but for creating so effective a spectacle that 'the blending is so happy and natural that no-one can distinguish which is exactly the old and which the new'. [43]

For a modern audience the vision of schoolboys marching in quasi-military formations and dressed in 'tribal' costume is deeply unsettling. Twentieth-century history has meant that any nationalist ritualistic organization of youth is inevitably interpreted according to certain codes and meanings. To suggest that St Enda's consciously promoted a fascist rhetoric would be anachronistic, as fascism as a political movement had not yet emerged at this point. However, the relationship that it promoted between power and display is deeply problematic, as it bears the seeds of many youth organizations that emerged in the inter-war years in Europe. St Enda's claims for the authority and political abilities of youth, its fetishization of the male body through costume and uniform, its interest in iconography and symbols, its attention to discipline and physical exercise, and its invention of an 'authentic' racial past were common features of European youth movements that later became recruited into fascist ideology.

St Enda's secured national identity to the body of the male youth and paraded youthful male bodies as a visual metaphor for the nation state. This practice was reflected in European-wide practices of annexing the 'physical culture' of masculinity to moral strength. Maintaining a healthy and fit body was seen as a way for young men to withstand the depravities and temptations of modern culture, therefore intensifying the perceived relationship between manliness and moral and spiritual superiority. The exhibition of Irish male youthfulness was part of a larger contemporary fascination with mass sports and physical culture across Europe and the United States. While on the one hand the pageantry and parade of history at St Enda's was part of a modern trend, on the other hand it is important not to disavow the sense of historical unease that surfaces when moral righteousness, male beauty and disciplined bodies are presented as being the epitome of nationalist masculinity. Perhaps the point to be made here is that it is too simple (as well as being historically lazy) to label St Enda's as an embryonic fascist organization, yet it is equally important to recognize that the school promoted certain troubling ideologies about the symbolic relationship between power and display. However, the St Enda's project of mapping history onto the present was consolidated by the revival of Gaelic games in the late nineteenth century. The promotion and resurgence of the native sports of hurling and Gaelic football played an important role in carving out a space for a wider Irish cultural renewal, but they also, significantly, provided another arena for the display of male identity.

7

Sport and Physical Culture: The GAA and the Fianna Éireann

The manipulation of athletic activities for social and moral ends was a lesson that Pearse had learned from the Gaelic Athletic Association (the GAA) and imperial youth movements. The GAA had already been in operation for over twenty years by the time St Enda's was founded in 1908. The GAA's promotion of national sports was crucial to ideologies of athletic masculinity which were in circulation at the school. From the outset the GAA had itself successfully mapped an imperialist sporting ethos onto a nationalist model, while the later Fianna Éireann youth organization, whilst ostensibly fashioning itself on the ancient boy troupe of Eamhain Macha, was formed in response to the success of the patriotic English Boy Scout movement. As is evidenced by the history of the GAA, the ability to appropriate imperial forms for nationalist ends was not a talent peculiar to Pearse, but at St Enda's he displayed a particular gift for reinventing modern ideas as ancient Irish ones.

The motivating force behind the foundation of the GAA in 1884 owes much to imperial discourses on the moral and physical health of men. W. F. Mandle argues that the GAA was forced to recognize, consciously or not, that certain 'features of Victorian sport . . . [with] its emphasis on morality, on health, on organisation, codification and competition' had much in common with the social and moral aims of nationalism.[1] The benefits of the discipline of sport had long been recognizable to imperial administrations. Treatises on the redemptive nature of sport were consistently advocated in rhetoric on 'character' during the latter half of the nineteenth century by pedagogues who considered 'the games field as the medium of moral indoctrination'.[2] The collective yet competitive nature of sports coupled with the discipline and rigour demanded of sportsmen promoted sport as a way of teaching rules and systems of organization, creating a fitter yet more disciplined body and creating bonds with local and native populations. Brian Stoddart claims that the contribution of sport to the maintenance of the Empire was impressive, suggesting that sport as 'a cultural bond had considerable force, conveying through its many forms a moral and behavioural code that bonded the imperial power' together.[3]

Debates on the benefits of sport were imported into nationalism as treatises on the benefits of Gaelic sports to physical fitness, morale and community became widespread.[4] Late Victorian ideas of 'character' were echoed in nationalist fears for the degradation and moral lassitude of the native spirit. Furthermore the antiquity of Gaelic games, particularly of hurling, was used as evidence of an Irish dynastic heritage and nationalist genealogy. As Mandle observes: 'Much of what the GAA regarded as distinctive about the meaning of its games was merely the result of the substitution of the word "Ireland" for "Britain" or "England"'.[5] Given the importance of sport in keeping the Empire together and considering Britain's role in the modern development of sport it was only a matter of time before a conflict between 'native' and 'anglicized' sports arose.[6] Mandle's contention that there are many 'uncanny parallels' between the development of sport within the GAA and within the British Empire is borne out by the way in which the meaning of Gaelic games was moralized and heightened, so that it was used as a symbol of national allegiance and the declaration of 'national distinctiveness'.

The GAA's primary aim was not, as is commonly thought, only the revival of Gaelic games, although that was one of the ancillary aims of the organization and later became its central focus. Instead, the GAA was concerned with *access* to sport, particularly for working-class and labouring men, and to promote physical fitness, community values and athletic spirit. Michael Cusack, the GAA's founder, had previously been involved in setting up a number of athletic and hurling societies. A teacher by profession, he ran a well-known crammer's institute, Cusack's Academy, in Dublin and encouraged his pupils to engage in physical exercise in their spare time. Originally from Clare, Cusack had seen at first hand the decline of native sports in the western counties in post-Famine times due to a combination of low community morale, poor physical health and emigration. He was angered and frustrated by the fact that most sporting days were organized by the local gentry, who promoted the more 'genteel' sports of horse-riding and cricket at the expense of athletic competitions and Gaelic matches. The rise of cricket in the 1860s, encouraged by local gentry and patronized by members of the community loyal to the Crown, threatened to overshadow Gaelic games and proved to be a motivating factor for Cusack in founding the GAA.[7]

Cusack was convinced that the dominance of 'imperial' sports was designed to degrade Irishmen by 'inveigling them into varieties of sporting competition in which they might readily be defeated'.[8] In a series of three articles in the *Irish Sportsman*, a leading sporting publication in 1881, Cusack outlined the need for an indigenous, non-sectarian, non-class-biased athletic body.[9] Deploring the decline in 'athletic spirit', Cusack voiced the anxiety that lack of bodily fitness could lead to a fall in public morals. In arguing that lack of public morals would have far-reaching consequences for the nation Cusack was, intentionally or not, echoing similarly stated imperialist concerns. Calling for a central public body to organize local and national competitions, Cusack argued that sport could erase political differences and could function as a bond of unity within a community. He pressed his point that unless communities took regional control of sporting events indigenous sports would be lost altogether.

By 1884 enough public and financial support was in place to found the GAA. However, in the early years after Parnell's death the organization was plagued by bitter infighting. The GAA faltered until the establishment of the Gaelic League in 1893 boosted its membership once again. Many GAA members had joined the League straight away and by the late 1890s there was a noticeable flow in the opposite direction. In many of the smaller towns around the country it was common for the local Gaelic League branch to set up a hurling or football club.[10] Apart from boosting support for the GAA in urban areas, the Gaelic League contributed an administrative expertise, an increased organizational network and an increase in middle-class support. The fortunes of the GAA, administrative and financial, showed a marked improvement from 1901 onwards. The growth of the GAA after 1901 owed much to the popularity of the Gaelic League, which contributed to the increase of the playing of Gaelic games and the popularity of hurling and football as spectator sports, as well as the development of a modified form of hurling – camogie – for women players.

The close links between the GAA and the non-sectarian Gaelic League encouraged a more mixed membership (urban and rural, lay and clergy, male and female, Catholic and Protestant) than had been seen in the GAA previously. The League brought a different kind of member into the GAA. Prior to the establishment of the League the GAA was largely patronized by tenant farmers and agricultural workers in rural areas and by tradesmen, barmen and shop assistants in the towns. However, the League introduced a new stratum of non-manual workers, teachers, civil servants, clerks and local officials, which helped to popularize Gaelic games in urban, middle-class areas.

The growing popularity of Gaelic games meant that it was only a matter of time before the GAA began a campaign to introduce hurling and football into boys' schools. In 1910 the GAA founded a junior league and the success of their efforts can be measured by the fact that in 1911 the first Colleges All-Ireland was played and the Sigerson and Fitzgibbon university cups were established in football and in hurling.

The rules for Gaelic football had been standardized in 1901, but there is evidence that some form of the game had been played in

Ireland since the sixteenth century.[11] The game of hurling, however, held a different place in the nationalist imagination. In hurling the GAA did have an ancient sporting tradition to draw upon and a game which 'need not be pale, or even robust, imitations of the inventions of imperial power'.[12] Hurling was an aristocratic sport and crowned as the 'sport of kings' and was most famously played by Cúchulainn, who supposedly died around AD40. However, legend suggests that the game is even older and that the Battle of Moytura, *circa* 2000BC, was preceded by a fierce hurling game.[13] The game survived in its present form and Marcus de Búrca provides evidence of the game being played countrywide throughout the seventeenth and eighteenth centuries.[14] The decline of 'native' games after the Famine was severe but not enough to drive hurling and football to extinction. The disintegration of local communities, the emigration of droves of young men and an overall slump in physical health and morale were coupled with direct or indirect bans by local authorities and government officials on indigenous games. The reasons varied from the need to discourage insobriety and violence to a fear of Gaelic games operating as a front for nationalist insubordinates. There are other sports claimed as traditionally Irish, handball and road-bowling among them, but none of them had the distinct attractions of hurling.[15]

The importance of sport to cultural unity lies not only within the game as it was played but in the sporting occasion as national spectacle. Sport as physical activity and collective ritual became part of the language of nationalism, as spectator and participator shared equally in the concepts of leadership, heroism and physical strength, all within a national sporting context. As an instructive medium, sport was central in promoting values of masculinity, teamwork and heroism and was perceived to ward off moral degeneration and physical decline.

Whilst the GAA was gathering popularity in Ireland the debate over masculinity and physical fitness was dramatically heightened in England by the outbreak of the Boer War in 1899. Military revelations about the feeble state of men's health and the poor performance of British soldiers in the war shocked the War Office and Members of Parliament.[16] Since 1902 and the end of the Boer War anxieties about masculinity, performance and 'Englishness' were deployed in discourses on health, sociology, the military and medicine throughout the British press.[17] Demoralization after Boer victories gave rise to alarming suggestions that the English race might be physically deteriorating and so the government formed an Inter-Governmental Committee on Physical Deterioration, which published its findings in 1904. Prior to this, British Army reports produced figures which suggested that 60 per cent of men were physically unfit for military service.[18] Figures for any perceived decline in Irish manhood do not seem to be available; in 1907 Dr John Story in the *Dublin Journal of Medical Science* laments the fact that, although there are statistics relating to the physical degeneration of the population at large, there are 'no statistics whatsoever' about the state of Irish physical health.[19] However, Story does cite evidence that Irish manhood was in physical decline; rejections from the British Army had risen dramatically in the early years of the century.[20] Committees and sub-committees of researchers were anxious to contradict widely held beliefs that men were in a state of decline, but the very existence of reports, inquiries and committees was enough to stimulate fears and lend weight to existing anxieties. Evidence of physical decline gave rise to fears of moral weakness and prompted a spate of popular and academic discourses about the need to encourage discipline and moral character in young men.

The anxiety over adult men's health and fitness inevitably focused concern on the calibre of physical instruction offered within schools. In 1900 the Department of Education in London issued a special report on boys' schooling outlining the importance of physical fitness in the formation of manhood.[21] The Board of Education was instructed to introduce physical education into schools in a more formalized fashion and so, between 1900 and 1910, most schools in Britain and Ireland were obliged to provide some form of physical exercise for their students. However, as Story notes, by 1909 a medical study of Irish schools showed there was an almost complete lack of organized physical fitness classes in Irish schools.[22] The perceived need for a physically fit male body was not only for military and labour reasons but as a further indication of a general moral discipline which was necessary for social order.[23] In schools the type of training introduced moved from an apparatus-based programme (the vault, the parallel bars) to a more militaristic exercise programme which included drilling, marching and responding to formation commands.[24] This latter type of training was known as the Swedish Method and was in use in St Enda's under the tutelage of Con Colbert. Since 1890 the Board of Education, in consultation with the War Office, had advocated 'military drill' as a form of physical training, so it was perceived to be impossible to separate military needs from physical training. Quite often the type of physical training in schools echoed that of military training camps, with an increased emphasis on discipline and order.

The establishment of the Boy Scout movement in 1908 in England may be framed within the national attempt to counteract anxieties about the depletion of the agency and virility of English manhood which had been in circulation since the tail-end of the century.[25] It further indicates a shift of energy away from the 'degenerated' adult male body to the formative, and malleable, body and character of the boy. Contemporary concerns with boyhood reveal an oppositional construction of the figure of the boy. On the one hand the boy was inscribed within romantic discourses on the child, which, as already argued, represented childhood as an imaginatively free, spiritually pure, place and was driven by a nostalgic yearning for a pre-lapsarian world. J. M. Barrie's *Peter Pan,* which was first published in 1904, is not merely an example of a romantic narrative about childhood but, more particularly, a narrative about boyhood as a 'Never-Never Land' where adult masculinity (and its attendant tensions) is constantly deferred.[26] However, the end of the Boer War and increased social concern about class unrest resulted in the emergence of the socially deviant category of the boy hooligan. The increase in discourses on hooliganism and spirited adolescence became part of an unstated need to attempt to control, or at least contain, 'boy nature'. The very notion of 'adolescence' as a discrete stage of development did not come about until 1904, when psychologist G. Stanley Hall published his massively influential work *Adolescence* and there emerged a quasi-scientific discourse, 'Boyology', which constructed 'a pedagogy for the making of boys into men'.[27]

'Boy life' became a convenient shorthand for the assumption that control over boys was 'the key to the future of nation and empire'.[28] The tensions between perceptions of the boy as romantic 'other' and as social deviant fixed attention on boyhood as a site of potential disaster as well as of nostalgic longing. Boys needed close monitoring in order to guard against the possibility that they would, like Peter Pan or the Lost Boys, refuse to 'grow up' (i.e. become free-spirited adolescents) and would fail to enter into the world of responsible adult masculinity. The interest in movements which channelled the energies of boys into profitable pursuits, whether it be the GAA or the Boy Scouts, can be understood in broader terms by making connections between the individual body and the collective body. Anxieties about uncontrollable male behaviour were linked to the health of the body politic, revealing how much contemporary society perceived the male body and national collectivity to be one and the same thing. In order to safeguard public morality and national vigour the male body must be morally strong and physically fit. It is no coincidence that it was in the Edwardian era that a vogue for male body-building (the literal 'construction' of the body) became widespread.

The enormous success of the Boy Scout movement as a response to the perceived needs of 'boy life' aroused interest in England and Ireland as well as elsewhere.[29] The *Irish Nation,* in an article in 1909, mused on the possible social benefits which might accrue to the nation if a similar organization were to be formed in Ireland. Whilst acknowledging the physical benefits of the GAA the author nevertheless urged a nationalist version of the youth organization which trains 'youths and men in habits of obedience and discipline, and teach[es] them to honour and glory in the British Empire'.[30] He argued that the formation of a youth organization which might work in conjunction with the GAA would 'draw around them the boys of each district' who 'smoke, loaf about and read penny horribles'. The advantages of such an organization would be to reach boys who 'could be reformed and taught the duties of citizenship' and who would benefit from a youth movement which sought to 'organise them, teach them the glory of perfect health, [and] the dangers of smoking and bad publications physically'.[31] Irish-Ireland's interest in youth movements was particularly informed by the fears expressed in the nationalist press that anglicization, cheap publications and non-Irish culture contributed to the degeneracy of Irish youth.

Lord Baden-Powell wrote to Pearse in 1909 and, acting on Pearse's reputation as a headmaster and pedagogue, invited him to set up an Irish branch of the Boy Scouts.[32] Pearse refused the invitation, declining 'to make potential British soldiers out of Irish boys', but the idea stirred Constance Markievicz to urge the foundation of a parallel Irish Boy Scout movement.[33] On the initiative of Markievicz and Bulmer Hobson the Fianna Éireann was founded and the initial tenets of the organization were declared as the establishment of the independence of Ireland and 'the training of the youth of Ireland mentally and physically by scouting and military exercises, and Irish history and language'.[34]

Margaret Skinnider's autobiography maintains that it was Markievicz who came up with the name 'Fianna Éireann', since their stories 'of daring and chivalry' were those that would best appeal to boys.[35] Called after the ancient *macradh* of Eamhain Macha, the Fianna Éireann was established with a much more military, and ideological, agenda than its English and American counterparts. Along with instruction in scouting, shooting and tracking went nationalist history lessons and political indoctrination. The constitution of the Fianna reveals that the organization was formed along the lines of a political party rather than a national youth movement, since, for example, its members could be court-martialled.[36] The Fianna Song, written by an unnamed Fianna boy, illustrates the evangelical and military slant of the organization. The second verse reads: 'Break the bonds of slavery/O Great God, it cannot be/That Gaels could ever bend the knee/To England, their oppressor'.[37]

The Fianna's objective was 'to re-establish the independence of Ireland' by means of 'teaching scouting and military exercises, Irish history and the Irish language'. Boys swearing into the Fianna had to promise 'to work for the independence of Ireland' and 'never to join England's armed forces'.[38] There was a strict dress code of two recommended uniforms (of Irish manufacture), which functioned to create a visual bond between the boys and to instil a disciplinary pride in individual and communal appearance. The first uniform was a 'kilt uniform' with a dark green kilt and saffron cloak worn over a green jersey, and the second was a 'knicks uniform' of olive-green shirt, navy-blue knicks, and dark-green felt hat.[39] Dress regulations provided explicit instructions on how knives, haversacks and coats should be strapped and carried. The Fianna flag (Plate 22) of a rising sun on a blue background was similar in design to the St Enda's school flag and was ordered to be carried 'on all public parades and demonstrations'.[40] The Fianna badge was a circular brooch with an inset sun pierced sideways by a sword or rapier (Plate 23).

The *Fianna Handbook* of 1914 contains a frontispiece by Constance Markievicz showing a figure of indeterminate sex, which might be either (or both) angel and warrior with eyes uplifted (Plate 24). He, or she, holds a sword heavenward in what might be taken for reverent supplication. The other-worldly figure is poised against a rising sun with a replica sun symbol emblazoned on the chest. The styling of the costume is obviously meant to suggest the ancient Fianna of Ireland, but there is a medieval feel to the image, which is complemented by the leg-bindings, the loose tunic and the crown. The effect suggests a multiplicity of allegorical readings for the figure as youth, as spirit, as nation, as truth, as liberty, as sacrifice and so on. The iconography of the rising sun suggests liberation, but as a nationalist image it could also be read as the sun finally setting on the British empire.[41] The same edition of the *Fianna Handbook* has an illustrated cover of an unquestionably male warrior (Plate 25). Arms outstretched, he stands on the brow of a rugged rocky outcrop and brandishes a shield and a spear. The birds circling overhead and the wind blowing through his cloak contribute to a reading of victorious defiance and a rugged masculinity which is absent from Markievicz's ethereal figure. The combination of the two images underpins the juxtaposition of manly adventure and of nationalist ideology that marks all of the Fianna publications.

The first *Fianna Handbook* of 1909 carried essays by Markievicz, Casement, Hyde and Pearse all outlining different historical and ideological aspects of the Fianna. It was in this handbook that Casement's essay on chivalry appeared. Markievicz's essay carried an appeal to 'the best and noblest of Ireland's children to win Freedom . . . at the price . . . of suffering and pain'.[42] Markievicz's appeal to 'Ireland's children' was, in reality, a call to duty to the nation's boys although she did unsuccessfully agitate for the inclusion of girls into the Fianna ranks. A female organization, Clan Maeve, was founded in 1923 at the instigation of Markievicz and Nora Connolly, daughter of James. Pearse's essay, 'The Fianna of Fionn', is an historical overview of the origins of the movement, with particular emphasis on the importance of continuing the ancient tradition of militarism and patriotism.

The actual instructional content of the *Fianna Handbook* differed little from contemporary manuals used by the Boy Scouts. There were extensive sections on first-aid, drilling, camping, outdoor cooking, knot-tying and survival techniques. Illustrations from the *Handbook* demonstrating the formation of drills and marches are similar to Edwardian scouting representations and do not show boys dressed in either of the recommended Fianna uniforms. The disparity between the energy and virility of the individual Fianna warrior featured on the front cover of the *Handbook* and the uniformity of the 'Company Drill' as illustrated within the *Handbook* is quite striking. The illustration accompanying the instructions for 'Rifle Exercise' features young men dressed in the quasi-military clothing that was familiar throughout European youth movements at this time (Plate 26).[43]

The emphasis on national character, national history and national manliness within the Fianna Éireann was already so deeply implicated in the curriculum of St Enda's that some past pupils later wondered if there had been a branch of the Fianna Éireann at the school.[44] In the 1960s it was officially declared that, whether or not there had actually been an official branch at St Enda's, any boy by virtue of his attendance at the school alone was automatically deemed to have been a member of the Fianna Éireann and was therefore entitled to medals and certificates of service.[45] In fact the school records show that a troupe of the Fianna Éireann was set up in St Enda's in 1910, 'with the object of encouraging moral, mental, and physical fitness'.[46] Eamonn Bulfin and Desmond Ryan, two of the most senior boys, organized the St Enda's boys into a local Fianna Éireann club. They called it 'An Chraobh Ruadh', or 'The Red Branch', after the heroes of the Ulster cycle. Con Colbert had joined the school as the physical fitness master in the autumn of 1910 and he gave his first lessons in 'military foot drill' and code-signalling that November. Colbert had attended the very first meeting of the Fianna Éireann in August 1909 and was later instrumental in recruiting a number of the older boys into the Irish Republican Brotherhood. Among the activities in which the boys engaged were rifle-shooting, boxing, signalling, first aid, drill, ambulance work, mountain marches and gymnastics.

A photograph dating from this period shows Colbert conducting a drilling lesson in the school's optimistically named gymnasium (Plate 27). Colbert, like the boys, is kilted: the boys are dressed in dark kilts and light-coloured jumpers decorated with the school crest, while Colbert is more formally dressed in a brass-buttoned short jacket, which was one of the official uniforms of the Fianna Éireann. The exercises seem more callisthenic than military, since the boys are stretching with their arms behind their heads, but the presence of an uileann piper, and the kilted figures, suggests that the combination of music and exercise was a newly constructed 'native' form of drilling. The kilt functioned as an authentic Irish 'costume' as well as a quasi-military uniform. Parents of the boys were encouraged to dress their sons in kilts (as a 'distinctively national form of dress') or, at the very least, Irish-made clothing. Willie Pearse almost always wore a kilt or some version of 'Gaelic costume' and Thomas MacDonagh and Pearse liked to wear kilts as ordinary wear.[47] Generally, the wearing of kilts by Irish-Irelanders was not uncommon and in his autobiography Frank O'Connor recalls how kilts were objects of sartorial envy, since 'no one could suspect the loyalty of a boy who wore a kilt'.[48]

It is hardly surprising that, as a nationalist youth movement with military overtones, the Fianna Éireann placed a premium on physical fitness and was especially dedicated to the playing of Gaelic games. A 1913 article in the *Irish Homestead,* whilst expressing wariness at the increasing militarization of the Fianna, nevertheless complimented the movement on its historic roots and admired the physical rigour of its regime. Making the by now commonplace connection between physical and moral fitness, the author invoked a nostalgia for the 'models of physical beauty' which were the men of the ancient Fianna.[49] Those 'long-haired warriors, tall, graceful [and] skilled in every bodily exercise' were the perfect complement of 'healthy, vigorous human body' and 'healthy, vigorous mind' and contrasted startlingly with 'the slouching products of our modern civilisation'. What the modern Fianna Éireann offered was the promise of 'the old chivalrous ideas, the old physical fitness, [and] the old manliness'.[50]

From the outset St Enda's sought to promote a heady mix of physical activity, adventure (routed through history and mythology) and moral fibre. The importance of 'Physical Culture' for promoting teamwork, friendship and discipline amongst boys was noted in the first school prospectus of 1908. Devoting a special paragraph to its significance, the document outlined the many opportunities for sporting and outdoor activities that the school offered. Stressing the importance of physical fitness, the Prospectus emphasized that 'Physical Culture' taught the boys 'to prize bodily vigour, grace and cleanliness'. The special lessons of the sporting ground were designed to foster a 'system of organisation and discipline' which would be beneficial 'towards [developing] a sense of civic and social duty'.[51]

The school boasted exemplary instruction in the ancient arts of hurling and football and the promise to create 'from the purely pedagogic view . . . as Irish a school [as] can possibly be made' was founded on the belief that 'an Irish school, like an Irish nation, must be permeated through by Irish culture'.[52] Irish mythology and legend is full of the outstanding sporting exploits of Fionn Mac Cumhaill, Cúchulainn and Diarmuid and the men of ancient Ireland provided St Enda's with formidable heroes. Given Pearse's personal and abiding fascination with Cúchulainn's legendary prowess on the battle and sporting fields it was not surprising that, for a man so uninterested in playing sports, hurling should capture Pearse's imagination. Football never possessed the legendary power of hurling – after all, the GAA had standardized football as recently as 1901. Pearse's interest was not so much the game of hurling itself as its history and the continuing tradition of an ancient, authentic form. In many ways hurling stood as a metaphor for the best of ancient aristocratic Ireland being imported into contemporary culture. The appeal of hurling lay in its long and illustrious past, a past, as Mandle has pointed out, that 'extended into legend and fantasy'.[53] For a school founded on the principles of 'effort on the part of the child itself, struggle, self-sacrifice, [and] self-discipline', the romance and history of hurling or any other native arts were irresistible.[54]

Despite the prospectus' emphasis on sporting activities, the school's first sporting grounds were not added until three months after the school opened. Although the boys were playing hurling as part of the school curriculum from January 1909 onwards it was not until June that they played (and won) their first competitive hurling match.[55] After the very first term at St Enda's, Pearse wrote that nothing had given him greater pleasure than to see the school develop its 'athletic side'. Stating that St Enda's, boys 'must now be amongst the best hurlers and footballers in Ireland', he invoked Wellington's dictum that the battle of Waterloo was won on the playing fields of Eton and proposed the St Enda's boys to be capable of winning any battle for Ireland: 'When it comes to a question of Ireland winning battles, her main reliance must be on her hurlers. To your camáns, O boys of Banba'.[56]

By the time St Enda's moved to Rathfarnham in 1910, the GAA had initiated its junior league for schools. The new grounds at the Hermitage boasted twenty-five acres of hurling and football fields.[57] Pearse was pleased with the added amenities that the Hermitage could offer, saying that Cullenswood House had been too suburban and that the grounds offered 'no scope for that outdoor life . . . which ought to play so large a part in the education of a boy'.[58] After two years he was already talking about the fine tradition of hurling at St Enda's and in October the hurling team won the new Dublin Juvenile Hurling competition while the Gaelic football team were the holders of the Dublin Schools Cup (Plate 28). Pearse had been one of many in favour of initiating an inter-collegiate league and the first championships were inaugurated in November 1910, leading to an outbreak of 'passion for hurling and football' amongst the pupils. St Enda's did well, only losing in hurling and football in the finals.

The celebration of 'bodily vigour', 'purity' and 'manly self-reliance' in the school's prospectus sits easily alongside the equally valued virtues of 'kindness', 'chivalry', 'truth' and 'social duty'. Although sport was undeniably useful in the pursuit of 'character', for Pearse the ancient games represented a visual and potent connection to the time of Cúchulainn and Fionn Mac Cumhaill. Echoing a general feeling amongst Irish-Irelanders that the St Enda's boys were the modern embodiment of ancient Ireland, Pearse's comments on watching a hurling match in 1910 reveal his fantasy that he was actually watching Cúchulainn play.[59] The physicality and speed of hurling, as opposed to football or handball, and its cultural and historic connections to ancient Ireland led Pearse to consider it as a more authentically masculine game. His wish to have the boys instructed further in boxing, fencing, marching, wrestling, swimming and shooting is linked to his admission that 'every day I feel more certain that the hardening of her boys and young men is the work of the movement for Ireland'.[60]

Pearse's particular admiration of school hurling matches was focused less on the style of game but, as is evidenced in match reports, on the form and the beauty of the boys who played it.[61] One such account, written in 1910, fails to record the school's opponents or even the winning score, but instead Pearse describes his admiration for the white-bodied 'light boyish figures' on the pitch, with their deftness of touch, grace and swift beauty.[62] His reminiscences about watching the boys play focus on 'the admiration of onlookers' at the sight of the 'whiter and slighter' bodies of the St Enda's boys in full flight. Praising a number of his favourite pupils for their speed and skill he described Frank Burke as having 'the daring of Cúchulainn' and commented that Burke resembled the mythic hero 'in his size and his darkness'. The physical dexterity and athletic fitness of the boys in their 'leaping', 'towering', 'lightning' and 'breathless' playing secured victory for the school, and the rallying cry was 'like Cúchulainn's battle-fury when Laegh reviled him'.[63] The voyeuristic pleasure evidenced in Pearse's eyewitness accounts of watching the slender white bodies of the hurlers leads, inevitably, to a consideration of how the idea of the boy was eroticized by Pearse at St Enda's. The emphasis within Pearse's writings on the beauty, grace and sexual naïvety of young male bodies does not sit as easily with modern readers as Pearse's fanciful pageants and reinventions of Celtic traditions. Nevertheless, the eroticizing of boys and boys' culture at St Enda's is inextricably linked to Pearse's reworkings of history, tradition and physical culture.

8

The Erotics of Boyhood

A poignant, but strangely unsettling, photograph shows some St Enda's boys bathing in a river *circa* 1909. The image, like many others, was sold as a commercial postcard to raise the public profile of the school. Presumably the picture, 'The Boys' Bathing Pool', was intended to illustrate the combination of boyhood freedom and 'physical hardening' which was so assiduously promoted at the school (Plate 29). A reading of the image hovers between the sense of an interrupted moment of boys at play and a more formal portrait, evidenced by the stylized posing in which some of the boys are engaged. A number of the boys stand with arms folded across their chests, while others stretch their arms behind their heads in a movement reminiscent of the drilling exercises in the gymnasium. The photograph may be read as a pastoral scene where the boys' nakedness is displayed as an indication of their freedom or, alternatively, that their nakedness dramatizes the vulnerability of their tender flesh.

To a modern viewer this voyeuristic photograph presents an ambiguity that was almost certainly absent for a contemporary audience. It also focuses attention on the question of Pearse's attraction to young boys, a question I will return to later in this chapter. During the 1890s the boys-bathing theme was a popular one in photography as well as in painting.[1] However, the theme of boys bathing was an equally popular image within the less respectable photographic interests of Edwardian visual culture. For example, the literary and artistic movement of Uranism looked to the worlds of Ancient Greece and Rome as its cultural touchstone – eroticized homosocial bonds between men, lamented lost youth – and is marked by its romantic voyeurism and production of poems, drawings, paintings and photographic 'art studies' eulogizing male beauty. The Uranists are described as being 'a body of enthusiastic paedophiles' who used 'a stream of pamphlets, poems, drawings, [and] paintings . . . to argue the attractions and 'impeccable morality of boy-love'.[2] The Uranists were devoted to the worship of young male beauty whilst stressing chastity and abstinence, but such highmindedness was often impossible to sustain.[3] This styling of erotic photographs in the late nineteenth and early twentieth centuries owed much to the concept of fine-art studies and to the influence of classical models on the arrangement and composition of male subjects. Photography allowed newly available erotic images of men and boys based on fine-art conventions to be reproduced and circulated, so that by the late 1890s the photographic image was the currency of erotic voyeurism.[4] It is impossible to know how widely the work of the Uranists was known. Some of their writings and pictures were circulated privately, but many were in the public domain and were consumed as complementary to existing Edwardian narratives of male friendship. The cultural historian Paul Fussell suggests that the Uranist and popular depiction of boys bathing may be traced to the influence of Walt Whitman's *Song of Myself*, first published in 1855, which exploited the homoerotic possibilities of watching young men bathing.[5] Throughout the latter half of the century images of young men bathing (whether in literature, photography or painting) came to be understood as a statement about the intensity of male friendship and camaraderie as well as its more subtle eroticized undertones.[6] Before the First World War many erotic Uranist poems were indistinguishable from poems in public circulation and poems produced during the war unwittingly eulogized male beauty and the vulnerability of male flesh after the Uranist style.[7]

The Edwardian cult of athleticism (including military endeavour) and its corresponding eroticization of young men owes much to the popularity of Greek culture across Europe in the late nineteenth century. The nineteenth-century fascination with Greek and Roman culture in Britain has been well documented.[8] For late nineteenth-century culture the Hellenic world privileged physical beauty, warriorship, rhetoric and athleticism, producing a model of eroticized masculinity. The importance of athleticism and heroism was easily imported into imperial discourses on service, duty and discipline. On the other hand, the emphasis on, and importance of, male beauty foregrounded the homoerotic appeal of the classical world.

The promotion of 'vitalistic manhood', which privileged the athletic and healthy body, as well as eroticizing bodies of male beauty, is rooted in the nineteenth century's fascination with classical antiquity. However, within narratives at St Enda's, and elsewhere in nationalist culture, it was ancient Ireland that offered a balance between male athleticism and male beauty. There are many references to the similarities between the physicality of Greek culture and ancient Ireland in Pearse's writing. In a lecture first given in 1906 and published as 'In First Century Ireland' in 1907, Pearse makes connections between the manliness of the ancient Greeks and the ancient Irish. In doing so he recasts the desired Hellenic body of late Victorian culture into the naturalized form of the Irish boy.[9] Pearse acknowledged P. W. Joyce's 1903 study, *A Social History of Ancient Ireland*,[10] as his 'most valuable mine of information' and maintained that in ancient Ireland the men were 'splendid specimens of manhood'. They were 'big boned and sinewy, but without an ounce of spare flesh; broad in the shoulder, thin in the flank' and 'as lithe as greyhounds'. Their physical endurance was legendary, since they could 'bear hunger and cold and thirst without complaint'.[11]

An attempt to ally ancient Ireland to ancient Greece was not uncommon in nationalist writing generally. Most obviously the connection is expressed in relation to Irish mythology and is part of the process of validating and legitimating the antiquity of Irish legend. Douglas Hyde makes numerous comparisons between the mythology of classical Greece and pre-Christian Ireland.[12] In 'The Necessity for De-Anglicising Ireland' he argues that Ireland is the last bastion of cultural purity since the demise of the classical civilizations of Greece and Rome.[13] T. W. Rolleston's edition of Irish myths and legends makes historical connections between the Celts and the Greeks suggesting that they were kindred peoples.[14] Although not published until 1922 it is difficult not to mention James Joyce's *Ulysses* in this context, since it contains the most brilliant, irreverent and imaginative connections between ancient Greece, Irish mythology and contemporary Ireland.

The importance placed on Greek and Latin in the public school system in the latter half of the nineteenth century meant that a knowledge of the classics, whether in literature, art or social polity, became part of the language of the educated man.[15] The popularity of particular types of athletic activity, especially track and field events, in the public schools was directly borrowed from the classical Greek tests for athletic fitness and strength. The nineteenth-century cult of heroic masculinity was adequately represented by the figure of the Greek warrior, who also displayed a youthful and athletic muscularity. The Victorian and Edwardian interpretation of the Greek warrior/athlete was informed by a complex network of historical, mythological and aesthetic discourses about masculine heroism and beauty. This was also, of course, the period in which the ancient Olympic Games were resurrected in 1896. The representation of the male nude within the nineteenth century corresponded with models commonly found within Greek culture, one of the most important being the model of the 'ephebe'.[16] The figure of the ephebe is understood to be a pubescent male aged approximately sixteen who is taken out of society and initiated into certain rituals of manhood as part of the experience of adolescence.[17] The ephebe was an adolescent on the threshold of adult life and was expected to show prowess in warrior skills and arms, as well as being an excellent athlete and sportsman.[18] The function of this specific period of Greek training (the ephebia) was to isolate the youth from his family (and especially from the influence of women) and to guide him through an intense course of education. The influence of ephebic training is found in the structure and organization of public schools that strongly echo the ephebia of ancient Greece. The physical sportsmanship, the all-male world, the sequestration of boys from female and domestic influences and the cult of manliness were all important pedagogical tools for guiding nineteenth-century boys through adolescence. The institution of the ephebia allowed for erotic relations between ephebes and between boys and older men, with potentially strong erotic elements, although such relationships were strictly governed in practice.[19]

From its inception St Enda's adapted certain qualities of imperial pedagogy and saw itself as a worthy rival to English public schools. The importance of classical studies in the St Enda's curriculum is also a testament to the influence of late Victorian and Edwardian values. However, what is more significant are the close similarities between the institution of the ephebia and the pre-Christian (and later Christian) practice of fosterage, which took boys out of their homes and brought them to a central, all-male, location to be instructed in the intellectual, emotional and physical skills of manliness. If the late Victorians borrowed from the Greek ephebia then Pearse's adaptation of the public-school system could legitimately be configured within an older, Irish, tradition. Therefore St Enda's, despite its similarities to English public schools, was able to occupy the high nationalist ground as a latter-day foster community in the Irish tradition. In a 1912 address to the Gaelic League, Pearse made some startling, and naïve, comparisons between the riches of ancient Greece and of ancient Ireland, claiming for Irish literature a clearer vision, greater humanity and deeper spirituality than Greek literature, whilst acknowledging the importance of Greek pedagogical ideals.[20] The traditions and practices of the ephebia are echoed in Pearse's talk on first century Ireland, which detailed the 'physical culture' of ancient Ireland.

According to Pearse's lecture the Greek emphasis on athleticism and warriorship was of equal importance to pre-Christian Ireland, which also valorized youthful masculinity and appreciated the 'natural' beauty of the nude male body. The idealization of Irish male beauty that is a feature of Pearse's writing can be framed within an understanding of ephebic adolescence but also within the late Victorian and Edwardian vogue for images of young men bathing or at play in the outdoors. According to Pearse ancient Irish men 'had a veritable passion for bathing' and, while 'a gambol in the river or lake was part of the recreation of every day', men often took communal baths together in specially designated areas of the household.[21] Youths wore little or no formal clothing and 'a cultured Gael' of these times 'would no more have been shocked at the sight of . . . a nude young lad' or of 'a nude athlete or warrior than would a cultured Greek of the days of Socrates'.[22] Like the Homeric heroes, according to Pearse, the warriors of the Red Branch 'often went nude into battle'.[23] Despite the cult of the male nude in fine art painting and photography around this time, Pearse was still able to state authoritatively that the 'modern . . . horror of comely nakedness' was a British and imperial invention and was proof of how alienated English masculinity had become from its natural state. Indeed Irish-Irelanders had a reputation for sleeping nude, presumably because it was the way of the old Gaels and possibly because it reaffirmed their masculinity.[24]

Physical tests of manliness assigned to the ephebia were also common to the boys of the ancient Fianna. The *macradh,* or boy troop of the Fianna community, were highly engaged in sport and 'are taught to swim, to perform various feats in the water, to run, jump, wrestle, dive, ride, and use their weapons'.[25] Like the warrior athletes of ancient Greece their entire education was directed 'towards making [the boys] strong and clever – brave and patient in war, gentle and courteous in peace'.[26] Like the ephebia the hypermasculinized ethos of the *macradh* produced a highly charged and eroticized arena for male display and spectatorship. Pearse's loving imaginings of the boys of ancient Ireland emphasizes their youthful comeliness, 'the glow of health on their cheeks', the 'flash of glee in their eyes' and their hair 'braided or floating loose behind them'.[27] The boys are described as 'sturdy', 'straight and true of limb', and 'quick of eye, foot, and hand'. Physically unselfconscious and boisterously energetic, the boys' favourite pastime was, according to Pearse, trying to 'tear off one another's clothes'.[28] Apparently Cúchulainn, Pearse's great hero, was the most accomplished member of the Red Branch at this particular game. According to Pearse, whereas the other boys 'could not as much as unloose the brooch which fastened his brat, [Cúchulainn] was able to tear off not merely the cloaks and tunics, but the kilts of any three!'[29] Pearse's description of Cúchulainn's antics is almost childishly gleeful, admiring the mischievousness of the *macaomh* in a way that disavows the homoerotics of the image. Nationalism made available a discourse of male heroism and sporting camaraderie in which it was possible for men to praise other men's bodies, to admire their prowess and skill and to express love for them as comrades and friends.

The complex influences of Edwardian homoerotic culture, overlapped with conventions of representations which readily circulated erotic images and poems to a sentimental, rather than a 'knowing', audience, make it difficult to know how best to read images and narratives produced within St Enda's. It also inevitably leads into the treacherous scholarly terrain of Pearse's homoeroticism and sexuality. Certainly there has always been, if not a cloud, then a shadow, hanging over the question of Pearse's attachment to boys' culture. His contemporaries worried about his isolation from women and his lack of interest in adult emotional attachments. Pearse's great friend Mary Hayden, who was some years older than him and played a sisterly, if not maternal, role in Pearse's affairs, expressed her concerns about Pearse's unmarried state in an undated letter *circa* 1903.[30] Hayden chided Pearse for remaining unmarried and, curiously, for shying away from the company of adult men, indirectly suggesting that Pearse was beginning to take on 'feminine' qualities. It is a playful and affectionate letter but one which suggests that the boundaries between the sexes must be rigorously maintained for fear of women becoming 'de-feminized' and of men becoming effeminized.

After Pearse's death there was a concerted attempt to explain his bachelorhood in terms of an earlier romantic heartbreak. Desmond Ryan's memoirs of Pearse make special reference to the impact of the death of Eibhlín (Eveleen) Nicolls, a Gaelic League colleague who drowned off the coast of Kerry in 1909. Nicolls had undoubtedly been a valued and admired friend of Pearse, but the posthumous attempt to make her into his secret fiancée is probably misplaced. Ruth Dudley Edwards' biography of Pearse finds no evidence that Nicolls and Pearse had had a personal romance. Even Louis Le Roux, Pearse's most ardent hagiographer, could not find any substance to the supposed attachment when he wrote his biography in the 1920s. Dudley Edwards notes that in the English version of Le Roux's book, translated by Desmond Ryan, the sense of the story of Nicolls and Pearse was altered to suggest a definite engagement between the pair and so 'the story of Eveleen Nicolls took up a permanent position in the Pearse story'.[31] In his memoir, *Remembering Sion*, Ryan recalls that on the day of Nicolls' funeral Pearse was upset and red-eyed and that in later years he realized that Pearse had been weeping for his 'dead love'.[32] The nature of Nicolls' death meant that her funeral was a highly charged and emotional event; she had drowned whilst trying to rescue another girl who was in difficulties. The selflessness of Nicolls' sacrifice, her bravery, her popularity as a lively colleague and her reputation as an enthusiastic Gaelic Leaguer heightened the sadness of the occasion and there was much rhetoric about the nature of her sacrifice and the consecration of her life to the service of Irish-Ireland.[33]

The 'romance' between Nicolls and Pearse, devised after both of their deaths, not only suggests the need to create an emotional past for Pearse but it also lays bare an anxiety (whether conscious or not) that his contemporaries felt about his sexuality. The careful 'heterosexualizing' of Pearse does not, of course, of itself indicate the 'fact' of his homosexuality, but it does suggest that *any* questions with regards to Pearse's sexuality were elided if not obscured after his death. It is only relatively recently that the sexual and affective specificity of Pearse's poetic and fictional writings have been directly addressed. Dudley Edwards' biography tackles with some authority the questions about Pearse's sexuality by referring to his delight in the physical beauty of boys.[34] Edwards is careful, however, to emphasize the unconscious nature of Pearse's attraction and his chaste asexuality. More recently, Sean Farrell Moran, Elizabeth Butler Cullingford, Eugene McCabe and Éibhear Walshe have been more forthcoming about Pearse's attraction to boys and the question of his sexuality. Cullingford has framed her critique of Pearse's work around the erasure of female voices in his fiction (except as allegorical representations of Ireland) and comments on the socio-sexual exclusivity of Pearse's actual and fictionally created male communities. Although she hints broadly, her article only refers obliquely to the implications of male homosocial community within a consideration of Pearse's sexuality.[35] McCabe names Pearse as 'a severely non-practising homosexual' while Walshe addresses the homoeroticism that is implicit in Pearse's writing.[36] Moran is the most forthright of all recent commentators; he is quite unequivocal in pointing to Pearse's deeply emotional and erotic attraction to young boys.[37]

The impulse to 'name' Pearse or to claim him as homosexual is problematic. This is not out of any hesitation to acknowledge Pearse's undeniably eroticized view of young boys and boys' culture but a reluctance borne out of the fact that to ascribe a sexual identity to Pearse is seen to be articulating a central 'truth' about him. Michel Foucault has warned against essentializing sexual identity as if to know the details of a person's sexual behaviour is to have access to 'the most real' aspect of his or her identity.[38] Anxious biographers and historians have attempted to elide or completely ignore the question of Pearse's homoerotic gaze, but it would be equally unscholarly to determine to name and fix Pearse's sexual identity as gay. There are a number of reasons for this. First of all, the specific nature and details of Pearse's sexual behaviour seems secondary to his larger legacy and my purpose here is not to unearth the 'truth' (if any) about Pearse's sexual behaviour. Indeed it is questionable why such information is so keenly sought after. Secondly, the category of homosexual is a recently constructed social identity and one which would not have been available to Pearse, so it is inappropriate to consider him to have been a gay man in the sense that is now commonly understood.[39] However, that does not mean that there was not in existence a set of relationships, practices, codes and subcultures which accord with the modern-day notion of a gay identity. It is merely debatable whether or not Pearse can be 'named' as homosexual in a contemporary sense. Thirdly, the eroticizing of boys and boys' culture which is evident in Pearse's works, and which to modern readers may be seen as 'proof' of Pearse's homosexuality, is framed within heterosexual Edwardian narratives on male physical beauty and friendship as well as in the more 'knowing' discourses on Uranism, erotica and Greek culture. There is an important distinction to be made between the homosexual as a social and sexual subject and the tenderness for male homosocial culture as expressed in the multitude of references to male camaraderie, athleticism and aesthetic and religious sentiments on boyhood found within Edwardian cultural life. Finally, the refusal to 'fix' Pearse's sexuality within the categories of contemporary definition should be not be seen as an unwillingness to deal with Pearse's homoeroticism, which is quite a different issue. The refusal to label Pearse with a neat either/or sexual identity is informed by considerations of the fluidity of sexual identity as well as the necessity to separate sexual acts from sexual desire.

Lack of documentary evidence and the limitations of research methodologies make it impossible to determine whether Pearse practised or thought about same-sex relationships. Given his orthodox Catholic background, his highly principled, highly disciplined life and the sheltered conservative social circles in which he moved, it seems highly unlikely that Pearse envisaged the possibility of sexual relations between men. The trial and death of Oscar Wilde happened within Pearse's adult lifetime, yet there is no mention of Wilde in any of Pearse's papers, although it seems unlikely that he could have been unaware of Wilde's fate. It is entirely possible that Pearse was ignorant of the language or practice of homosexuality and where he might have gained such information is unclear. It must also be acknowledged that perhaps Pearse suppressed the possibility of having *any* kind of sexual relationship. However, to suggest that Pearse was unlikely to have been homosexually active is not to disregard other questions about homoerotic desire as being redundant.

A reading of Pearse's poetry clearly demonstrates how Pearse's view of boys and boys' culture was filtered through the lens of homoerotic desire. There are a number of poems penned by Pearse which focus on the body of a young boy as a symbol of innocence, purity or sacrifice. His 1914 collection, *Songs of Sleep and Sorrow*, contained twelve poems, six of which had been previously published. Three of them, 'Long to Me Thy Coming', 'A Rann I Made' and 'Christ's Coming', fuse erotic longing with Christian symbolism. In 'Christ's Coming' the poet waits like a lover for the arrival of Christ and in 'Long to Me Thy Coming' the body of Christ is yearned for with an almost intensely felt physical pain. 'A Rann I Made' is written in the form of an elegiac love poem and addressed to 'my love', 'the rider', 'the high king', 'the king of kings' and 'ancient death'. As a love poem it echoes the phrasing of the Bible's *Song of Solomon*, with the poet's vision of 'the dark of thy house, tho' black clay' described in longing terms as 'sweeter . . . than the music of trumpets'. This was not the only poem in the collection that spoke of death. 'O Lovely Head' has been taken by some critics as proof of Pearse's love for Eveleen Nicolls, but since it was written five years after her death this seems unlikely. Pearse tended to respond to specific events either during or immediately after the event, for example his poem 'On the Strand of Howth', which records his feelings about Willie living in Paris. What is interesting about 'O Lovely Head' is that it is the only poem in which Pearse addresses a woman who is not a maternal or allegorical figure. However, the 'lovely head' is quite dead and the woman is being gnawed by 'slender worms'.

Three of the poems in the *Songs of Sleep and Sorrow* collection take as their subject the poet's longing for a particular child or what that child represents. 'I Have Not Garnered Gold' venerates the simplicity of childhood, where the poet, eschewing love, fortune and fame, pleads that God will ensure that the poet's name is inscribed on the 'heart of a child'. The poem echoes Cúchulainn's famous declaration that he cared not for fame or for deeds but only that his name should live after his death. 'In To a Beloved Child' the poet is bewitched by a child's laughing mouth but in foretelling a sorrowful future for the child is tortured by the thought of the child weeping. He imagines the 'lovely face' whose 'brightness shall grow grey' and the 'noble head' which will 'bow with sorrow'. The sadness in store for the child might be the process of ageing but is more likely, given Pearse's preoccupation with unhappy endings, to be tragic death. A literary review of Pearse's writing on and for children assumes, interestingly, that the child at the centre of the poem 'To a Beloved Child' is a girl.[40] The reviewer suggests that Pearse's ability to foretell the child's future is, in fact, a prophesy of his own death: '[Pearse] sees [the child's] happy life clouded with sorrow; he sees the laughing mouth twitching in pain; he sees the sparkling eyes welling up in tears, and he breaks out into lamentation'.[41] The romantic investment in the spiritual integrity and insight of the child is here extended to Pearse after his martyred death.

The most striking example of the fusion between the paternal and the erotic gaze is found in Pearse's poem 'Little Lad of the Tricks'. This poem is used by McCabe as 'evidence' of Pearse's sexual proclivities.[42] It is a highly sexualized love poem to a young boy and even Pearse's contemporaries were concerned when they read it. Both Joseph Plunkett and Thomas MacDonagh (who was certainly more worldly-wise than Plunkett) were dismayed by the poem's frankly erotic content and carefully suggested to Pearse how the poem might be misconstrued, although the poem had been accepted for publication and was published to general acclaim in *An Claidheamh Soluis* in 1909.[43] Pearse was greatly offended and upset and it is worth quoting the poem in its entirety to understand both Pearse's naïveté and his friends' alarm.

> Little lad of the tricks,
> Full well I know
> That you have been in mischief:
> Confess your fault truly.
>
> I forgive you, child
> Of the soft red mouth:

I will not condemn anyone
For a sin not understood.

Raise your comely head
Till I kiss your mouth:
If either of us is the better of that
I am the better of it.

There is a fragrance in your kiss
That I have not found yet
In the kisses of women
Or in the honey of their bodies

Lad of the grey eyes,
That flush in thy cheek
Would be white with dread of me
Could you read my secrets.

He who has my secrets
Is not fit to touch you;
Is not that a pitiful thing,
Little lad of the tricks?

To a modern reader the poem is startlingly sexual and disturbingly pederastic. It is worth noting that, although Ruth Dudley Edwards' biography of Pearse draws attention to the homoeroticism of this very poem, she neglects to quote the final two verses, which are perhaps the most damning. The chastisement of the child for 'a sin not understood' is set uneasily against the confession that the poet has secrets which would make him unfit to touch the child. It is difficult not to read this poem as a sexual encounter between an adult and a child. The adult who, after kissing the child, is the one who 'is the better of it' acknowledges that his 'secrets' might inspire dread and fear in the boy if the child were to understand what they mean. The boy's 'comely head', his 'soft red mouth' and the 'fragrance' of his kiss compare more than favourably with the 'kisses of women' and the 'honey of their bodies'. Walshe maintains that it is impossible to read this poem and argue that Pearse was unaware of its sexual content. What is the 'mischief' to which the child must confess? The tone is too knowing and too self-conscious to be seen as a rhyme about the charms of boyhood.[44] What is the 'secret' that the poet has which makes him unfit to touch the child? Certainly the poem fits into conventions of affective and homoerotic poetry which were in circulation at this time. Fussell documents how devotional poems and narratives to young men and boys tended to fixate on themes of innocence, vulnerability and charm but were generally overwhelmingly chaste.[45]

Given the poem's content and tone it is difficult, if almost impossible, to defend it against accusations of pederasty. Pearse's frequent use of the word 'lad' in many contexts might support Walshe's claim that the poem is not as innocent as it seems. Paul Fussell's excavation of the origins of the word 'lad' suggests that it had a particular meaning in homoerotic verse. A. E. Housman's *A Shropshire Lad* had been in constant circulation since it was first published in 1896, although its enormous popularity was not secured until the beginning of the First World War. According to Fussell the success of the book was in the increase of interest in the theme of 'beautiful suffering lads', which was sanctioned by the war but which had already been a popular theme throughout the first decade of the century.[46] Fussell argues that the word 'lad', channelled through Housman, acquired a specific erotic meaning of 'a beautiful brave doomed boy'.[47] The use of the word 'men' was understood to be a neutral term of attachment, 'boy' was a little more emotionally warm, but the term 'lad' was highly emotionally and erotically charged. Pearse's use of the word 'lad' in 'Little Lad of the Tricks' and the affective and sexualized language of that poem corresponds to its popular usage in Britain at that time. 'Lads' were overwhelming fair-haired and, as discussed in an earlier chapter, the equation of blondness with special spiritual and moral beauty was in keeping with Victorian religious and popular iconography, an attribute exemplified in Pearse's writings by the figure of Íosagán. However, unlike the golden-haired child of Victorian culture, the Edwardian use of the word 'lad' did not necessarily signify a child. A 'lad' could be a youth or man who was sexually available or at the very least a potential lover.[48] It is impossible to say whether or not Pearse was aware of the different nuances of meaning between 'lads' and 'boys', but he has a distinction of his own between the *macaomh* (as 'lad') and the boy.

Pearse commonly uses the term 'boy' to depict not merely a chronological stage of development but also a spiritual and emotional state of mind. 'A boy', asserted Pearse in a 1909 article, 'is the most interesting of all living things'.[49] 'A love of boys, of their ways, of their society' and 'the desire to help as many boys as possible become good men' was Pearse's self-confessed primary motivation in establishing St Enda's.[50] The beauty of boys and boys' culture lay in their 'winning ways', their 'aloofness', their passion, their mystery, their gaiety, their earnestness and their promise.[51] There is a slight, but discernible, difference between a 'boy' and a *macaomh*. Historically, the *macaomh* is, of course, Cúchulainn, but the meaning of the word *macaomh* corresponds very closely to the Edwardian understanding of the 'lad' as a 'beautiful, brave doomed boy'. The particular meaning of 'lad' was compounded by the experience of the First World War, even though Pearse remained largely ignorant of its specific horrors. It is important, therefore, to understand the corresponding meanings of 'lad' and *macaomh* as conceived in the decade before the war. The privileging of boys' culture within Edwardian literary narratives meant that the imaginative availability of a figure like Cúchulainn was a perfect parallel to the romantic and eroticized 'lad'. Cúchulainn was the perfect combination of the vulnerable and sensitive boy and the physically aggressive warrior 'lad'. Fussell notes how, even before the First World War, 'soldier boys' carried an erotic *frisson* which was provided by their youth, their cleanliness, their athleticism, their willingness for sacrifice and a fetishistic attention to military uniform.[52] Within nationalist culture the 'lads' were latter-day incarnations of the *macaomh* and the 'soldier boys' were members of the Fianna Éireann. Fussell suggests that homoerotic interest in the figure of the soldier collapsed the patriotic ideals of duty, manliness and sacrifice within a rhetoric of Hellenic beauty and desire.[53]

In 1913 Pearse recorded a dream he had had over four years previously on the opening of the school.[54] In the dream Pearse saw a youth 'standing alone upon a platform above a mighty sea of people'. In the dream Pearse understood that the boy was destined to die and as he watched him he admired his bare white throat, his smile and the hair on his forehead stirred by the wind. Recounting the dream Pearse described the exhilaration and excitement he felt as the same as watching his beautiful boys playing hurling. The boy was actually a pupil at the school, but Pearse never revealed his name. Before the boy was due to die another pupil climbed the scaffold, embraced his comrade and tended to his friend 'in an act of immense brotherly charity and loyalty'. The dream was immensely vivid and Pearse was inspired by the vision to tell his pupils that he could not hope for 'a happier destiny' for any of them 'than to die . . . in the defence of some true thing', since, as Peter Pan says, 'to die will be a very big adventure'.[55]

There are a number of doomed beautiful boys who appear in Pearse's fictional writings; two of them, Íosagán and Eoineen of the Birds have already been discussed. The figure of the sacrificial boy is most prevalent in Pearse's dramatic writings, perhaps because the theatrical form allowed for the public performance and collective visualization of a young boy's death. *Owen* is a short drama that was written in Irish, but published in English in the magazine *Fianna* in 1915 and was performed twice. The performances took place at a *céilí* in the Mansion House and at a Gaelic League winter *céilí* during 1913 somewhere in Dublin, but there are little or no details of the events or of the players. *Owen* is set in the west of Ireland, Pearse's favourite psychological and ideological terrain, and the child players wore local *báinín* clothing and the long trousers favoured by children in the Gaeltacht.[56] *The King*, *The Master* and *Owen* all feature idealistic boys who sacrifice themselves (or are sacrificed) in service to a set of ideals. The three plays share a highly charged fixation with the idealism, purity and beauty of boyhood and young adolescence. Unlike *The King* and *The Master*, the short play *Owen* is set in the 1860s at the time of the Fenian risings. Written before *The Master* it shares many of the themes of that play as well as developing ideas that were already found in *The King*, which had been written in 1912.

Young Owen hears stories about the courage of Irish Fenian rebels daily from his village schoolmaster, who also teaches the boys about military strategy and how to maintain effective fire cover if under artillery attack. A passing ballad singer comes to the school to pass on a covert message to the master, who is being sought for Fenian activities. When two men step outside in order to make plans, the young boys take over the classroom and Owen, obviously a born leader, pretends to be the master. The teacher returns and finding the class in uproar keeps Owen behind after school as a punishment. It becomes apparent that the master has been told to go on the run for his own safety and, forgetting about the schoolboy in the corner, he begins to pack his personal things, musing aloud to himself about his future. Stooping to uncover a cache of arms underneath the schoolroom floorboards, he suddenly realizes that young Owen is watching him intently. The master decides to confide in the boy, then shows him how to load a rifle and tells him that 'there are men in every place in Ireland, that are going out to fight tonight'. Owen offers to be his master's mascot, or rifle-bearer, or even drummer-boy, but the teacher declines and swears Owen to secrecy about his illegal activities. They swear an oath of allegiance and shake hands. As Owen turns to leave he sees a number of policemen coming towards the school. The master escapes out the back window while the boy remains in the school to try to deter the men. He barricades the doors and windows and loads the rifle. The policemen hammer at the door and start to break it down. Owen takes aim and fires. A volley from outside matches his single shot and hits the child repeatedly. The policemen break into the school and kneeling beside Owen's dead body realize 'that it's only a little lad'.

Owen is an allegorical expression of Pearse's growing militarism, but it displays a familiar sentimentality about the inspirational nature of a young boy's zeal and courage. The sacrificial boy, like Iollann Beag in *The Master* and Giolla na Naomh in *The King*, is framed within nationalist allegory but is also understood in those narratives on boyhood, idealism and purity of purpose which were circulated within Edwardian imperial culture. A photograph published in *Fianna* magazine in December 1915 shows Desmond Carney as Owen (Plate 30). Carney is kneeling with a rifle at his shoulder, dramatizing the moment when Owen fired the first shot to save his teacher. It is unclear whether this photograph was taken at an actual production of the play or whether it was posed at some other time. Carney of course also played the part of the sacrificial Giolla na Naomh in *The King* at least a year previously and it is his image that so closely resembles the school motto of the Fianna warrior. Carney's body, or at least his image, was used to display the shining innocent faith of pagan/Christian boyhood, a contemporary boy-hero and a figurative representation of an abstract school code.

Carney may or may not have played the part of Iollann Beag in *The Master* in 1915. He was still in attendance at St Enda's but accounts of the production do not record the name of the key player. *The Master*, as discussed in an earlier chapter, is thematically similar to *The King*, but the figure of the Giolla na Naomh lacks the erotic gaze that frames the characterization of Iollann Beag. Elizabeth Butler Cullingford sees in *The Master* 'evidence' of Pearse's 'scoutmasterly obsession with little boys' and suggests that the interaction between the boys 'voices all of our suspicions' about Pearse's 'extraordinary *naïveté*' regarding the homoeroticism of his gaze.[57] Iollann Beag's exceptional beauty is cause for comment by the other boys, as is the master's special treatment of the boy whose 'fair cheek . . . reddens when the Master speaks to him'. They note that the master does not chastise him when he is late or inattentive and the others suggest that this is because Iollann Beag is 'only a little lad'. Maine, the most boisterous and cheeky of the boys, says that Iollann Beag is 'more like a little maid' than a boy. The others dispute this feminizing of Iollann Beag, who is an accomplished sportsman and hurler, and point out that 'you wouldn't call him a little maid when you'd see him strip to swim a river'. All are in agreement that, although he has 'a high manly heart', he has 'a beautiful white body'. It is for this special physical beauty, suggests Maine, that Iollann Beag is loved by all of the community, including the master. Being an all-male community 'we have no woman here' continues Maine, and so 'make love' (meaning here to use the speech of a lover) 'to our little Iollann' instead. One of the boys laughs and disputes this interpretation of Iollann's attraction, arguing that he had struck the boy for playing a trick on him. Maine has the last word on Iollann's appeal: 'men sometimes thrash their women . . . it is one of the ways of loving'.

Abigail Solomon-Godeau, in her study on representations of masculinity, has argued convincingly that in homosocial societies the absence of female bodies enables an internal division to occur within ideologies of masculinity. This means that often, in all-male communities, a male body takes on the representative or emotional qualities of femininity.[58] This feminized masculinity is not to be confused with effeminacy, which is deeply threatening to male identity, since it suggests a loss or diminishing of manhood.[59] The figure of Iollann Beag is decidedly not female, but he is feminized in order to allegorize boyhood in a way which is outside the acceptable boundaries of dominant masculinity. Iollann Beag's innocence, sensitivity and reverence for 'natural' religion is similar to the other-worldiness of Íosagán. However, Íosagán is understood, and expressly stated, to be Christ in the form of a boy. Whereas Iollann Beag is a child who by virtue of *being a boy* carries a natural or innate spirituality that is ordinarily associated with femininity. Solomon-Godeau's contribution to this debate is her suggestion that the space of pleasure and eroticism that is vacated by femininity is filled by an idealized and eroticized male figure. She argues that within nationalist narratives the pleasure and erotic investment usually invested in the female form becomes displaced onto a child-like body.[60]

Within nationalist narratives the female body is seen as an allegorical symbol of the nation, but the male body possesses full political citizenship and is understood to *be* the nation. The figure of the boy hovers somewhere in between symbol and political reality. He represents the promise of manhood (and therefore citizenship) and remains, while still a child, closely associated with the maternal and the domestic. The young male body therefore is, on the one hand, a physically 'real' active body but, on the other hand, he may function as a symbol of femininity and of erotic beauty. It is because of this ambiguity that the image of a beautiful young boy may serve as an ideal national form.

The nationalist community's encouragement of the production and consumption of the image of the eroticized, sacrificial male ideal (from Joseph Campbell, to Pearse, to Beatrice Elvery) suggests that it found nothing particularly provocative about the bodies of young boys. Indeed young boys had become almost conventional signs within certain nationalist narratives. It is therefore difficult to talk about Pearse's attraction to 'real' boys in any knowledgeable way, since the 'idea' of a boy was intensely emotionally and spiritually affecting for him. This is not to deny the homoerotics of Pearse's gaze but to attempt to understand his inexperience in sexual matters. It is important to bear in mind when reading Pearse's plays and poems the extent to which he was perceived as chaste and naïve by his contemporaries. MacDonagh's and Plunkett's concern with the sexualized content of 'Little Lad of the Tricks' is in itself an indication of Pearse's ignorance of alternative interpretations. Although inevitably part of the hagiographic process, Pearse is described in memoirs and reminiscences as a shy, gentle, unworldly and priest-like man by those who knew him.[61] The curious mix of romantic longing, passionate sacrifice and valorizing of boyhood adventure that is found in Pearse's rhetoric bespeaks a quality of childishness in his own character. His attachment to boys' culture and his apparent lack of interest in emotional or sexual adult relationships is not perhaps so much an indication of an adult erotic attachment to boys as the desire to *be* a boy.

In spite of his many other social commitments and Gaelic League activities, it is clear that Pearse was at his happiest at school and in the company of his brother and family. The Pearse brothers were particularly close and Mary Brigid's biography of Patrick suggests that they shared the usual family jokes as children but that these persisted into adulthood. They were odd children, however; both

Willie and Patrick liked 'to masquerade as different, strange, rather eccentric people – principally females' and present themselves at the front door.[62] However, even as adult men the brothers still liked to dress up and play tricks on each other; at one time Willie, dressed as a beggar woman, was imperiously ordered from St Enda's by Pearse before he realized the joke. The Pearse brothers treated each other affectionately and were inseparable. Even as adults they spoke to each other in a childish gibberish or baby dialect that was described by Ryan, Pearse's most ardent fan, as 'weird in the extreme'.[63] Sean Farrell Moran's psychological, and humanizing, profile of Pearse sketches a man with an uncertain sense of adulthood. He sees Pearse as socially inadequate, physically awkward and at times painfully shy, yet egotistical and vain. The cast in his eye and his tendency to stammer increased his sense of social inferiority in the world represented by Yeats and Lady Gregory. The security of his position within his family, where he was clearly adored by his mother and sisters, the certainty of his role within the school and the ease with which he inhabited the world of boy-heroes and legendary adventures suggests that Pearse often found adulthood overwhelming and complex and that he was much more comfortable in the world of childhood.[64]

However, these are not the assessments of Pearse in which current society is interested. In discussions of Pearse across a broad range of media, from television documentaries and newspaper articles to academic scholarship, the topic that resurfaces again and again is the question of Pearse's sexuality.[65] Given his tremendous output, his long-lasting influence and his intellectual calibre, it seems a wry irony that one of Pearse's legacies to the Irish populace is a debate on his sexual identity. The question of Pearse's sexuality disguises the more problematic issue of why it is important for us to possess this information, as if, as Foucault says, in the possession we know the 'truth' about him. A closer consideration of public interest in Pearse's sexuality involves unpacking the layers of confusion that often arise within an understanding of the difference between homoerotic, homosexual and paedophile. The homoerotic is a love and desire for the same sex that is primarily filtered through a visual or literary sensibility and is not usually understood to involve sexual acts. Homosexuality is a socio-sexual identity that may or may not be defined in terms of sexual activity with the same sex. Paedophilia is a much more closely defined activity expressed as a sexual interest in, and engagement with, children.

The unease surrounding Pearse's sexuality which has become a feature of public and media interest in Pearse in recent years needs to be addressed in the context of these three, sometimes overlapping but quite different, categories of sexual behaviour. It is possible, therefore, that the need to 'know about Pearse' is not, in most cases, motivated by a desire to 'out' a national hero but is an attempt to articulate the discomfort that arises from a consideration of his writings. This is to say that, in general, people do not have a difficulty with the knowledge that Pearse was a homosexual man who sublimated his erotic desire for the male body into his work, his writing and his politics. The question that dare not speak its name is whether or not Pearse was a paedophile. However, to be a homosexual man is not the same as being a paedophile. For older generations who grew up respecting the venerated status of Pearse within the Irish state the very conjunction of the words Pearse and paedophile may seem treasonable, yet today it is the unarticulated subject which continues to circle around any debate about Pearse's life.

The persistent interest in Pearse's sexuality is perhaps more suggestive of our own anxieties about men's relationships with children and has little to do with the facts of Pearse's life. Pearse's dedication to boys, his love of boys' culture and his poetic declarations of desire for the young male body certainly suggest homoerotic tendencies, but they do not indicate any sexual activity between him and his pupils which would have made him a paedophile. It was the sublimation of Pearse's sexuality that produced such a remarkable interweaving of discourses on aesthetics, martyrdom, masculinity and nationhood, which found literary, visual and dramatic expression in the highly eroticized figure of the *macaomh*.

9

'What if the Dream Come True?': After the Revolution

Between 1908 and 1916 a generation of boys passed through St Enda's; the school's objective in 'awakening a spirit of patriotism' and forming 'a sense of civic and social duty' amongst its pupils was complemented, in part, by the nationalist pedigree of many of those boys. At the beginning, in 1908, Pearse's dream of a liberal (and Catholic), bilingual and natively Irish educational institution had not been linked to a political vision for the establishment of a nation state. The early years, between 1908 and 1912, formed the most productive and inspiring period of the school in all regards – culturally, educationally and ideologically. By 1912 the glory days of St Enda's were over. The school was still highly regarded in nationalist circles but the immediacy and freshness of the school's vision, which had been so apparent to many in 1908, seemed a little jaded some years later and Pearse's increasing militarism caused disquiet.

The school had moved from its premises in Cullenswood House, Ranelagh, to the more distantly situated location of the Hermitage in Rathfarnham in the school year 1910–11. The school's distance from the city resulted in a drop in the number of day pupils who attended and whose parents were reluctant for their sons to become boarders. From an attendance roll of 130 boys in the school year 1909–10, the number of pupils had dropped to seventy by 1910–11. Pearse's increased involvement with politics outside school life took its toll on disenchanted parents and children so that after 1912–13 the numbers of pupils remained below sixty. In the final year of the Hermitage, 1915–16, there were only twenty-eight boys in the senior years.

After 1912 the school began to feature less prominently in Pearse's vision for the future. Instead of promoting the school as the microcosm of a utopian nation Pearse's attention was drawn away from the school as a model by his desire for the establishment of a nation state. It is difficult to pinpoint where the shift from micro to macro began but it was hastened by the collapse, in 1912, of St Ita's school, the female counterpart to St Enda's. St Ita's had been struggling financially for some time and when it eventually folded Pearse was left with an administrative headache, and a mountain of debts and bad feeling. Pearse had hoped to sell the school to one of the teachers, Louise Gavan Duffy, but the plans fell through almost at the last moment. The collapse of St Ita's was calamitous for Pearse's involvement with St Enda's in a number of ways. First of all it exacerbated the financial strains on the boys' school that were already at breaking-point; it highlighted Pearse's managerial weaknesses and the increased administrative duties drew him away from teaching.[1] In the longer term the financial situation of St Enda's necessitated a fundraising trip to America in 1914, where Pearse's revolutionary appetite was sharpened, heralding the demise of the school.

The Dublin Lock-Out of 1913 and its disastrous consequences for workers, the formation of the Irish Volunteers in November 1913, Pearse's initiation into the secret military organization, the Irish Republican Brotherhood (IRB), in December 1913 and the threat of a European war escalated Pearse's political activism. His three-month trip to America on behalf of the school was particularly significant. Pearse's sojourn in America was a baptism of fire in the complexities of Irish-American republicanism and he soon discovered that his audiences were less interested in St Enda's than in the newly formed Volunteers. The incendiary events of 1913 made Pearse's speeches on the 'Irishing' of education seem almost quaint.

According to Dudley Edwards, from quite early in his tour Pearse began to rely heavily on his association with the Volunteers in order to introduce the topic of St Enda's.[2] As the tour wore on Pearse's fundraising efforts began to take on an American slant: sponsors and donors were offered classrooms named after them or plaques erected in the school building detailing their beneficence.

The American tour was not a financial success. Despite a punishing schedule and the proceeds of the gate at a Gaelic football match in Celtic Park, New York, he returned to St Enda's with less than he had hoped to collect. However, Pearse returned from America with a new agenda. There had been little interest in him as the headmaster of St Enda's, but he had achieved public affirmation of his power as an orator and public speaker. Dudley Edwards suggests that America altered Pearse's vision of himself from schoolmaster to political figure. She argues that for Pearse 'it was no longer a question of whether there should be a revolution – only a question of when'.[3]

Unbeknown to Pearse a number of his pupils had been initiated into the IRB some months before Pearse himself was recruited. Desmond Ryan, Frank Burke and Eamonn Bulfin (three of Pearse's faithful 'dogs'), as well as Joseph Sweeney, were accepted into the IRB by Con Colbert some time early in 1913. Ryan recalls that Colbert involved lots of IRB boys in the 1913 St Enda's fête in Jones's Road in order to swell the numbers of the marching formations – a fact of which the Pearse brothers were unaware. According to Ryan, Colbert was admired by the brothers as the living incarnation of Napoleon, but Colbert was disdainful of their hero-worship. He considered the Pearse brothers naïve in the extreme; when accepting their compliments as to the professionalism of the St Enda's boys Colbert found it difficult to believe that they were unaware that he had been drilling the boys in the city hall with the IRB for months.[4] After Pearse returned from America Ryan recalls the headmaster's 'worship of military discipline' becoming 'fanatical to the point of absurdity'.[5] What Ryan called Pearse's 'Napoleonic complex' intensified and he maintained that his kinship with Napoleon was evident in his 'excess of sentiment', his recklessness of action and his inability to see beyond a given set of circumstances.[6] Padraic Colum also remarked on Pearse's 'devotion to the Corsican' and notes that Pearse claimed to own a lock of Napoleon's hair.[7]

While Pearse was penning *The Wandering Hawk*, an IRB group of past pupils, under the supervision of the chemistry teacher Peter Slattery, were constructing home-made bombs in the basement at St Enda's. By that time Desmond Ryan, Frank Burke and Eamonn Bulfin were students at University College Dublin but were living at St Enda's and were involved in part-time teaching and administrative work at the school. Ten past pupils in attendance at the university formed a St Enda's University Group and it was this band of youthful idealists who 'manufactured canister grenades of a crude type' and 'moulded buckshot', which was loaded into primed cartridges.[8]

By the time of the Easter Rising in 1916, more than two hundred men from the Rathfarnham Company of the Irish Volunteers joined Pearse in the GPO, although not all of them were from St Enda's. Joseph Sweeney recalls that when the split in the Volunteers had occurred in September 1914 the Rathfarnham Company, 'practically to a man', backed Pearse against the more moderate Redmondites.[9] Over thirty St Enda's pupils (past and current) volunteered to be with Pearse in the GPO. For a school whose attendance lists had dwindled to less than sixty in the preceding years this represents a significant number of youthful revolutionaries. The youngest of them, Eunan McGinley, was only sixteen at the time and was a republican casualty of the Civil War. There was only one St Enda's boy killed during the Rising, Gerald Keogh, who was running messages for the rebels when he was gunned down by a sniper outside Trinity College. However, the toll for St Enda's was high: out of the fourteen men executed in 1916, five of them – Pearse, Willie Pearse, Thomas MacDonagh, Con Colbert and Joseph Plunkett – were connected to the school.

Most of the St Enda's boys arrested after the Rising were interned in Frongoch in North Wales until December 1916. Mrs Pearse, Margaret and Mary-Brigid were left to run St Enda's. The school moved back to its old premises in Cullenswood House, since the

Hermitage had been commandeered by the British Army after the Rising. Joseph MacDonagh, brother of Thomas, became headmaster when St Enda's reopened in the autumn of 1916.[10] Feelings were running high and by Christmas of that year returning internees were even more fiercely convinced of Pearse's vision than ever. Brian Joyce and Frank Burke returned from Frongoch early in 1917 to take up their old teaching duties. However, MacDonagh was arrested in late 1917 and his place was taken by Peter Slattery, the inventive chemistry teacher.

By 1919 the school was relocated once again in the Hermitage and, when Slattery left, his place was taken by Frank Burke, one of the original 'Dogs', who became headmaster in 1923. The school was not a success. The flair and vision of Pearse was sorely missed and while the Pearse family struggled to fill up teaching hours the women lacked Patrick's gift for teaching. Prior to the Pearse brothers' deaths the women's involvement in the intellectual life of the school had been minimal and they were ill-equipped to contribute to the broad and liberal curriculum. One pupil who attended in 1917 recalls being taught zealous catechism and little else.[11]

The Pearse women had always been pious, but after 1916 their religious fervour reached new heights and there were those who resented Mrs Pearse's and her daughters' presumption that they had a monopoly on Pearse's memory and on personal bereavement.[12] Even though Tom Clarke had been the instigator and strategist behind the revolutionary events at Easter, posthumously Pearse's role in the Rising supplanted all of the other leaders. Dudley Edwards maintains that the high profile of Pearse was due, in part, to the public perception of the needlessness of Willie's execution, and also to the publicity surrounding Mrs Pearse. The veneration of the mothers of the republican dead reached its zenith in the years immediately following the Rising, to the extent that Mrs Pearse was elected to Dáil Éireann in 1919. She voted against the Treaty in the name of her dead sons, was a member of the first Executive of Fianna Fáil and was elected to the Senate in the 1920s.[13] However, she, and her daughter Margaret after her, were never political animals but were manipulated shamelessly by the emergent Fianna Fáil party, which hijacked Pearse for the republican cause.[14]

After the War of Independence and the signing of the Treaty in 1921 many ex-St Enda's boys joined the republican forces and bitterly opposed partition. It remains a matter of debate as to whether or not Pearse would have supported the Treaty. While his mother was adamant that he would not have, people closer to him, like Desmond Ryan, were not so sure.[15] Public uncertainty as to whether or not Pearse would have settled for the Treaty resulted in the situation – peculiar to civil wars – where brothers and friends fought on opposing sides. Two of these were Eoin MacNeill's sons, who had been educated together in Rathfarnham. Niall MacNeill fought on the pro-Treaty side during the Civil War, while his brother Brian was a member of the republican forces and was murdered early in 1922 by a pro-Treaty brigade. It was at this time that the loyal band of 'Dogs' split politically, with Ryan supporting the Treaty.

The establishment of the Free State saw a large number of old boys serving in the army and government and many others contributed to the public life of the fledgling state as teachers, lawyers, doctors and writers. Frank Burke and Brian Joyce returned to St Enda's to teach and Burke remained the headmaster until the school's closure in 1935. Joe Sweeney, who had fought on the pro-Treaty side during the Civil War, became a major-general in the Irish Army. Two brothers of Eunan McGinley, Conor and Diarmuid, formed careers as a prominent architect and as the president of Conradh na Gaeilge respectively. At least six old boys became doctors, among them were Fred and Vincent O'Doherty – brothers who had been admired for their athletic skills at St Enda's. There was also a handful of lawyers, some of them more prominent in the state's affairs than others. Norman and Kenneth Reddin, Rory O'Hanrahan and Joseph Thunder all dedicated their legal abilities to public service. Desmond Ryan, Denis Gwynn and John Dowling made careers in journalism and writing. Ryan's particular role in preserving Pearse's papers, writing his biography and committing his memoirs of St Enda's to paper deserve special mention. There is no record of any ex-pupil entering religious orders, although many past pupils chose to serve as lay teachers in Catholic schools.

Burdened by mounting debts and outstanding payments, the school limped on for some years. Pearse had died intestate and the financial affairs of the school were in disarray. A campaign was started to buy the Hermitage outright and the building passed into the hands of the family in 1920. A fundraising trip to America brought Mrs Pearse home with over $10,000 in 1924, but the Pearse family had never been good at managing money and St Enda's went further into decline over the next few years. The numbers of pupils hovered between sixteen and thirty and the school only faintly echoed the vivacity of its early days. Mrs Pearse died in 1932 and when the school finally closed in 1935 it was possibly a relief to those who had experienced the school at its most successful.

The high profile of many old boys in the new state, coupled with the status accorded to Mrs Pearse as the most exalted of Irish mothers contributed to the intensive veneration of Pearse during the 1920s. The new Department of Education, anxious to secure the primacy of the Irish language in the curriculum, was restricted in its choice of suitable texts in Irish. Pearse's literary works, which were written in a very simple Irish, proved to be perfect curricular material and as a result his Irish texts appeared on school syllabi nationally. His memoirs of St Enda's, which had been published in *An Macaomh*, was a set text for the Kilkenny County Council scholarship, which posed the question 'Why would you like to visit Sgoil Éanna?' In addition, Pearse's early lectures on Irish literature (delivered to the Gaelic League when he was only seventeen) became required reading at teacher training colleges.[16]

Dudley Edwards maintains that the prominence of Pearse in the curriculum made his name familiar to schoolchildren countrywide and further secured his status as the most venerable of the dead martyrs.[17] It is interesting to note that the fictional works of Pearse which were chosen for publication and distribution in the schools were predominantly drawn from his early collection of stories, *Íosagán*. The tales of Eoineen Beag, Íosagán and the many other good and ethereal children of Pearse's early works were used as pedagogic devices to instruct children in moral purity, religious observance and discipline. The determined emphasis on the innocence of Pearse's child characters led some to make analogies between the innate spirituality of children and the posthumous holiness of Pearse. An article in *The Irish Monthly* in 1922 made a reverential connection between the spiritual beauty of children and the otherworldliness of Pearse.[18] Many civil servants employed by the Department of Education were devoted admirers of Pearse who advocated a nationalist curriculum along the lines of Pearse's educational manifesto 'The Murder Machine'. Teachers were recommended to study Pearse's collected writings and to inculcate 'the continuity of the separatist idea from Tone to Pearse'.[19] It was almost impossible for teachers struggling with overcrowded classrooms, shortages of textbooks, and badly equipped schools to satisfy the Department's demand to 'Gaelicize' education with measured judgement. Instead, Pearse's complex and liberal ideas on pedagogy became reduced to a narrowly focused religious and nationalist orthodoxy that lacked the flair and creativity of his initial vision for Irish education.

With only one exception, extant memoirs of past pupils remain overwhelmingly positive about their time at St Enda's. Kenneth Reddin complimented the school's commitment to its pupils, the feeling of being involved with something new and innovative and the stimulating and exciting intellectual atmosphere engendered there.[20] Milo McGarry recalled his schooldays with fondness and was particularly grateful for the emphasis on literature and the dramatic arts.[21] The dissenting voice comes from Denis Gwynn, who had been one of Pearse's favourite pupils and certainly one of his most academically gifted. Gywnn was the son of Stephen Gwynn, the Redmondite MP, and both father and son heeded Redmond's call for Irishmen to join the British Army in 1914. At this time Gwynn was a classics scholar at University College Dublin. In 1923 Gwynn published a fiercely critical article on Pearse's 'celtic imperialism' in the *Dublin Review* attacking the narrow vision of Pearse's revolutionary philosophy.[22] Gwynn accused Pearse of developing St

Enda's 'into a more or less precariously established institution' and of deliberately using the school as 'an instrument to provide himself with the nucleus of a band of young politicians who would follow him to the scaffold as the political successor of Wolfe Tone and Robert Emmet'.[23] He was critical of the insularity of Pearse's social and political life maintaining that Pearse was not open to influences beyond a small circle of friends. Although Gwynn had left St Enda's at the end of the 1910 school year he asserted that after 1912 the many brilliant teachers who had contributed to the school had moved on and that as a result the intellectual life of the school became enervated and narrow. Gwynn's bitterness in 1923 at what he considered 'the training ground' of St Enda's was bewildering to those who had been at school with him. Desmond Ryan accused Gwynn of a total lack of humour and a selective memory about his time at St Enda's, remarking that Gwynn had held Pearse in exceptionally high regard when he attended the school.[24] It is perhaps easy to forgive Ryan's bewilderment at Gwynn's vitriol, for Ryan could not have understood the impossible position that Gwynn, and many like him, found himself in after the 1914–18 war. Gwynn had joined the British Army in good faith in 1914 believing that Ireland would be rewarded with Home Rule. With the benefit of historical hindsight it is possible to appreciate the devastation and horror that Gwynn most certainly witnessed in France but then to return to an Ireland which was exulting in heroic martyrdom, and to be marginalized because of his own contribution, must have been extremely difficult.

There were others who had been indirectly involved with St Enda's who had their own epitaphs to write. While W. B. Yeats lamented Pearse's political extremism he nevertheless mourned the passing of a fine educator. Yeats remembered Pearse as the man who 'kept a school' and 'rode our wingèd horse'[25] but also as the man who declared 'that in every generation/must Ireland's blood be shed'.[26] Even General Blackadder, after condemning Pearse to death, remarked to the Countess of Fingall that Pearse was one of the finest men he had ever met and that it was no 'wonder that his pupils adored him'.[27]

The question of Pearse's legacy and the success of St Enda's remains open for discussion. Dudley Edwards has famously described the life and ambitions of Pearse as 'a triumph of failure' and she unambiguously suggests that the vision of St Enda's was never realized, since, for example, many of the boys left the school without any competent degree of fluency in Irish, which had been one of its most important founding principles. Certainly the educational philosophy of the school cast a long shadow over the emergent Department of Education and continues to hold its own against modern, libertarian schooling. The more difficult evaluation is the one of Pearse himself. Others have written on Pearse's political legacy, but Pearse continues to court controversy as either a radical visionary or a fanatical bigot.[28] It is not in dispute that he was a gifted and dedicated teacher and that he was responsible for putting into place an enlightened and liberal curriculum at St Enda's. His driven energy is evident in his prolific output, from his days as the editor of *An Claidheamh Soluis* to his time at St Enda's. He was an indefatigable worker for the Irish language and for nationalism for all of his adult life. As a private individual he was deeply committed to his family and his faith and it is not in doubt that he was a man of sincere conviction, a thoughtful son and brother and a kind and generous friend. It is a humbling process to acknowledge all that he managed to achieve in his thirty-six-year span.

The legacy of the cult of boyhood is less clear. The boy as national symbol seems to have faded from nationalist imagery after 1916. As it was not only Pearse who had used the figure of the boy to promote ideals of nationhood, it would be overly simplistic to argue that the boy as icon died with Pearse. Instead the image of the mother appears to have a stranglehold as *the* image of Ireland, at the expense of a variety of other female representations, in the immediate years after the Rising. The symbol of the mother had always been popular within nationalist writing and imagery, but after 1916 the prevailing mood ensured that the fusion of religious orthodoxy and national martyrdom privileged images of Ireland as a grieving mother. Most obviously the image of Ireland as mother was mapped onto Catholicism's interest in the Virgin Mother and made it easy to map one image of a bereaved mother onto another. The disappearance of the boy as a symbol for nation cannot easily be explained, for he could have co-existed quite easily with the newly dominant image of mother. Perhaps it came about because the image of the boy was so often perceived as representing the political future, a sort of citizen in waiting, rather than as an abstract symbol of Ireland. The boy therefore functioned as a very powerful representation of revolution and progress. Maybe it is for this very reason that the image of the boy largely disappeared after the revolutionary events of 1916. Could it be that the War of Independence and the Civil War fractured identities so much within Irish society that the revolutionary boy could no longer represent a shared ideal of citizenship? This would also explain why the image of Ireland as mother became so potent: the mother gives birth to all the children of the nation and sees no difference between them. Given the divisive political climate of post-revolutionary Ireland, it was no longer clear whose child the revolutionary boy was. The image of the boy, of Pearse's beloved *macaomh,* functioned most powerfully and visibly in pre-revolutionary Ireland because he represented a promise of what had not yet been achieved and, through him, it was possible for a generation to imagine a future without boundaries.

Today the Hermitage, the site of St Enda's most happy and successful years, is a museum dedicated to the life and educational work of Patrick Pearse. Cullenswood House has recently been renovated and is now functioning as a *gaelscoil.* In some ways there could be no finer epitaph for St Enda's than to be remembered as both school and museum. As an educational experiment it was radically inspiring to generations of young men and continues to be upheld as an ideal in nationalist pedagogy. However, the figure of the *macaomh* – the brave, beautiful, sacrifical warrior/scholar – is perhaps more fittingly consigned to the quietness of a museum.

Bibliography

Akenson, Donald. *The Irish Education Experiment: The National System of Education in the Nineteenth Century.* London: Routledge & Kegan Paul, 1970.

Aldrich, Robert. *The Seduction of the Mediterranean: Writing, Art and Homosexual Fantasy*. London and New York: Routledge, 1993.

Altbach, Philip, and Gail Kelly. *Education and Colonialism.* New York and London: Longman, 1978.

Anderson, Benedict. *Imagined Communities: Reflections on the Origin and Spread of Nationalism.* London: Verso, 1983.

Anderson, David, and David Killingray (eds.). *Policing the Empire: Government Authority and Control 1830–1940.* Manchester: Manchester University Press, 1991.

Andrew, John. *A Paper Landscape: The Ordnance Survey in Nineteenth Century Ireland.* Oxford: Oxford University Press, 1975.

Armstrong, John. *Nations Before Nationalism.* Chapel Hill: University of North Carolina Press, 1982.

Arnold, Matthew. *The Study of Celtic Literature.* 1869; repr. London: David Nutt, 1910.

Aronwitz, Stanley and Henry Giroux. 'Teaching and the Role of the Transformative Intellectual'. *Education Under Siege.* London: Routledge & Kegan Paul, 1985.

Ashcroft, Bill, Gareth Griffiths and Helen Tiffin (eds.). *The Post-Colonial Studies Reader.* London and New York: Routledge, 1995.

Atkinson, Norman. *Irish Education: A History of Educational Institutions.* Dublin: Allen Figgis, 1969.

Badinter, Elisabeth. *On Masculine Identity.* Trans. Lydia Davis. New York: Columbia University Press, 1995.

Bahktin, Mikhail. 'Discourse in the Novel'. *The Dialogic Imagination.* Ed. Michael Holquist. Austin: University of Texas Press, 1981.

Barker, Francis, Peter Hulme and Margaret Iversen (eds.). *Colonial Discourse/Post-Colonial Theory.* Manchester: Manchester University Press, 1994.

Barry, Reverend Albert. *Lives of the Irish Saints.* Dublin: James Duffy, n.d.

Barthes, Roland. *Camera Lucida: Reflections on Photography.* London: Fontana, 1984.

Battersby, Christine. *Gender and Genius: Towards a Feminist Aesthetics.* London: The Women's Press, 1989.

Beckson, Karl. *London in the 1890s: A Cultural History.* New York and London: W. W. Norton & Company, 1992.

Benjamin, Walter. 'The Work of Art in the Age of Mechanical Reproduction'. *Illuminations.* New York: Schocken Books, 1969; 217–51.

____. 'Theses on the Philosophy of History'. *Illuminations.* New York: Schocken Books, 1969; 253–63.

____. 'A Small History of Photography'. *One Way Street and Other Writings.* London: New Left Books, 1979; 240–57.

Bernstein, Basil. 'The Social Construction of Pedagogic Discourse' and 'Education, Symbolic Control and Social Practices'. *The Structuring of Pedagogic Discourse: Class, Codes and Control.* London and New York: Routledge, 1990; 133–218.

Betterton, Rosemary. *Looking On: Images of Femininity in the Visual Arts and Media.* London and New York: Pandora, 1987.

Best, Richard Irvine (ed.). *Bibliography of Irish Philology and of Printed Irish Literature.* Dublin: Department of Agriculture and Technical Instruction, 1913.

____ (ed.). *A Bibliography of the Publications of Kuno Meyer.* Dublin: National Library of Ireland, 1923.

____ (ed.). *A Bibliography of Irish Philology (1913–14).* Dublin: National Library of Ireland, 1942.

Bhabha, Homi K. 'A Question of Survival: Nations and Psychic States'. *Psychoanalysis and Cultural Theory.* Ed. James Donald. London: Macmillan, 1991: 89–103.

——. 'Race Time and the Revision of Modernity'. *Oxford Literary Review*, No. 13, 1991.

——. 'DissemiNation: Time, Narrative, and the Margins of the Modern Nation'. *Nation and Narration.* London and New York: Routledge, 1990; 291–322.

——. *The Location of Culture.* London and New York: Routledge, 1994.

Bharucha, Rustom (ed.). *Theatre and the World: Performance and the Politics of Culture.* London: Routledge, 1993.

Birley, Derek. *Sport and the Making of Britain.* Manchester and New York: Manchester University Press, 1993.

——. *Land of Sport and Glory: Sport and British Society 1887–1910.* Manchester and New York: Manchester University Press, 1995.

Bolger, Patrick. *The Irish Co-operative Movement: Its History and Development.* Dublin: Institute of Public Administration, 1977.

Boscagli, Maurizia. *Eye on the Flesh: Fashions of Masculinity in the Early Twentieth Century.* Oxford: Westview Press, 1996.

Bose, Abinash Chandra. *Three Mystic Poets: A Study of William Butler Yeats, AE and Rabindranath Tagore*. Norwood Editions, 1977.

Bourke, Joanna. *Dismembering the Male: Men's Bodies, Britain and the Great War.* London: Reaktion Books, 1996.

Bowe, Nicola Gordon (ed.). *Art and the National Dream: The Search for Vernacular Expression in Turn of the Century Design*. Dublin: Irish Academic Press, 1993.

Boyd, Ernest. *Ireland's Literary Renaissance.* London: Maunsel, 1916.

Boyle, Reverend John. *Cuimhne Colmcille.* Dublin: M. Gill & Sons, 1898.

Bratton, J. S., Richard Allen Cave, Breandan Gregory, Heidi J. Holder and Michael Pickering (eds.). *Acts of Supremacy: The British Empire and the Stage, 1790–1930.* Manchester: Manchester University Press, 1991.

Bristow, Joseph. *Empire Boys: Adventures in a Man's World.* London: Harper Collins, 1991.

Brown, Malcolm. *The Politics of Irish Literature: From Thomas Davis to W. B. Yeats*. Seattle: University of Washington Press, 1972.

Brown, Father Stephen. 'Irish Fiction for Boys'. *Studies*, No. 7 (1918), 665–670.

____ 'Irish Ficton for Boys.' *Studies*, No. 8 (1919), 469–472.

Brown, Terence. *Ireland: A Social and Cultural History, 1922–1985*. London: Fontana, 1981.

____ (ed.). *Celticism*. Amsterdam Studies on Cultural Identity. Amsterdam and Atlanta, GA: Rodopi, 1996.

Bryson, Lucy, and Clem McCartney. *Clashing Symbols: A Report on the Use of Flags, Anthems and Other National Symbols in Northern Ireland*. Belfast: The Institute of Irish Studies, Queen's University, 1994.

Bryson, Norman. *Vision and Painting: The Logic of the Gaze*. New Haven: Yale University Press, 1983.

____. 'Géricault and "Masculinity"'. *Visual Culture: Images and Interpretations*. Eds. Bryson, Holly, and Moxey. Hanover, NH, and London: Wesleyan University Press, 1994.

Burgin, Victor. 'Looking at Photographs'. *Thinking Photography*. Ed. Victor Burgin. London: Macmillan Education, 1982: 142–153.

Butler, Judith. *Gender Trouble: Feminism and the Subversion of Identity*. London and New York: Routledge, 1990.

____. *Bodies That Matter*. London and New York: Routledge, 1993.

Butler Cullingford, Elizabeth. '"Thinking of Her . . . as . . . Ireland": Yeats, Pearse and Heaney'. *Textual Practice*, Vol. 4, No. 1, 1990; 1–21.

Byrne, Michael. *The Vocational Education Movement: The Midland Experience*. Tullamore: Offaly VEC, 1980.

Cairns, David and Shaun Richards. *Writing Ireland: Colonialism, Nationalism and Culture*. Manchester: Manchester University Press, 1988.

Campbell, Joseph. *The Gilly of Christ*. Illustrations by Ada Wentworth Shields. Dublin: 1907.

____. *The Man Child*. Dublin: Loch Press Booklets No. 1, 1907.

Canning, Kathleen. 'Feminist History After the Linguistic Turn: Historicizing Discourse and Experience'. *Signs: Journal of Women in Culture and Society*, Vol. 19, No. 2, Winter 1994; 368–404.

Carlyle, Thomas. *On Heroes, Hero-Worship and the Heroic in History*. London: 1840; repr. London: Dent, 1967.

——. *Past and Present*. London, 1843.

Carnoy, Martin. *Education as Cultural Imperialism*. New York: Longman, 1974.

Casey, Daniel J. and Robert E. Rhodes (eds.). *Views of the Irish Peasantry 1800–1916*. Hamden, CT: Archon Books, 1977.

Casteras, Susan. *Victorian Childhood*. New York: Abrams, 1986.

——. *Images of Victorian Womanhood in English Art*. London and Toronto: Fairleigh Dickinson Associated Press, 1987.

Castle, Kathryn. *Britannia's Children: Reading Colonialism through Children's Books and Magazines*. Manchester: Manchester University Press, 1996.

Chatterjee, Partha. *Nationalist Thought and the Colonial World: A Derivative Discourse*. Minneapolis: University of Minnesota Press; repr. 1993

——. *The Nation and Its Fragments: Colonial and Postcolonial Histories*. Princeton: Princeton University Press, 1993.

Chiari, Joseph. *The Aesthetics of Modernism*. London: Vision, 1990.

Chodorow, Nancy. *The Reproduction of Mothering: Psychoanalysis and the Sociology of Gender.* Berkeley: University of California Press, 1978.

Clarke, Brenna Katz. *The Emergence of the Peasant Play at the Abbey Theatre*. Theatre and Dramatic Studies No. 12. UK: Bowker Publishing Company, 1987.

Clarke, J. C. Critcher and R. Johnson (eds.). *Working Class Culture*. London: 1979.

Clery, Arthur. 'The Gaelic League, 1893–1919'. *Studies* No. 8, 1919; 398–408.

Coldrey, Barry. *Faith and Fatherland: The Christian Brothers and the Development of Irish Nationalism 1838–1921*. Dublin: Gill and Macmillan, 1988.

Collier, John. *Visual Anthropology: Photography as a Research Method.* New York: Holt, Rhinehart and Winston, 1967.

Collini, Stefan. *Public Moralists, Political Thought and Intellectual Life in Britain 1850–1930.* New York and Oxford: Oxford University Press, 1991.

Colum, Mary. *Life and the Dream.* New York: 1947.

Colum, Padraic. 'The Destruction of the Hostel'. *An Macaomh,* Vol. 2, No. 3, Christmas 1910; 25–38.

——. *A Boy in Eirinn.* Harrap, 1913.

——. *The King of Ireland's Son.* New York: Harrap, 1916.

——. *The Children of Odin.* Harrap, 1922.

——. *Three Plays.* Dublin: Allen Figgis, 1963.

Colum, Padraic, and Mary Colum. *The Irish Rebellion of 1916 and its Martyrs.* New York: The Devin-Adair Company, 1916.

Commissioners of Irish Education. *Palles Report.* 1899.

Comyn, David. *The Youthful Exploits of Finn.* Dublin: Gill, 1896.

Connolly, Nora. *The Unbroken Tradition.* New York: 1918.

Coolahan, John. *Irish Education: Its History and Structure.* Dublin: Institute of Public Administration, 1981.

Corcoran, Timothy. 'The Native Speaker as Teacher'. *Irish Monthly,* No. 51, 1923; 187–90.

Corkery, Daniel. *The Hidden Ireland: A Study of Gaelic Munster in the Eighteenth Century.* Dublin: Gill and Macmillan, 1924.

——. *The Fortunes of the Irish Language.* Cork: Mercier Press, 1954.

Costello, Peter. *Clongowes Wood: A History of Clongowes Wood College, 1914–1989.* Dublin: Gill and Macmillan, 1989.

Coveney, Peter. *The Image of Childhood. The Individual and Society: A Study of the Theme in English Literature.* London: Penguin, 1957.

Coxhead, Elizabeth. *Lady Gregory: A Literary Portrait.* London: Macmillan, 1961.

Cronin, Sean. 'Nation building and the Irish Language Revival Movement'. *Eire,* Vol. 13, No. 1, 1978.

Crowley, Tony. 'Bahktin and the History of the Language'. *Bakhtin and Cultural Theory.* Eds. Ken Hirschkop and David Shepherd. Manchester: Manchester University Press, 1989.

Curthoys, M. C. and H. S. Jones. 'Oxford Athleticism 1850–1914: A Reappraisal'. *History of Education*, Vol. 24, No. 4, December 1995; 305–17.

Curtis, Edmund. *A History of Ireland.* London: Methuen, 1936.

Curtis, L. P. *Apes and Angels: The Irishman in Victorian Caricature.* Washington: Smithsonian Institution Press, 1971.

Dalsimer, Adele M. (ed.). *Visualising Ireland: National Identity and the Pictorial Tradition.* London: Faber and Faber, 1993.

Daly, Mary and David Dickson. *The Origins of Popular Literacy in Ireland: Language and Education Development 1700–1920.* Dublin: Anna Livia, 1990.

Dawe, Gerald and John Wilson Foster (eds.). *The Poet's Place: Ulster Literature and Society.* Belfast: Institute of Irish Studies, Queen's University, 1991.

Dawson, Graham. *Soldier Heroes, British Adventure, Empire and the Imagining of Masculinities.* London and New York: Routledge, 1994.

Davis, Thomas. 'Our National Language'. *Prose Writings of Thomas Davis.* Ed. T. W. Rolleston. London: Camelot, 1890; 165.

Deane, Seamus. *Celtic Revivals: Essays in Modern Irish Literature 1880–1980.* London and Boston: Faber and Faber, 1985.

Debord, Guy. *Society of the Spectacle.* London: Black and Red, 1970; repr. London: Rebel Press, AIM Publications, 1987.

De Búrca, Marcus. *The GAA: A History of the Gaelic Athletic Association.* Dublin: Cumann Lúthchleas Gael, 1980.

De Freine, Seán. *The Great Silence.* Cork: Mercier Press, 1978.

Dennis, Alfred. 'A Memory of P. H. Pearse'. *Capuchin Annual,* 1942; 259–62.

Diamond, Irene, and Lee Quinby (eds.). *Feminism and Foucault: Reflections on Resistance.* Boston: Northeastern University Press, 1988.

Diprose, Rosalyn and Robyn Ferrell (eds.). *Cartographies: Poststructuralism and the Mapping of Bodies and Spaces.* Sydney: Allen & Unwin, 1991.

Dirks, Nicholas (ed.). 'Introduction: Colonialism and Culture'. *Colonialism and Culture.* Ann Arbor: University of Michigan Press, 1992; 1–25.

Dirks, N., Geoff Eley and Sherry Ortner (eds.). *Culture/Power/History: A Reader in Contemporary Social Theory.* Princeton: Princeton University Press, 1994.

Dollimore, Jonathan. *Sexual Dissidence: Augustine to Wilde, Freud to Foucault.* Oxford: Clarendon Press, 1991.

Donlon, Patricia. 'Irish Children's Fiction'. *Linen Hall Review,* Autumn 1985; 12–13.

Dowling, Linda. *Hellenism and Homosexuality in Victorian Oxford.* London and Ithaca, New York: Cornell University Press, 1994.

Dowling, P. J. *The Hedge Schools of Ireland.* Cork and Dublin: Mercier Press, 1968.

Doyle, Katherine. 'The Irish Language as a Curricular Element in Irish Primary Education in the Period 1831–1935'. Unpublished M.Ed thesis, Dublin University, Trinity College, 1983.

Druckery, Timothy. 'From Dada to Digital: Montage in the Twentieth Century'. *Aperture,* No. 136, Summer 1994.

Dudley Edwards, Ruth. *Patrick Pearse: The Triumph of Failure.* London: Victor Gollancz, 1977; repr. Dublin: Poolbeg Press, 1990.

Dunleavy, Gareth W. and Janet Egleson Dunleavy. *Douglas Hyde: A Maker of Modern Ireland.* Berkeley: University of Calfornia Press, 1991.

Durcan, Thomas Joseph. *History of Irish Education from 1800.* Bala, Wales: Dragon Press, 1972.

Dutton, Kenneth. *The Perfectible Body: The Western Ideal of Physical Development.* London: Cassell, 1985.

Dyhouse, Carol. *Girls Growing up in Late Victorian and Edwardian Society.* London: Routledge & Kegan Paul, 1981.

Edelstein, T. J., Richard Born and Sue Taylor (eds.). *Imagining an Irish Past: The Celtic Revival 1840–1940.* Chicago: The David and Alfred Smart Museum of Art, University of Chicago, 1992.

Edwards, Elizabeth (ed.). *Anthropology and Photography 1860–1920.* London: Royal Anthropological Institute, 1992.

Elliot, Robert. *Art and Ireland.* New York and London: Kennikat Press, 1902.

Eyler, Audrey and Robert F. Garrett (eds.). *The Uses of the Past: Essays on Irish Culture.* Newark: University of Delaware Press, 1988.

Fahy, F. A. 'A Gaelic League Catechism'. Gaelic League Pamphlets, No. 5, 1900.

Fairweather, Eugene. *The Oxford Movement.* New York and Oxford: Oxford University Press, 1964.

Fanon, Frantz. *Black Skin, White Mask.* London: McKibbon & Kee, 1968.

Farragher, Seán, and Annraoi Wyer. *Blackrock College, 1860–1995.* Dublin: Paraclete Press, 1995.

Farren, Sean. 'Irish Model Schools 1833–1870: Models of What?' *History of Education*, Vol. 24, No. 1, 1995; 45–60.

Faulkner, Peter. *William Morris and W. B. Yeats.* Dublin: 1962.

Faxon, Alicia Craig. *Dante Gabriel Rossetti.* Oxford: Phaidon Press, 1989.

Fear Faire. 'Irish in and out of the Intermediate'. *Irish Educational Review,* No. 3,1910; 410–12.

Feeney, William J. *Drama in Hardwicke Street: A History of the Irish Theatre Company.* London and Toronto: Fairleigh Dickinson University Press, 1984.

Fianna Éireann Handbook. Dublin, 1909; repr. 1914.

Fingall, Elizabeth, Countess of. *Seventy Years Young*. Dublin: Lilliput Press, 1991.

Fishman, Joshua. 'The Impact of Nationality on Language Planning'. *Language in Socio-Cultural Change*. Selected and introduced by Anwar S. Dil. Stanford: Stanford University Press, 1972.

——. *Language and Nationalism.* Rowley, MA: 1973.

Forbush, William. *The Coming Generation.* London: n.p., 1912.

——. *Guide Book to Childhood.* London: n.p., 1921.

Fortner, Robert S. 'The Culture of Hope and the Culture of Despair: The Print Media and Nineteenth-Century Irish Emigration'. *Eire,* Vol. 13, No. 3, Fall, 1978; 32–48.

Foster, R. F. *Paddy and Mr Punch: Connections in Irish and English History.* London: Allen Lane, 1993.

Foster, John Wilson. 'Certain Set Apart: The Western Isle in the Irish Renaissance'. *Studies*, Winter 1977; 265.

Foucault, Michel. *Discipline and Punish: The Birth of the Prison.* Trans. Alan Sheridan. London: Penguin, 1977.

——. *Language, Counter-Memory, Practice.* Ed. D. F. Bouchard. New York: Cornell University Press, 1977

——. *The History of Sexuality: Volume I.* London: Penguin, 1978.

——. 'Truth and Power'. *Power/Knowledge: Selected Interviews and Other Writings 1972–1977.* Ed. Colin Gordon. New York: Pantheon, 1980; 109–33.

——. 'The Order of Discourse'. *Untying the Text.* Ed. Robert Young. London: Routledge & Kegan Paul, 1981.

Fox, Geoffrey. *Children's Literature in Education.* London: Heinemann Educational Books, 1976.

Fox, Moireen. 'Some aspects of the Celtic Movement'. *Irish Review,* Vol. 2, 1912; 553–56.

Frazier, Adrian. *Behind the Scenes: Yeats, Horniman and the Struggle for the Abbey Theatre.* Berkeley: University of California Press, 1990.

Fried, Michael. *Absorption and Theatricality: Painting and Beholder in the Age of Diderot.* Berkeley: University of California Press, 1980.

Friel, Brian. *Translations.* London: Faber and Faber, 1981.

Fullerton, R. 'The Place of Irish in Ireland's Education'. *Irish Educational Review,* Vol. 5, 1912; 456–66.

——. 'What Is the Good of It: A Word to Our Young Priests'. *Catholic Bulletin,* No. 4, 1914.

——. *The Prudence of St Patrick's Irish Policy.* Dublin: O'Brien and Ards, 1916.

Furlong, Alice. *Tales of Fairy Folks, Queens and Heroes.* 1909.

Fussell, Paul. *The Great War and Modern Memory.* London: Oxford University Press, 1975.

Gainor, Ellen (ed.). *Imperialism and Theatre: Essays on World Theatre, Drama and Performance.* London and New York: Routledge, 1995.

Geertz, Clifford. *The Interpretation of Cultures.* London: Hutchinson, 1975.

Giddens, Anthony. *The Consequences of Modernity.* Stanford: Stanford University Press, 1990.

Gilbert, Sandra and Susan Gubar, *The Madwoman in the Attic: The Woman Writer and the Nineteenth-Century Literary Imagination.* New Haven: Yale University Press, 1979.

Giles, H. (ed.). *Language, Ethnicity and Intergroup Relations.* London: Academic Press, 1977.

Gilman, Sander L. *Seeing the Insane: A Cultural History of Psychiatric Illustration.* London: Wiley, 1985.

Gilroy, Paul. *The Black Atlantic: Modernity and Double Consciousness.* London and New York: Verso, 1993.

Girouard, Mark. *The Return to Camelot: Chivalry and the English Gentleman.* New Haven: Yale University Press, 1981.

Giroux, Henry. 'Paulo Freire's Approach to Radical Educational Theory and Practice'. *Ideology, Culture and the Process of Schooling.* London: The Falmer Press, 1981; 127–41.

——. *Border Crossings: Cultural Workers and the Politics of Education.* London and New York: Routledge, 1992.

Glandon, Virginia E. 'The Irish Free Press and Revolutionary Irish Nationalism 1900–1922'. *Eire,* Spring 1981; 21–33.

Glenavy, Beatrice. *Today We Will Only Gossip.* London: 1964.

Goldstein, Laurence. 'The Spectacle of his Body'. *Michigan Quarterly Review,* Vol. XXXXIV, No. 4, Fall 1995; 681–702.

Goldstrom, Joachim. *The Social Context of Education 1808–1870: A Study of the Working Class School Reader in England and Ireland.* Shannon: Irish University Press, 1972.

Gordon Bowe, Nicola. *The Life and Work of Harry Clarke.* Dublin: Irish Academic Press, 1989.

—— (ed.). *Art and the National Dream: The Search for Vernacular Expression in Turn-of-the-Century Design.* Dublin: Irish Academic Press, 1993.

Gordon Bowe, Nicola and Elizabeth Cumming, *The Arts and Crafts Movements in Dublin and Edinburgh, 1885–1925.* Dublin: Irish Academic Press, 1997.

Gore, Jennifer. *The Struggle for Pedagogies.* London and New York: Routledge, 1993.

Gorham, Deborah. *The Victorian Girl and the Feminine Ideal.* London: Croom Helm, 1982.

Gorman, Sheila. 'Dichotomy, Boundary and Paradox: Aspects of the Psychology and Sociology of the Uniforms of the British Military with Particular Reference to the Royal Irish Fusiliers in the Great War, 1914–1918'. Unpublished M.A. thesis, National College of Art and Design, 1991.

Gramsci, Antonio. *Selections from the Prison Notebooks.* Eds. Quintin Hoare and Geoffrey Nowell Smith. London: Lawrence and Wishart, 1971.

——. 'Language, Linguistics and Folklore'. *Selections from Cultural Writings.* Eds. David Forgacs and Geoffrey Nowell-Smith, trans. William Boelhower. London: Lawrence and Wishart, 1985.

Greene, David. *The Irish Language.* Dublin and Cork: 1966.

——. 'Robert Atkinson and Irish Studies'. *Hermathena,* C 11, Spring 1966; 6–15.

——. *Writing in Irish Today.* Dublin and Cork: Mercier Press, 1972.

Gregory, Lady Augusta. *Cúchulainn of Muirthemne: The Story of the Men of the Red Branch of Ulster.* Dublin: John Murray; New York: Scribners, 1902.

——. *Poets and Dreamers.* Dublin: John Murray; New York: Scribners, 1903.

——. *Gods and Fighting Men.* Dublin: John Murray; New York: Scribners, 1904.

——. *The Kiltartan Poetry Book.* Dublin: Cuala Press, 1918.

Grote, Georg. *The Gaelic League 1893–1993.* Germany: Waxmann, 1994.

Gwynn, Denis. 'Patrick Pearse'. *Dublin Review,* January/March 1923; 92–105.

——. *The Life and Death of Roger Casement.* London: Jonathan Cape, 1930.

——. *Edward Martyn and the Irish Revival.* London: Jonathan Cape, 1930.

Gwynn, Stephen. 'Irish Education and Irish Character'. *Moral Instruction and Training in Schools: Report of an International Enquiry. Volume I.* London: Longmans, Green & Co., 1908; 465–80.

Gwynn, Mrs Stephen. *Stories from Irish History Told for Children.* Illustrated by George Morrow and Arthur Donnelly. Dublin and Cork: Browne & Nolan, 1904.

Haddon, A. C. and C. R. Browne. 'The Ethnography of the Aran Islands'. *Proceedings of the Royal Irish Academy,* 2nd and 3rd Series, 1891–1893; 452–505.

Haddon, A. C. 'Photography and Folklore'. *Folklore,* Vol. 6, 1895; 222–24.

Hagan, Edward A. *'High Nonsensical Words': A Study of the Works of Standish O'Grady.* New York: The Whitson Publishing Company, 1986.

Halén, Widar. *Dragons from the North.* Dublin and Bergen: 1995.

Hall, Donald (ed.). *Muscular Christianity: Embodying the Victorian Age.* Cambridge: Cambridge University Press, 1994.

Harbison, Peter, Homan Potterton and Jeanne Sheehy. *Irish Art and Architecture.* London: n.p., 1978.

Hayden, Mary and George A. Moonan. 'Literature and Language in the Nineteenth Century'. *A Short History of the Irish People.* Dublin: Talbot Press, 1921.

Hechter, Michael. *Internal Colonialism: The Celtic Fringe in British National Development, 1536–1966.* London: Routledge and Kegan Paul, 1975.

Helferty, Seamus and Raymond Refaussé. *Directory of Irish Archives.* Dublin: Irish Academic Press, 1993.

Heidegger, Martin. *The Question Concerning Technology.* Trans. William Lovitt. Harper & Row, New York: 1977.

Hertz, Neil. 'Medusa's Head: Male Hysteria under Political Pressure'. *Representations,* Vol. 4, Fall 1983; 27–54.

Hewison, Robert (ed.). *New Approaches to Ruskin.* London, Boston and Henley: Routledge and Kegan Paul, 1981.

____. *Future Tense: A New Art for the Nineties*. London: Methuen, 1990.
Hilliard, David. 'UnEnglish and Unmanly: Anglo-Catholicism and Homosexuality'. *Victorian Studies*, Vol. 25, Winter 1982.
Hindley, Reg. *The Death of the Irish Language: A Qualified Obituary.* London: Routledge, 1990.
Hirsch, Julia. *Family Photographs: Content, Meaning and Effect.* New York and Oxford: Oxford University Press, 1989.
Hirschkop, Ken. 'Bahktin and Cultural Theory'. *Bahktin and Cultural Theory.* Eds. Ken Hirschkop and David Shepherd. Manchester: Manchester University Press, 1989.
Hobsbawm, Eric. *Nations and Nationalism since 1780: Programme, Myth and Reality.* Cambridge: Cambridge University Press, 1990.
Holland, C. H. (ed.). *Trinity College Dublin and the Idea of a University.* Dublin: Trinity College Press, 1991.
Hollis, Patricia. *Women in Public, 1840–1900: Documents of the Victorian Women's Movement.* London and Boston: Allen & Unwin, 1979.
Holloway, Joseph. *The Abbey Theatre: A Selection from his Unpublished Journal 'Impressions of a Playgoer'.* Eds. Robert Hogan and Michael J. O'Neill. New York: Carbondale, 1967.
Holweck, Reverend F. G. *A Biographical Dictionary of the Saints.* London and Missouri: B. Herder Book Co., 1924.
Holzapfel, Rudi. 'A Summary of Irish Literary Periodicals from 1900 to the Present Day'. Unpublished M.Litt. thesis, Trinity College, Dublin, 1964.
Horne Peter and Reina Lewis (eds.). *Outlooks: Lesbian and Gay Sexualities and Visual Cultures.* London and New York: Routledge, 1996.
Houghton, Walter. *The Victorian Frame of Mind, 1830–1870.* New Haven and London: Yale University Press, 1957.
Hull, Eleanor (ed.). *The Cúchulainn Saga in Irish Literature.* Grimm Library, 1898.
____. *The Silver Bough in Irish Legend.* 1901.
____. *The Saga Book of the Viking Club.* 1903.
____. *Pagan Ireland.* Dublin: Gill, 1904.
____. *The Story of Deirdre.* 1904.

——. *Early Christian Ireland.* Preface by Alfred Nutt. Dublin: Gill, 1905.

——. *A Textbook of Irish Literature to the Sixteenth Century.* 1906.

——. *Cúchulainn the Hound of Ulster.* Dublin: Harrap, 1909.

——. *The Poem Book of the Gael: Translations from Irish Gaelic Poetry into English Prose and Verse.* 1912.

——. *The Northmen in Britain.* Dublin: Harrap, 1913.

Humphreys, Alexander J. *New Dubliners: Urbanisation and the Irish Family.* London and New York: Routledge and Kegan Paul, 1966.

Hunt, Peter and Dennis Butts. *Children's Literature: An Illustrated History.* Oxford: Oxford University Press, 1995.

Hutchinson, John. *The Dynamics of Cultural Nationalism: The Irish Revival and the Creation of the Nation State.* London and Boston: Allen & Unwin, 1987.

Hyam, Ronald. *Empire and Sexuality: The British Experience.* Manchester: Manchester University Press, 1990.

Hyde, Douglas. *The Religious Songs of Connacht.* 1893–4; repr. in Ó Conaire, Brendán (ed.). Dublin: Irish Academic Press, 1985.

——. *A Literary History of Ireland: From Earliest Times to the Present Day.* Fisher Unwin, 1899; repr. edited and with introduction by Brian Ó Cuív. London: Ernest Benn Limited; New York: Barnes and Noble, 1967.

——. 'An Naomh Ar Iarraidh – The Lost Saint'. Trans. Lady Augusta Gregory. *Samhain,* 1902.

——. 'Half-Holiday Lecturers at St Enda's: Dr Douglas Hyde on the Language Movement'. *An Macaomh,* Vol. 12, 1909; 50–51.

——. 'My Memories of the Irish Revival'. W. G. Fitzgerald (ed.). *The Voice of Ireland.* Dublin and London: Virtue, 1923; 454–446.

——. 'The Irish Language Movement: Some Reminiscences'. *Gaelic Churchman,* No. 6, 1924; 306–07, 317–18, 328–29, 340–41, 352–53.

——. 'A Plea for the Irish Language'. *Douglas Hyde: Language Lore and Lyrics.* Ed. Brendán Ó Conaire. Dublin: Irish Academic Press, 1986; 74–80.

———. 'The Necessity for De-Anglicising Ireland'. *Douglas Hyde: Language Lore and Lyrics*. Ed. Brendán Ó Conaire. Dublin: Irish Academic Press, 1986; 153–70.

Hynes, Samuel. *The Edwardian Turn of Mind*. London: Oxford University Press, 1968.

Inglis, Brian. *Roger Casement*. London: Hodder and Stoughton, 1973.

Innes, Catherine. *Women and Nation in Irish Literature and Society 1880–1915*. London: Harvester Wheatsheaf, 1993.

Jacobs, Joseph. *Celtic Fairy Tales*. Illustrated by J. D. Batten. London: David Nutt, 1892.

Jeffrey, Keith (ed.). *An Irish Empire? Aspects of Ireland and the British Empire*. Manchester and New York: Manchester University Press, 1996.

Joyce, Patrick W. *A Social History of Ancient Ireland*. 2 vols. London, 1903; repr. Dublin, 1913.

Joynt, Maud. 'The Future of the Irish Language'. *New Ireland Review*, Vol. 13, 1900; 193–99.

Kearney, Richard. 'Postmodernity, Nationalism and Ireland'. *History of European Ideas*, Vol. 16; Nos. 1–3; 147–55.

———. *Myth and Motherland*. Derry: Field Day Pamphlet, 1984.

Keating, Carla (ed.). *Horace Plunkett and Co-operatives*. Cork: UCC Bank of Ireland Collective, 1983.

Keating, Geoffrey. *History of Ireland*. 3 vols. London: Irish Texts Society, 1902–1914.

Keating, Paul. 'National Self-Images and the Internalisation of Tastes, Values and Demands: The Case of Ireland'. *World Futures*, Vol. 33, No. 1–3, 1992; 121–31.

Keith, Jeffrey (ed.). *An Irish Empire? Aspects of Ireland and the British Empire*. Manchester and New York: Manchester University Press, 1996.

Kennedy, Robert. *The Irish: Emigration, Marriage, and Fertility*. London: 1978.

Kenney, James F. 'Modern Scholarship and the Gaelic Revival'. *Sources for the Early History of Ireland*. Volume I. New York: Columbia University Press, 1929.

Kestner, Joseph A. *Masculinities in Victorian Painting.* England: Scolar Press, 1995.

Kiberd, Declan. 'The Perils of Nostalgia: A Critique of the Revival'. *Literature and the Changing Ireland.* Ed. P. Connolly. Gerrard's Cross: Colin Smythe, 1980.

——. 'The War Against the Past'. *The Uses of the Past.* Eds. Audrey Eyler and Robert Garratt. Delaware University Press, 1988.

——. *Synge and the Irish Language.* 2nd ed. London: Macmillan Press, 1993.

——. *Inventing Ireland: The Literature of the Modern Nation.* London: Vintage, 1996.

Kincaid, James. *Child-Loving: The Erotic Child and Victorian Culture.* New York and London: Routledge, 1992.

Kissane, Noel. *The Irish Face.* Dublin: National Library of Ireland, 1986.

Knapp, James. 'Primitivism and Empire: John Synge and Paul Gaugin'. *Comparative Literature,* Vol. 41, No. 1, 1989; 53–68.

Kosofsky Sedgwick, Eve. *Between Men: English Literature and Male Homosocial Desire.* New York: Columbia U.P., 1985.

——. *Epistemology of the Closet.* Great Britain: Harvester Wheatsheaf, 1991.

Kruger, Barbara and Phil Mariani (eds.). *Remaking History.* Discussions in Contemporary Culture 4. Seattle: Bay Press, 1989.

Larmour, Paul. *The Arts and Crafts Movement in Ireland.* Belfast: Friar's Bush Press, 1992.

Leahy, Arthur. *The Sick Bed of Cuchulainn.* London: 1905.

——. *Heroic Romances of Ireland.* London: 1905–6.

Lee, Joseph. *The Modernisation of Irish Society 1848–1918.* Dublin: Gill and Macmillan, 1973; repr. 1989.

Lee, Timothy. *The Value of the Irish Language and Irish Literature.* Limerick: O'Connor Press, 1901.

Leerssen, Joep. *Mere Irish and Fíor-Ghael: Studies in the Idea of Irish Nationality, Its Development and Literary Expression Prior to the Nineteenth Century.* Cork: Cork University Press in association with Field Day, 1996.

———. *Remembrance and Imagination.* Cork: Cork University Press in association with Field Day, 1996.

Lennon, Michael J. 'Douglas Hyde'. *The Bell,* No. 166, 1951; 46–54.

Le Roux, Louis. *Patrick H. Pearse.* Translated and adapted by Desmond Ryan. Dublin: Phoenix, 1932.

Lester, DeeGee. *Irish Research: A Guide to Collections in North America, Ireland and Great Britain.* Bibliographies and Indexes in World History No. 9. Connecticut: Greenwood Press, 1987.

Lincoln, Bruce. *Discourse and the Construction of Society: Comparative Studies of Myth, Ritual and Classification.* New York and Oxford: Oxford University Press, 1989.

Lloyd, David. *Nationalism and Minor Literature.* Berkeley: University of California Press, 1988.

Loftus, Belinda. 'In Search of a Useful Theory'. *Circa,* No. 40, Summer 1988; 17–23.

———. 'Colouring: The Black and White'. *Circa,* No. 40, Summer 1988; 26–31.

———. *Mirrors: William III and Mother Ireland.* Dundrum, Co. Down: Picture Press, 1990.

Luddy, Maria and Cliona Murphy (eds.). *Women Surviving: Studies in Irish Women's History in the Nineteenth and Twentieth Centuries.* Dublin: Poolbeg Press, 1990.

Lusted, D. 'Why Pedagogy?'. *Screen,* No. 275, 1986.

Lyons, F. S. L. *Ireland Since the Famine.* London: Fontana Press, 1971.

Mac Aodha, Breandán S. 'Was This a Social Revolution?' *The Gaelic League Idea.* Ed. Seán O'Tuama, Cork and Dublin: Mercier Press, 1972; 20–30.

Mac Auslan, MacMhuirich. 'The Cultural Liquidation of Celtica: The Message of Patrick Pearse' *The Celtic Experience: Past and Present.* Ed. F. G. Thompson. Dublin: Celtic League, 1972.

McClintock, Anne. 'Family Feuds: Gender, Nationalism and the Family'. *Feminist Review,* No. 44, Summer 1993; 61–80.

———. *Imperial Leather: Race, Gender and Sexuality in the Colonial Conquest.* London and New York: Routledge, 1995.

McClintock, H. F. and John Dunbar. *Old Irish and Highland Dress.* Dundalk: Dundalgan Press, 1950.

McCone, Kim. *Pagan Past and Christian Present in Early Irish Literature.* Maynooth: An Sagart, 1990.

McDonagh, Thomas. *Literature in Ireland: Studies Irish and Anglo-Irish.* Dublin: Talbot Press, 1916.

McGarry, Milo. 'Memories of Sgoil Éanna'. *Capuchin Annual,* 1930; 35–41.

McGrath, Fergal. *Education in Ancient and Medieval Ireland.* Dublin: Special Publications, 1979.

McKenna, Stephen. *Memories of the Dead.* Dublin: 1916.

McKenzie, John (ed.). *Imperialism and Popular Culture.* Manchester: Manchester University Press, 1986.

McLaren, Peter and Colin Lankshear. *The Politics of Liberation: Paths from Freire.* London and New York: Routledge, 1994.

MacLeod, David. *Building Character in the American Boy: The Boy Scouts, YMCA, and their Forerunners, 1870–1920.* Madison: University of Wisconsin Press, 1983.

McLeod, Hugh. *Religion and Society in England 1850–1914.* Basingstoke: Macmillan Press, 1996.

Mac Réamoinn, Seán (ed.). *The Pleasures of Gaelic Poetry.* London: Allen Lane, 1982.

Mackey, James. *Religious Imagination.* Edinburgh: Edinburgh University Press, 1987.

Maguire, Reverend E. (ed.). *'Cuímnhe Coluimcille', or The Gartan Festival, being a Record of the Celebration Held at Gartan, on the 9th June, 1897, the Thirteenth Centennial of Saint Columba.* Dublin: M. Gill & Son, 1898.

Mancoff, Debra. *The Arthurian Revival in Victorian Art.* New York: Garland, 1990.

Mandle, W. F. *Irish Culture and Nationalism 1750–1950.* London: Macmillan Press, 1983.

——. *The Gaelic Athletic Association and Irish Nationalist Politics 1884–1924.* London: Christopher Helm; Dublin: Gill and Macmillan, 1987.

Mangan, J. A. *Benefits Bestowed: Education and British Imperialism.* Manchester: Manchester University Press, 1988.

____ (ed.). *Making Imperial Mentalities: Socialisation and British Imperialism.* Manchester: Manchester University Press, 1990.

____ (ed.). *The Cultural Bond: Sport, Empire, Society.* London: Frank Cass, 1992.

____. *The Imperial Curriculum: Racial Images and Education in the British Colonial Experience.* London and New York: Routledge, 1993.

Mangan, J. A. and W. J. Baker. *Sport in Africa: Essays in Social History.* London and New York: Routledge, 1987.

Mangan, J. A. and James Walvin (eds.). *Manliness and Morality*. New York: St Martin's Press, 1987.

Marantz, Sylvia. *The Art of Children's Books.* New York and London: Garland Press, 1995.

Martin, F. X. (ed.). *The Easter Rising 1916 and University College, Dublin.* Dublin: Browne and Nolan, 1966.

____ (ed.). *Leaders and Men of the Easter Rising: Dublin 1916.* London: Methuen, 1967.

Martin, Stoddard. *From Wagner to the Waste Land: A Study of the Relationship of Wagner to English Literature.* London and Basingstoke: Macmillan, 1982.

Massy, Richard. *Analytical Ethnography: The Mixed Tribes in Great Britain and Ireland Examined and the Political, Physical and Metaphysical Blunderings on the Celt and Saxon Exposed.* London: Binns and Goodwin, 1855.

Megaw, Ruth and Vincent Megaw. *Celtic Art: From Its Beginnings to the Book of Kells.* London: Thames and Hudson, 1989.

Memmi, Albert. *The Colonizer and the Colonized.* London: Earthscan Publications; 1967, repr. 1990.

Minh-ha, Trinh T. 'Documentary Is/Not a Name'. *October*, Vol. 52, Spring 1990.

Mitchell, Juliet and Ann Oakley (eds.). *The Rights and Wrongs of Women.* Harmondsworth: Penguin, 1976.

Moran, D. P. *The Philosophy of Irish Ireland.* Dublin: James Duffy, 1905.

Moran, Sean Farrell. *Patrick Pearse and the Politics of Redemption: The Mind of the Easter Rising, 1916.* Washington DC: The Catholic University of America Press, 1994.

Murphy, Father James. *Nos Auteum: A History of Castleknock College.* Dublin: Gill and Macmillan, 1996.

Mulvey, Laura. 'Visual Pleasure and Narrative Cinema', *Screen*, Vol. 14, No. 3, Autumn 1975.

Nandy, Ashis. *The Intimate Enemy: The Loss and Recovery of Self Under Colonialism.* Delhi: Oxford University Press, 1983.

——. *The Illegitimacy of Nationalism: Rabindranath Tagore and the Politics of Self.* Delhi: Oxford University Press, 1994.

Nash, Catherine. 'Remapping and Renaming: Cartographies of Identity, Gender and Landscape in Ireland'. *Feminist Review*, No. 44, Summer 1993; 39–57.

——. 'Embodying the Nation: The West of Ireland Landscape and Irish National Identity'. *Tourism in Ireland: A Critical Analysis.* Eds. Michael Cronin and Barbara O'Connor. Cork: Cork University Press, 1993.

Nead, Lynda. *The Female Nude: Art, Obscenity and Sexuality.* London: Routledge, 1992.

Neale, Steve. 'Masculinity as Spectacle: Reflections on Men and Mainstream Cinema'. *Screen*, Vol. 24, No. 6, November/December 1983; 2–16.

Nic Shiubhlaigh, Máire. *The Splendid Years: Recollections of Máire Nic Shuibhlaigh.* Dublin: James Duffy, 1935.

Nockles, Peter. *The Oxford Movement in Context.* Cambridge: Cambridge University Press, 1994.

Norman, Diana. *Terrible Beauty: A Life of Constance Markievicz 1868–1927.* London: Hodder & Stoughton, 1987.

Norstedt, Johann. *Thomas MacDonagh: A Critical Biography.* Charlottesville: University Press of Virginia, 1980.

Nowlan, Kevin (ed.). *The Making of 1916: Studies in the History of the Rising.* Dublin: Stationery Office, 1969.

Nutt, Alfred. *Cuchulainn: The Irish Achilles.* London: Nutt, 1900.

O'Brien Johnson, Toni and David Cairns (eds.). *Gender in Irish Writing*. Buckingham: Open University Press, 1991.
Ó Buachalla, Séamus (ed.). *The Letters of P. H. Pearse*. Gerrard's Cross: Colin Smythe, 1980.
——. *The Literary Writings of Patrick Pearse*. Dublin and Cork: Mercier Press, 1979.
—— (ed.). *A Significant Irish Educationalist: The Educational Writings of P. H. Pearse*. Dublin and Cork: The Mercier Press, 1980.
——. 'Educational Policy and the Role of the Irish Language from 1831–1981': *European Journal of Education*, Vol. 19, 1984; 75–92.
O'Casey, Sean. *Drums Under the Windows*. London: Macmillan, 1945; repr. New York: Carroll and Graft Publishers, 1984.
Ó Conaire, Brendán (ed.). *Douglas Hyde: Language Lore and Lyrics*. Dublin: Irish Academic Press, 1986.
Ó Conaire, Pádraig Óg. 'Cuimhní Scoil Éanna'. *Cuimhní na bPiarsach*. Dublin: 1958.
O'Conor Eccles, Charlotte. *Simple Advice: To be Followed by All who Desire the Good of Ireland and Especially by Gaelic Leaguers*. Dublin: Gaelic League, 1905.
O'Connor, Anne and Susan Parkes. *Gladly Learn and Gladly Teach: Alexandra College and School 1866–1966*. Dublin: Blackwater Press, 1984.
O'Connor, Barbara and Michael Cronin (eds.). *Tourism in Ireland: A Cultural Analysis*. Cork: Cork University Press, 1993.
O'Connor, Frank. *An Only Child*. London: Macmillan, 1961.
——. *The Backward Look: A Survey of Irish Literature*. London: Macmillan, 1967.
O Cuív, Brian (ed.). *A View of the Irish Language*. Dublin: Stationery Office, 1969.
O'Curry, Eugene. *On the Manners and Customs of the Ancient Irish*, 3 Vols. A series of lectures edited with an introduction by W. K. O'Sullivan. London: Williams and Newgate; New York: Scribners, 1873.
O'Donoghue, D. 'Nationality and Language'. *Irish Man-Irish Nation*. Ed. Columban League. Cork: Mercier Press, 1947; 20–28.

O'Driscoll, Robert (ed.). *The Celtic Consciousness*. Dublin: The Dolmen Press, 1982.

Ó Dubhthaigh, Fiachra. *A Review of the Contribution of Sir Patrick Keenan to the Development of Irish and British Colonial Education.* Unpublished M.Ed. thesis, Trinity College, Dublin, 1974.

Ó Fearáil, P. *The Story of Conradh na Gaeilge*. Dublin: Clódhanna, 1975.

O'Grady, Standish James. *History of Ireland: The Heroic Period.* Volume 1. Sampson and Low, London: 1878.

____. *History of Ireland: Cúchulainn and His Contemporaries.* Volume II. London: Sampson and Low, 1879.

____. *The Flight of the Eagle.* London: Lawrence & Bullen, 1892; repr. Dublin: Talbot Press, n.d.

____. *Finn and His Companions.* Illustrations by Jack Butler Yeats. London: T. Fisher Unwin, Children's Library, 1892.

____. *The Coming of Cuculain.* London: T. Fisher Unwin, 1894.

____. *Lost on Du Carrig: Or 'Twixt Earth and Ocean.* London and Paris: Cassell, 1894; repr. Dublin: Talbot Press, n.d.

____. *The Chain of Gold: A Boy's Tale of Adventure on the Wild West Coast of Ireland.* London: Unwin, 1895; repr, Dublin: Talbot Press, n.d.

____. *The Masque of Finn.* Dublin: Sealy, Bryers & Walker, 1907.

____. *The Triumph and Passing of Cúchulainn.* Illustrated by Patrick Tuohy. London: T. Fisher Unwin, 1920

Ó hAodha, Ciarán. 'Bilingualism as an Objective in Education in Ireland, 1843–1941'. Unpublished M.Ed thesis, Trinity College, Dublin, 1982.

O'Hehir, C. J. 'The Problem of Nationality'. *Studies*, No. 2, 1913.

Ó hÓgáin, Daithí. *Fionn Mac Cumhaill: Images of the Gaelic Hero.* Dublin: Gill and Macmillan, 1988.

O'Kane, Finola. 'Nurturing a Revolution: Patrick Pearse's School Garden at St Enda's'. *Garden History*, Vol. 28, No. 1, 2000.

O'Leary, Philip. 'What Stalked Through the Post Office: Pearse's Cúchulainn'. Proceedings of the Harvard Celtic Colloquium vol III (1983).

Ó Luing, Seán. *Kuno Meyer.* Dublin: Geography Publications, 1991.

O'Malley, Ernie. *On Another Man's Wound*. London: Kimble and Bradford, 1936.

Ó Muimhneacháin, A. *An Claidheamh Soluis: Thirty Years of the Gaelic League*. Dublin: Gaelic League Pamphlet, 1955.

O'Neill, Eamonn. 'Patrick Pearse: Some Other Memories'. *Capuchin Annual*, 1935; 217–22.

Osborne, Charles. *The Complete Operas of Wagner: A Critical Guide*. London: Victor Gollancz, 1992.

O'Shannon, Cathal (ed.). *Souvenir of the Golden Jubilee of the Fianna Éireann*. Dublin: 1959.

Ó Tuama, Seán (ed.). *The Gaelic League Idea*. Cork and Dublin: The Mercier Press, 1972.

Owens, Craig. 'The Discourse of Others: Feminism and Postmodernism'. *Postmodern Culture*. Ed. Hal Foster. London: Pluto Press, 1985.

Parker, Andrew, Mary Russo, Doris Sommer and Patricia Yeager (eds.). *Nationalisms and Sexualities*. London and New York: Routledge, 1992.

Pateman, Carole. *The Disorder of Women: Democracy, Feminism and Political Theory*. Polity Press, 1989.

Pearse, Senator Margaret M. 'Patrick and Willie Pearse'. *Capuchin Annual*. 1943.

Pearse, Mary Brigid (ed.). *The Home Life of Pádraig Pearse*. Cork and Dublin: Mercier Press, 1934.

Pearse, P. H. *Íosagán agus Sgéalta Eile*. Dublin: Conradh na Gaedhilge, 1907.

____. *In First Century Ireland*. Dublin and Cork: Talbot Press, 1907.

____. *An Sgoil: A Direct Method Course in Irish*. London: Maunsel, 1913.

____. *The Complete Works of P. H. Pearse: Songs of the Irish Rebels and Specimens from an Irish Anthology; Some Aspects of Irish Literature: Three Lectures on Gaelic Topics*. Dublin: Phoenix, 1924.

____. *The Complete Works of P. H. Pearse: Political Writings and Speeches*. Dublin: Phoenix, 1924.

____. *The Complete Works of P. H. Pearse: Plays Poems Stories*. Dublin: Phoenix, 1924.

——. *The Complete Works of P. H. Pearse: The Story of a Success*. Ed. Desmond Ryan. Dublin: Phoenix, 1924.
——. *The Complete Works of P. H. Pearse: Scríbhinní.* Dublin: Phoenix, 1924.
——. *The Literary Writings of Patrick Pearse.* Ed. Séamus Ó Búachalla. Dublin and Cork: Mercier Press, 1979.
——. *Selected Poems.* Ed. Dermot Bolger; introduction by Eugene McCabe and Íar-Fhocal by Michael Davitt. Dublin: New Island Books, 1993.
Perchak, Andrew and Helaine Posner (eds.). *The Masculine Masquerade: Masculinity and Representation.* Massachussetts: The MIT Press, 1995.
Poliakov, Leon. *The Aryan Myth.* New York: Basic Books, 1971.
Poovey, Mary. *Uneven Developments: The Ideological Work of Gender in Mid-Victorian England.* Chicago: University of Chicago Press, 1988.
Pultz, John. *Photography and the Body.* London: The Everyman Art Library, 1995.
Rafael, Vicente L. 'Nationalism, Imagery, and the Filipino Intelligentsia in the Nineteenth Century'. *Critical Inquiry*, Vol. 16, No. 3, Spring 1990; 591–611.
Reade, Brian (ed.). *Sexual Heretics: Male Homosexuality from 1850 to 1900.* New York: Coward McCann, 1971.
Reddin, Kenneth. 'A Man Called Pearse'. *Studies*, June 1943; 241–51.
Reeves, Dr. *Life of St Columba.* Dublin: Irish Archaeological and Celtic Society, 1857.
Reinelt, Janelle G. and Joseph R. Roach (eds.). *Critical Theory and Performance.* Ann Arbor: University of Michigan Press, 1992.
Renan, Ernest. 'What Is a Nation?' 1882; repr. in *Nation and Narration.* Ed. Homi K. Bhaba. London and New York: Routledge, 1990; 8–22.
——. *The Poetry of the Celtic Races, and Other Studies.* 1896. Translated with introduction and notes by William G. Hutchison. New York and London: Kennikat Press, 1970.

Rhodes, Colin. *Primitivism and Modern Art.* London and New York: Thames and Hudson, 1994.

Richards, Jeffrey (ed.). *Imperialism and Juvenile Literature.* Manchester and New York: Manchester University Press, 1989.

Ridgeway, William. *The First Shaping of the Cuchulainn Saga.* London: Henry Frowde, 1905.

Rockett, Kevin, Luke Gibbons and John Hill. *Cinema and Ireland.* London: Routledge, 1987.

Rolleston, T. W. *The High Deeds of Finn and Other Bardic Romances of Ancient Ireland.* Illustrated by Stephen Reid. London: George Harrap, 1910.

——. *Myths and Legends of the Celtic Race.* London: Harrap, 1911; repr. Guernsey: Gresham Publishing Company, 1996.

Roper, Michael and John Tosh (eds.). *Manful Assertions: Masculinities in Britain since 1800.* London and New York: Routledge, 1991.

Rosenthal, Michael. *The Character Factory: Baden Powell and the Origins of the Boy Scout Movement.* New York: Pantheon; London: Collins, 1986.

Ruskin, John. *Collected Works.* Ed. E. T. Cook and A. D. O. Wedderburn. London, 1902–12.

Russell, George (Æ). 'The Dramatic Treatment of Heroic Literature'. *Some Irish Essays.* Dublin: Maunsel Press, 1906.

——. *Co-operation and Nationality.* Dublin: Maunsel Press, 1912.

Ryan, Desmond (ed.). *The Story of a Success: Being a Record of St Enda's College September 1908 to Easter 1916.* Dublin and London: Maunsel Press, 1917.

——. *A Man Called Pearse.* Dublin and London: Maunsel Press, 1919.

——. *Remembering Sion: A Chronicle of Storm and Quiet.* Edinburgh: 1934.

——. 'Pearse, St Enda's College, and the Hounds of Ulster'. *Threshold,* Vol. I, Autumn 1957; 54–58.

——. 'St Enda's: Fifty Years After'. *Dublin University Review,* Vol. II, No. 3, 1958; 82–89.

Ryan, W. P. *The Pope's Green Island.* Edinburgh: Ballantyne, Hanson & Co., 1912.

Sadler, Sir Michael Ernest. *Special Report on Preparatory Schools for Boys: Their Place in English Secondary Education*. London: HMSO, 1900.

——. 'The School in Some of its Relations to Social Organisation and National Life'. *Sociological Papers. Vol II*. London: Macmillan, 1906; 123–39.

——. 'Training for Citizenship'. An address delivered at an Educational Conference of the Co-Operative Union, 20 May 1907. Manchester: Co-Operative Printing Society, 1907.

—— (ed.). *Moral Instruction and Training in Schools: Report of an International Enquiry*. 2 volumes. London: Longmans, Green & Co., 1908.

Said, Edward. *Culture and Imperialism*. London: Vintage, 1993.

Saunders, Norah and A. A. Kelly. *Joseph Campbell, Poet and Nationalist 1879–1944: A Critical Biography*. Dublin: Wolfhound Press, 1988.

Scholes, Alex. *Education for Empire Settlement*. London: Longmans Green, 1932.

Scott, Joan Wallach. *Gender and the Politics of History*. New York: Columbia University Press, 1988.

Sekula, Allan. 'On the Invention of Photographic Meaning'. *Thinking Photography*. Ed. Victor Burgin. London: Macmillan Education, 1982; 84–109.

——. 'The Body and the Archive'. *October*, Spring/Summer 1987; 3–63.

Seltzer, Mark. *Bodies and Machines*. New York and London: Routledge, 1992.

Seton-Watson, Hugh. *Nations and States: An Enquiry into the Origins of Nationalism and the Politics of Nationalism*. Colorado: Westview Press, 1977.

Sexton, Sean. *Ireland: Photographs 1840–1930*. Introduction by J. J. Lee and text by Carey Schofield. Lawrence King Publishing, 1994.

Sheehy, Jeanne. *The Rediscovery of Ireland's Past: The Celtic Revival 1830–1930*. London: Thames and Hudson, 1980.

Showalter, Elaine. *The Female Malady: Women, Madness and English Culture 1830–1980.* London: Virago, 1988.
——. *Sexual Anarchy: Gender and Culture at the Fin de Siècle.* London: Bloomsbury, 1991.
Sigerson, George. *Bards of the Gael and Gall: Examples of the Poetic Literature of Erinn, Done into English After the Metres and Modes of the Gael.* London: 1897; repr. Dublin: Talbot Press, 1925, with a preface by Douglas Hyde.
Sinha, Mrinalini. *Colonial Masculinity: The 'Manly' Englishman and the 'Effeminate Bengali' in the Late Nineteenth Century.* Manchester: Manchester University Press, 1995.
Skinnider, Margaret. *Doing My Bit for Ireland.* New York: Century, 1917.
Smith, Gary (ed.). *Walter Benjamin: Philosophy, History, Aesthetics.* Chicago: University of Chicago Press, 1989.
Smith, Paul (ed.). *Boys: Masculinities in Contemporary Culture.* Oxford: Westview Press, 1996.
Smith-Rosenberg, Carroll. *Disorderly Conduct: Visions of Gender in Victorian America.* New York: Oxford University Press, 1985.
Smyth, Ailbhe. 'The Floozie in the Jacuzzi'. *Feminist Studies*, Vol. 17, No. 1, 1991; 7–11.
Snoddy, Theo. *Dictionary of Irish Artists: 20th Century.* Dublin: Wolfhound Press, 1995.
Solomon-Godeau, Abigail. 'The Legs of the Countess'. *October*, Spring/Summer 1987; 66–107.
——. *Male Trouble: A Crisis in Representation.* London: Thames and Hudson, 1997.
Sontag, Susan. *On Photography.* Harmondsworth: Penguin, 1978.
Spivak, Gayatri Chakravorty. *Outside in the Teaching Machine.* London and New York: Routledge, 1993.
Squiers, Carol (ed.). *The Critical Image: Essays on Contemporary Photography.* Seattle: Bay Press, 1990.
Squire, Charles. *The Boy Hero of Erin.* 1907.
Staff, Frank. *The Picture Postcard and Its Origins.* London: Lutterworth Press, 1966.

Stafford, Fiona. *William Morris: A Life for Our Time.* London: Faber and Faber, 1994.

Stavenow-Hidemark, Elisabet. 'Viking Revival and Art Nouveau: Traditions of Excellence'. *Scandanavian Modern Design, 1880–1980.* Ed. David Revere McFadden. New York: Harry Abrams, 1982; 4769.

Steadman, Carolyn. *Strange Dislocations: Childhood and the Idea of Human Interiority 1780–1930.* London: Virago Press, 1995.

Stephenson, Andrew. *Visualising Masculinities.* London: Tate Gallery, 1992.

Stoddart, Brian. 'Sport, Cultural Imperialism, and Colonial Response in the British Empire'. *Comparative Studies in Society and History,* Vol. XXX, 1988; 649–73.

Stokes, Margaret. *Early Christian Art in Ireland.* London: Chapman and Hall, 1887.

Story, Dr John. 'Physical Deterioration and a Remedy'. *Dublin Journal of Medical Science,* 1 June 1909.

——. 'Medical Inspection of Schools and School Children'. Address to the Statistical and Social Inquiry Society of Ireland, 1912.

Suleri, Sara. *The Rhetoric of English India.* Chicago: University of Chicago Press, 1992.

Sussman, Herbert. *Victorian Masculinities: Manhood and Masculine Poetics in Early Victorian Literature and Art.* Cambridge: Cambridge University Press, 1995.

Sweeney, Joseph. *The Easter Rising: 1916 and University College, Dublin.* Dublin: Browne & Nolan, 1966.

Tagg, John. *The Burden of Representation: Essays on Photographies and Histories.* London: Macmillan Education, 1988.

Tagore, Rabindranath. *The Post Office.* Madras: The Macmillan Company of India, 1914.

——. *Nationalism.* London: Macmillan, 1917; repr. 1991.

Thewelweit, Klaus. *Male Fantasies.* Volumes 1 and 2. Cambridge: Polity Press, 1939.

Thomas, Nicholas. *Colonialism's Culture: Anthropology, Travel and Government.* Cambridge: Polity Press, 1994.

Tickner, Lisa. *The Spectacle of Women.* London: Chatto & Windus, 1987.

——. 'Men's Work? Masculinity and Modernism'. *Visual Culture: Images and Interpretations.* Eds. N. Bryson, M. A. Holly and K. Moxey. Hanover and London: Wesleyan University Press and University Press of New England, 1995; 42–82.

Tierney, Michael. 'What Did the Gaelic League Accomplish? 1893–1963'. *Studies*, Vol. 52, 1963; 337–47.

Torgovnick, Marianna. *Gone Primitive: Savage Intellects, Modern Lives.* Chicago and London: University of Chicago Press, 1990.

Trivedi, Hanish. *Colonial Transactions: English Literature and India.* Manchester: Manchester University Press, 1995.

Trumpener, Katie. *Bardic Nationalism: The Romantic Novel and the British Empire.* Princeton: Princeton University Press, 1997.

Turner, Bryan S. *The Body and Society: Explorations in Social Theory.* Oxford and New York: Basil Blackwell, 1984.

Turpin, John. 'Cúchulainn Lives On'. *CIRCA*, No. 69, Autumn 1994; 6–11.

Ua Gallchobhair, L. 'The Children of P. H. Pearse'. *Irish Monthly*, March 1922; 120–24.

Vance, Norman. *The Sinews of the Spirit: The Ideal of Christian Manliness in Victorian Literature and Religious Thought.* Cambridge: Cambridge University Press, 1985.

Vernant, Jean Pierre. *Mortals and Immortals.* Princeton: Princeton University Press, 1991.

Viswanathan, Gauri. *The Masks of Conquest: Literary Study and British Rule in India.* Oxford and New Delhi: Oxford University Press, 1983.

Walby, Sylvia. *Theorizing Patriarchy.* Oxford: Blackwell, 1990.

Wallis, Mick. 'Pageantry and the Popular Front: Ideological Production in the Thirties'. *New Theatre Quarterly*, Vol. 10, No. 38, May 1994; 132–56.

Walsh, J. A. 'A Comparative Analysis of the Reading Books of the Commissioners of National Education and the Christian Brothers, 1831–1900'. Unpublished M.A. thesis, University College, Dublin, 1983.

Walshe, Éibhear (ed.). Sex, *Nation and Dissent in Irish Writing.* Cork: Cork University Press, 1997.

Ward, Margaret. *Unmanageable Revolutionaries: Women and Irish Nationalism.* London: Pluto Press; Dingle, Co. Kerry: Brandon Press, 1983.

Warner, Marina. *Alone of All Her Sex: The Myth and the Cult of the Virgin Mary.* New York: Knopf, 1976.

Waters, Martin. 'Peasants and Emigrants: Considerations of the Gaelic League as a Social Movement'. *Views of the Irish Peasantry 1800–1916.* Eds. Daniel J. Casey and Robert E. Rhodes. Hamden, CT: Archon Books, 1977; 160–77.

Weekes, Jeffrey. *Against Nature: Essays on History, Sexuality and Identity.* London: Rivers Oram Press, 1991.

West, Máire. 'Kings, Heroes and Warriors, Aspects of Children's Literature in Ireland in the Era of Emergent Nationalism'. *Bulletin of John Rylands University Library of Manchester (BJLR)*, Vol. 76, No. 3, Autumn 1994; 165–84.

West, Trevor. *Horace Plunkett: Co-operation and Politics: An Irish Biography.* Gerrard's Cross: Colin Smythe, 1986.

Whitehead, Clive. 'The Medium of Instruction in British Colonial Education: A Case of Cultural Imperialism or Enlightened Paternalism?' *History of Education*, Vol. 24, No. 1, 1995; 1–15.

Willey, Basil. *Nineteenth Century Studies.* Cambridge: Cambridge University Press, 1949.

Williams, Raymond. *Marxism and Literature.* Oxford: Oxford University Press, 1977.

——. *The Politics of Modernism.* London: Verso, 1989.

Wills, Clair. 'Language Politics, Narrative, Political Violence'. *Oxford Literary Review*, Vol. 13, 1991; 20–60.

——. *Improprieties: Politics and Sexuality in Northern Irish Poetry.* Oxford: Clarendon Press, 1993.

Wilson, Elizabeth. *The Sphinx in the City: Urban Life, the Control of Disorder, and Women.* London: Virago Press, 1991.

Wilson Foster, John. 'Certain Set Apart: The Western Island in the Irish Renaissance'. *Studies*, Winter 1977; 261–74.

———. *Fictions of the Irish Literary Revival: A Changeling Art.* Syracuse: Syracuse University Press, Dublin: Gill and Macmillan, 1987.

Wollen, Peter. *Raiding the Icebox: Reflections on Twentieth Century Culture.* London and New York: Verso, 1993.

Yeats, William Butler. *On Baile's Strand.* London: A. H. Bullen, 1904.

———. *Collected Poems of William Butler Yeats.* London and New York: Macmillan, 1957.

———. *Autobiographies.* London: Macmillan, 1966.

Young, Ella. *Celtic Wonder Tales.* Illustrated by Maud Gonne. Dublin: Maunsel, 1910.

Young, Robert. *White Mythologies: Writing History and the West.* London: Routledge, 1990.

Gaelic League Pamphlets

1. *The True National Ideal* by Michael O'Hickey (1898).
2. *The Case for Bilingual Education in the Irish-speaking Districts* (1900).
3. *Irish in the Schools*. Four letters by: Eoin MacNeill; Rev Dr M. O'Hickey; Norma Borthwick; Patrick Pearse (n.d.).
4. *Ireland's Battle for Her Language* by Edward Martyn (1900).
5. *Parliament and the Teaching of Irish: The Irish Language Debate in the House of Common on Friday, 21st July, 1900* (1900).
6. *Irishwomen and the Home Language* by Mary L. Butler (1901).
7. *A University Scandal* by Dr Douglas Hyde (1901).
8. *Bilingual Education* by Rev Dr D. D. Walsh, Archbishop of Dublin (1901).

9a. *Bilingual Instruction in National Schools* (1901).

9b. *The Future of Irish in the National Schools* by M. O'Hickey (1901).

10. *The Reign of Humbug* by Agnes O'Farrelly (1901).
11. *The Irish Language and Irish Intermediate Education I: Answers to Questions* (1901).
12. *The Irish Language and Irish Intermediate Education II: Evidence of Dr Mahaffy; Dr Delany, S.J.; Father Devitt, S.J.; Dr Bernard and Father Daly* (1901).

13. *The Irish Language and Irish Intermediate Education III: Dr Hyde's Evidence* (1901).
14. *The Irish Language and Irish Intermediate Education IV: Dr Atkinson's Evidence* (1901).
15. *The Irish Language and Irish Intermediate Education V: Foreign Testimony* (1901).
16. *The Irish Language and Irish Intermediate Education VI: Dr Hyde's Reply to Dr Atkinson* (1901).
17. *The Irish Language and Irish Intermediate Education VII: Dr O'Hickey's Reply to Dr Mahaffy, Mr Gwynn and Dr Atkinson* (1901).
18. *The Irish Language and Irish Intermediate Education VIII: Further Replies to Dr Atkinson, and Miscellaneous Documents* (1901).
19. *The Irish Language and Irish Intermediate Education IX: Father O'Leary, Dr Henebry, and Father O'Reilly on Dr Atkinson* (1901).
20. *The Irish Language and Irish Intermediate Education X: Further Miscellaneous Documents* (1901).
21. *The Irish Language Movement: Its Philosophy* by Patrick Forde.
22. *Bilingual Instruction in National School: The Prize Programme* (1901).
23. *Ireland's Defence – Her Language* by Reverend P. F. Kavanagh.
24. *The Threatening Metempsychosis of a Nation* by Reverend John Myles O'Reilly (1901).
25. *The Seven Hundred Years War* by P. H. Pearse.
    Lessons from Modern Language Movements: What Native Speech has Achieved for Nationality by William P. O Riain (1902).
26. *An O'Growney Memorial Lecture* by J. O'Donovan (1902).
27. *The Nationalisation of Irish Education* by M. O'Hickey (1902).
28. *The Irish Language Movement: Its Genesis, Growth and Progress* by M. O'Hickey (1902).
29. *Irish in University Education* (1902).
30. *The Possibilities of Irish Industry* by P. T. McGinley (1905).
31. *Ireland's Ideal* by Louisa E. Farquharson (1905).
32. *The Irish Battle of the Books* by Stanley Lane-Poole (1907).
33. *The Spirit of the Gaelic League* by George A. Moonan (1907).

34. *Facts about the Irish Language and the Irish Language Movement* by Mary Hayden (1910).

Newspapers and Periodicals

Bean na hÉireann
Catholic Bulletin, The
Capuchin Annual
Claidheamh Soluis, An
Department of Agriculture and Technical Instruction Journal
Derry Journal
Dublin Evening Mail
Dublin Magazine
Dublin Penny Journal
Dublin University Review
Éire-Ireland
Evening Herald
Fáinne an Lae
Fianna
Freeman's Journal
Gael, An
Gaelic Journal
Gaelic Union
Ireland's Own
Irish Ecclesiastical Record
Irish Freedom
Irish Gardening
Irish Homestead
Irish Independent
Irish Monthly
Irish Nation and Peasant
Irish Packet
Irish Review
Irish Sportsman
Irish Times
Irisleabhar na Gaeilge

Irishman, The
Journal of Irish Literature
Leader, The
Liverpool Catholic Herald
Macaomh, An
Our Boys
Samhain
Scoláire, An
Shamrock, The
Sinn Féin
Southern Cross
Studies
Threshold
United Ireland
United Irishman

Unpublished Materials and Manuscript Sources

Bloomer Papers, National Library of Ireland.

British Parliamentary Papers, Report of the Intermediate Education Board for Ireland, 1910–1912, Trinity College Library, Dublin.

Joseph Holloway Diaries, National Library of Ireland.

Thomas MacDonagh Papers MSS 10,843–58, National Library of Ireland.

Patrick Pearse Papers, National Library of Ireland.

William Pearse Papers, National Library of Ireland.

St Enda's Account Book 1908–1912, National Library of Ireland.

St Enda's Attendance Books 1908–1916, Pearse Museum, Rathfarnham, Dublin.

Miscellaneous papers, Brother Allen Library, North Richmond Street, Dublin.

Notes and References

Introduction

1. Partha Chatterjee, *The Nation and Its Fragments: Colonial and Postcolonial Histories* (Princeton University Press, 1993).
2. Letter from Roger Casement to Ballymena Academy declining a request for financial help. Quoted in Brian Inglis, *Roger Casement* (London: Hodder and Stoughton, 1973), 233.
3. W. P. Ryan, 'The Hero in the College', *The Pope's Green Island* (Edinburgh: Ballantyne Hanson & Co., 1912), 294.
4. Desmond Ryan, 'St Enda's: Fifty Years After', *Dublin University Review,* Vol. II, Nos. 3 & 4, 1958: 82.
5. Lord Alfred Douglas, *The Irishman,* January 1918 (Vol. III, No. 3). The quote is taken from William Bulfin's article 'Sgoil Éanna', which was published in *An Claidheamh Soluis* on 13 January 1912.

1 Beginnings

1. Editorial by John Henry, *An Claidheamh Soluis,* 12 September 1908.
2. 'By Way of Comment', *An Macaomh,* Vol. 1, No. 1, Midsummer 1909.
3. 'By Way of Comment', *An Macaomh,* Vol. 1, No. 1, Midsummer 1909.
4. Seamus Deane, 'Pearse: Writing and Chivalry', *Celtic Revivals: Essays in Modern Irish Literature 1880–1980* (London: Faber & Faber, 1985), 64.
5. See Albert Memmi, *The Colonizer and the Colonized* (London: Earthscan Publications, repr. 1990); Ashis Nandy, *The Intimate Enemy: The Loss and Recovery of Self Under Colonialism* (Delhi: Oxford University Press, 1994); Frantz Fanon, *Black Skin, White Mask* (London: McKibbon & Kee, 1968).
6. Arnold's study was published after the so-called 'first' Celtic Revival of the 1840s and was influenced by Ernest Renan's work, *The Poetry of the Celtic Races, and Other Studies* (trans. 1896). English interest in medievalism, complemented by the growth of Anglo-Catholicism, meant that Celtic art and early Celtic culture continued to enjoy the attention of Victorian enquiry. The Anglo-Catholic Oxford Movement of the 1830s and the church building that followed Catholic Emancipation in the same decade created an enormous demand for ecclesiastical art: stained glass, embroidery, metalwork and monumental sculpture. See Robert

Elliott, *Art and Ireland* (Dublin, 1902), and Jeanne Sheehy, *The Rediscovery of Ireland's Past: The Celtic Revival 1830–1930* (London: Thames and Hudson, 1980).

7. Arnold, *The Study of Celtic Literature*, 1869 (repr. London: David Nutt, 1910), 84.
8. Moran, 'The Future of the Irish Nation', *The Philosophy of Irish Ireland* (Dublin: James Duffy, 1905), 22.
9. See Elaine Showalter, *The Female Malady: Women, Madness and English Culture 1830–1980* (London: Virago, 1988); Sander L. Gilman, *Seeing the Insane: A Cultural History of Psychiatric Illustration* (London: Wiley, 1985); and Carroll Smith-Rosenberg, *Disorderly Conduct: Visions of Gender in Victorian America* (New York: Oxford University Press, 1985).
10. L. P. Curtis, 'Fenian Physiognomies', *Apes and Angels: The Irishman in Victorian Caricature* (Washington: Smithsonian Press, 1971), 89–93.
11. Belinda Loftus, *Mirrors: William III and Mother Ireland* (Dundrum, Co. Down: Picture Press, 1990), 44–60.
12. Richard Kearney suggests in *Myth and Motherland* (Field Day Pamphlet, 1984) that the appearance of the allegorical female form is concurrent with the history of dispossession in Ireland from the eighteenth century onwards (see pages 20–21). However, Loftus's work shows that the allegorical feminization of Ireland happened earlier than this (*Mirrors*, 48–50). The heightened visibility of images of Ireland after the eighteenth century may be attributable to the growth of print culture and increasing middle-class literacy.
13. The political theorist Carole Pateman has argued that in *all* political systems men are understood to form the body politic and are seen as individual citizens, while women, even if citizens, are often considered to embody abstract ideals about polity and their interests are grouped together as 'women' and not as citizens. Representations of Irish men and women would seem to bear out this distinction where men are seen as individuals and women are seen as allegories of something else. Pateman, *The Disorder of Women: Democracy, Feminism and Political Theory* (Oxford: Polity Press, 1989).
14. Moran, 'Is the Irish Nation Dying?', *The Philosophy of Irish Ireland*, 5.
15. Moran, 'Is the Irish Nation Dying?', *The Philosophy of Irish Ireland*, 4–5.
16. Moran, 'The Pale and the Gael', *The Philosophy of Irish Ireland*, 39.
17. The term is Ashis Nandy's and is understood as a strategic response to the feminizing processes of colonialism; see *The Intimate Enemy*, 10.
18. Pearse had not always been so appreciative of Celticism. Only thirteen when the Gaelic League was founded, Pearse was barely nineteen when Moran first began publishing his grievances about Celticism in 1898. Moran was obviously influential over the impressionable Pearse who, like Moran, denounced Anglo-Irish literature and the Celtic Twilight as being 'not-Irish'. In an 1899 letter to the Gaelic League newspaper *An Claidheamh Soluis* he called W. B. Yeats a 'mere English poet of the third or fourth rank' and condemned the Irish Literary Theatre as a sham. Letter to the Editor, *An Claidheamh Soluis*, 6 May 1899. However, Pearse has in his defence his youthful arrogance, and his later public revisions of his opinions suggest that his understanding of Irish-Ireland included an appreciation of Celticism and had moved away from Moran's narrowly focused criticisms.
19. Pearse, 'The Murder Machine', in *The Complete Works of P.H. Pearse: Political Writings and Speeches* (Dublin Phoenix, 1924) 9.
20. Mary Brigid Pearse (ed.), *The Home Life of Pádraig Pearse* (Dublin and Cork: Mercier Press, 1934; repr. 1979), 113.

21. Mary Brigid Pearse (ed.), *The Home Life of Pádraig Pearse*, 113.
22. See John Wilson Foster, 'Certain Set Apart: The Western Isle in the Irish Renaissance', *Studies* (Winter 1977), 265.
23. Pearse described his first trip to Aran in a plodding report that he wrote for *Fáinne an Lae,* 'Cuairt ar Arainn na Naomh' ('A Visit to Aran of the Saints'), 19 November 1898.
24. See Catherine Nash, 'Embodying the Nation: The West of Ireland Landscape and Irish National Identity', in Barbara O'Connor and Michael Cronin (eds.), *Tourism in Ireland: A Cultural Analysis* (Cork: Cork University Press, 1993), 86–112.
25. See Judith Butler, *Gender Trouble: Feminism and the Subversion of Identity* (London and New York: Routledge, 1990), and 'Critically Queer', in Butler's *Bodies That Matter* (London and New York: Routledge, 1993), 223–242.
26. Graham Dawson, 'The Blond Bedouin', in Michael Roper and John Tosh (eds.), *Manful Assertions* (London and New York: Routledge, 1991), 118.
27. Eve Kosofsky Sedgwick, *Between Men: English Literature and Male Homosocial Desire* (New York, 1985), 102.
28. Michael Roper and John Tosh (eds.), 'Historians and the Politics of Masculinity', *Manful Assertions: Masculinities in Britain since 1800* (London and New York: Routledge, 1991), 4.
29. 'The Murder Machine', *Political Writings and Speeches,* 25.
30. 'The Murder Machine', *Political Writings and Speeches,* 21.
31. 'The Murder Machine', *Political Writings and Speeches,* 21.
32. 'The Murder Machine', *Political Writings and Speeches,* 25.
33. 'The Murder Machine', *Political Writings and Speeches,* 33.
34. 'The Murder Machine', *Political Writings and Speeches,* 22–23.
35. For detailed descriptions of the schools of early Christian Ireland, see Douglas Hyde, *A Literary History of Ireland* (London: T. Fisher Unwin, 1899), 192–214.
36. Cullenswood House had been built in the eighteenth century for Bartholomew Mosse, the founder of the Rotunda Hospital. After St Enda's school relocated to Rathfarnham, the house was used by St Ita's School until its closure in 1912. During the War of Independence Cullenswood House was occupied by wives and families of IRA prisoners and it was known as a safe house. Ernie O'Malley, in his autobiography *On Another Man's Wound* (London: Kimble and Bradford, 1936), recalls how Michael Collins often slept in Cullenswood House when he was on the run.
37. St Ita's was named after the Irish saint from Waterford who was born around AD480. She was renowned for her wisdom and founded a monastery in Cill Íde, or Killeedy, Waterford. She also founded a school for boys and is said to have educated St Brendan. She was particularly known for her support of the educational rights of women. After St Enda's moved to the Hermitage in 1912 Gertrude Bloomer became the headmistress of St Ita's, which was designed as a sister school to St Enda's. The school was not a financial success although many prominent nationalist women were educated there, including Máire Bulfin, whose brother Eamonn attended St Enda's, Katherine (Kitty) Kiernan, Susie and Eileen Colum (who were related to Padraic Colum) and Eveline McGinley whose brothers also attended St Enda's. In 1917 Louise Gavan Duffy took over the running of the school and changed its name to Scoil Bhríde which is still running, although not at Cullenswood House.
38. 'The Schools', *An Claidheamh Soluis,* 7 March 1908.

2 Conquering Imperialism

1. Editorial, *An Claidheamh Soluis*, 18 April 1903.
2. For studies of colonial educational policies, see J. A. Mangan, *The Imperial Curriculum: Racial Images and Education in the British Colonial Experience* (London and New York: Routledge, 1993). For a discussion of English literary study as a regime of colonial power, see Hanish Trivedi, *Colonial Transactions: English Literature and India* (Manchester University Press, 1995), and Gauri Viswanathan, *The Masks of Conquest: Literary Study and British Rule in India* (New York: Columbia University Press, 1989).
3. John Coolahan, *Irish Education: Its History and Structure* (Dublin: Institute of Public Administration, 1981), 4.
4. For further reading on the Kildare Place Society and the Model School system, see Seán Farren, 'Irish Model Schools 1833–70. Models of What?', in *History of Education*, Vol. 24, No. 1, 1995, 45–60.
5. For further reading on the 1831 establishment of the national school system, see John Coolahan, *Irish Education*, 10–19. For an excellent overall history of the national school system in the nineteenth century, see Donald H. Akenson, *The Irish Education Experiment: The National System of Education in the Nineteenth Century* (London: Routledge & Kegan Paul, 1970).
6. For a general discussion on the ideological aims of school textbooks, see J. A. Mangan, 'Images for Confident Control: Stereotypes in Imperial Discourse', *The Imperial Curriculum*, 2–14.
7. Joachim Goldstrom, *The Social Context of Education 1808–1870: A Study of the Working Class School Reader in England and Ireland* (Shannon: Irish University Press, 1972).
8. Goldstrom, *The Social Context of Education*, 71–76.
9. John Coolahan, 'The Irish and Others in Irish Nineteenth-Century Textbooks', in J. A. Mangan (ed.), *The Imperial Curriculum*, 55.
10. Coolahan, 'The Irish and Others in Irish Nineteenth-Century Textbooks', *The Imperial Curriculum*, 54–63.
11. For a history of the 'payments by results' system see Fiachra Ó Dubhthaigh, *A Review of the Contribution of Sir Patrick Keenan to the Development of Irish and British Colonial Education.* Unpublished M.Ed. thesis, Trinity College, Dublin, 1974.
12. Coolahan, *Irish Education*, 28.
13. Coolahan, *Irish Education*, 30.
14. Reports of Commissioners on Intermediate Education (Palles) Final Report, H.C. 1899 (c. 9511), XXII.
15. Report of Dale and Stephens, H.C. 1905 (Cd. 2546) XXVIII. See Coolahan, *Irish Education*, 55–56.
16. Séamus Ó Buachalla (ed.), *A Significant Irish Educationalist: The Educational Writings of P. H. Pearse* (Dublin and Cork: Mercier Press, 1980), xxiv.
17. See Ó Buachalla, *A Significant Irish Educationalist*, xviii. Ó Buachalla refers to R. J. W. Selleck's study *The New Education* (London, 1968), which identifies six distinct groups within the New Education Movement: Practical Educationalists, Social Reformers, Naturalists, Hebartians, Scientific Educationalists and Moral Educationalists. In particular the Moral Education movement was allied to ideas about 'character' and national identity and 'was frequently seen as part of the process of nation building and national aggrandisement' (Ó Buachalla, xxviii).

18. Ó Buachalla, *A Significant Irish Educationalist,* xiv.
19. Pearse, 'The Murder Machine', *Political Writings and Speeches,* 8.
20. 'An Educational Programme', *An Claidheamh Soluis,* 7 November 1903.
21. 'An Educational Programme', *An Claidheamh Soluis,* 2 November 1903.
22. 'An Educational Policy', *An Claidheamh Soluis,* 12 December 1903.
23. Desmond Ryan, *The Story of a Success* (Dublin: Maunsel, 1917).
24. See Seamus Deane, *Celtic Revivals: Essays in Modern Irish Literature* (London and Boston: Faber and Faber, 1985).
25. Ruth Dudley Edwards, *Patrick Pearse: The Triumph of Failure* (London: Victor Gollancz, 1977), 106.
26. Séamus Ó Buachalla, *A Significant Irish Educationalist,* xiv.
27. See Breandán S. Mac Aodha, 'Was this a Social Revolution?' in Seán Ó Tuama (ed.), *The Gaelic League Idea* (Cork and Dublin: Mercier Press, 1972), 21.
28. By 1912 there were 18 Irish colleges, with the largest concentration in Connacht. The colleges operated primarily as summer schools, initiating the precedent for sending school groups to the Gaeltacht during holiday periods. The League school on the Tawan peninsula in Galway was run by a youthful Eamon de Valera.
29. 'The Connacht Irish School', *An Claidheamh Soluis,* 7 January 1905.
30. Letter from Eleanor Hull to Pearse, n.d. 1903, *Pearse Papers,* National Library of Ireland, MSS 21,054.
31. 'The Primary Schools', *An Claidheamh Soluis,* 26 December 1903.
32. 'Live Teaching in the Secondary School', *An Claidheamh Soluis,* 7 January 1905.
33. 'Textbooks', *An Claidheamh Soluis,* 5 November 1904.
34. 'The Philosophy of Education', *An Claidheamh Soluis,* 12 November 1904.
35. 'Irish in Secondary Schools', *An Claidheamh Soluis,* 18 November 1905.
36. Séamus Ó Buachalla, Introductory note to Letter 142, *The Letters of P. H. Pearse,* 119.
37. See Dudley Edwards, *Patrick Pearse: The Triumph of Failure,* 111–112. In 1906 League members Thomas O'Nowlan of Roscrea Cistercian College, Eoin MacNeill and Pearse had tentatively examined the idea of a full-time school for boys, since the League was already successfully running Gaeltacht summer schools.
38. Ó Buachalla (ed.), *Letters of P. H. Pearse,* 126.
39. Barry Coldrey, *Faith and Fatherland: The Christian Brothers and the Development of Irish Nationalism, 1838–1921* (Dublin: Gill and Macmillan, 1988).
40. 'The Secondary School: Thoughts and Suggestions', *An Claideamh* Soluis, 13 January 1906.
41. See J. A. Walsh, 'A Comparative Analysis of the Reading Books of the Commissioners of National Education and of the Christian Brothers, 1831–1900'. Unpublished MA thesis, University College, Dublin, 1983.
42. Coldrey, *Faith and Fatherland,* 57.
43. Mary Brigid Pearse (ed.), *The Home Life of Pádraig Pearse* (Dublin and Cork: Mercier Press, 1934), 34.
44. Desmond Ryan, *The Man Called Pearse* (Dublin and London: Maunsel and Company,1919).
45. 'Irish History in Intermediate Schools', *An Claidheamh Soluis,* 1 May 1909.
46. In 1838 and again in 1858 the government produced a special report urging the implementation of non-sectarian intermediate education that was bitterly opposed for ideological and practical reasons by Protestant and Catholic clergy alike. In

1870 the Powis Commission concluded that non-denominational education was not popular and control over schools came under the remit of the clergy.

47. 'Maynooth and Irish', *An Claidheamh Soluis*, 16 November 1907; 'The Situation at Maynooth', *An Claidheamh Soluis*, 23 November 1907; 'Maynooth', *An Claidheamh Soluis*, 30 November 1907; 'Dr Mannix and the Coiste Gnótha', *An Claidheamh Soluis*, 28 December 1907.

48. *The Letters of P. H. Pearse*, Letter to Patrick MacManus, 4 March 1908.

49. See 'Irish in Secondary Schools', 18 November 1905; 'The Secondary School', 25 November 1905; 'About the Intermediate', 9 December 1905; 'Live Teaching in the Secondary School', 6 January 1906; 'The Secondary School: Thoughts and Suggestions', 13 January 1906, for an idea of Pearse's increasing attention to the role of the teacher.

50. St Enda's nationalist curriculum differed significantly from leading Catholic private schools in Ireland. The prospectuses of Blackrock College, Clongowes Wood College and Castleknock College reveal them to be willing participants in a colonial educational system. Blackrock College, or the French College as it was known, was founded in 1860 by an order of French priests. The prospectus offers preparation for entry into 'the Ecclesiastical, Naval, Military or Engineering Colleges . . . and for the different departments of the Civil Service'. Irish was not offered in the school until the Gaelic Revival of the 1890s afforded it a brief popularity, although it was not made part of the core curriculum until the 1930s. Similarly, Gaelic games were introduced in the 1880s under the tutelage of the games master, Michael Cusack, the founder of the GAA, but fell from favour soon after and were not reintroduced to the school until the 1920s. A history of the school reveals that hundreds of alumni volunteered for service in the First World War, while only three are named as having been involved in the 1916 Rising (among them Eamon de Valera). Blackrock College's connections to France precluded any sympathy with rebels, who were perceived to be jeopardizing the success of the Allies in Europe. See Seán Farragher and Annraoi Wyer, *Blackrock College: 1860–1995* (Dublin: Gill and Macmillan, 1995). The Jesuit-run Clongowes Wood College was founded in 1814 and is one of the oldest private Catholic schools in the country. An historian of the school admits that the Gaelic Revival made little impact on the school and Irish was not favoured for inclusion in the curriculum by either teachers or parents. The Gaelic League's agitation for Irish to be a compulsory subject for matriculation was met by much hostility from the hierarchy. Irish was not taught as a curricular subject proper until 1934. Father Dinneen, a Gaelic scholar and League member, left the teaching staff in protest at the treatment of Irish. The school's contribution to imperial administrations is revealed by the numbers of alumni who served in the British military forces and as colonial governors and administrators in British territories in India, Africa and South America. The College celebrated 'Union Day' until the civil war. See Peter Costello's history of the College, *Clongowes Wood: A History of Clongowes Wood College, 1814–1989* (Dublin: Gill and Macmillan, 1989). Castleknock College was founded by the Vincentian fathers in 1835; however, the clerical influence in pedagogical practice precluded any experimentation with curriculum or flirtation with nationalist ideas. See Father James Murphy, *Nos Auteum: A History of Castleknock College* (Dublin: Gill and Macmillan, 1996). Many prestigious boarding schools started out as seminaries, including Newbridge College (founded in 1852) and the Patri-

cian College in Laois (founded in 1810). See *The Guide to Boarding Schools in Ireland,* (Mayo: Morrigan Books Company, 1983).

51. Ó Buachalla, (ed.), *Letters of P. H. Pearse,* Letter to Patrick MacManus, 4 March 1908, 128.
52. Ó Buachalla, (ed.), *A Significant Irish Educationalist,* xvi.
53. 'The Murder Machine', *Political Writings and Speeches,* 28.
54. 'The Murder Machine', *Political Writings and Speeches,* 11.
55. 'The Murder Machine', *Political Writings and Speeches,* 13.
56. 'The Murder Machine', *Political Writings and Speeches,* 14.
57. Originally Pearse had planned to name the school Scoil Lorcáin, in honour of the Catholic Archdiocese of Dublin; it is unclear why he changed the name, but perhaps he wished to signal his allegiance to St Enda's legacy of scholarship as well as marking his personal attachment to the Aran Islands and Íar Connacht. The fame and renown of Enda's settlements is detailed in Douglas Hyde's *A Literary History of Ireland* and was inspirational to the young Pearse, who, at the time of its publication in 1899, had just returned from his first trip to Aran.
58. Ruth Dudley Edwards, *Patrick Pearse: The Triumph of Failure* (London: Victor Gollancz, 1977), 111–112. In 1906 Gaelic League members Thomas O'Nowlan of Roscrea Cistercian College, Eoin MacNeill and Pearse had tentatively examined the idea of a full-time school for boys arising out of the success of the League's existing summer schools in the Gaeltacht.
59. *Prospectus,* Sgoil Éanna, 1908–9.
60. 'St Enda's School Gardens and Pleasure Grounds', *Irish Gardening,* Vol. VI, No. 60 (February 1911), 26. An article by Finola O'Kane, 'Nurturing a Revolution: Patrick Pearse's School Garden at St Enda's', *Garden History* (2000, No. 28, 1), discusses in detail the landscape design and Celtic influence on the gardens and lands at the Hermitage, pp 73–87.
61. Mrs Dryhurst, one of the founding members of the Irish Women's Franchise League, was a close friend of Muriel Gifford and her sisters Grace and Sidney and it was on one of her trips to St Enda's that she introduced the sisters to Thomas MacDonagh and Joseph Plunkett. Muriel later married MacDonagh, while Grace famously married Plunkett on the eve of his execution in the chapel at Kilmainham Gaol. Sidney Gifford gained a reputation as a political activist and suffragist. As a journalist she wrote under the name 'John Brennan' and she penned an article on St Enda's for *Bean na hEireann* proposing the establishment of a similar school for girls. 'Ought Irishwomen have political equality with men?', *Bean na nEireann.* No. 15 (1909).
62. 'October 17, 1908 – Annála na Sgoile', *An Macaomh.* Vol. 1, No. 1, Midsummer 1909.
63. Mac Ruaidhrí was illiterate and dictated his works for transcription. He was the author of the collection of folktales *Bréaga Eireann* and *Ean an Cheoil Bhinn* as well as other stories which were collected and published by Douglas Hyde. He also authored a life of Hugh O'Neill. He was well known as a *seanchaí* and storyteller and won six gold medals for oratory at the Oireachtas competitions.

3 Saints and Scholars

1. 'Passion Play in Dublin', *Irish Times,* 3 April 1911.
2. Desmond Ryan, 'A Retrospect', *The Story of a Success* (Dublin, 1917), 102–108.

3. Ryan, *The Story of a Success,* 107–108.
4. Ryan, *The Story of a Success,* 108.
5. Joseph Holloway, 7 April 1911, Holloway Diaries, National Library of Ireland.
6. Mary Colum, *Life and the Dream* (London: Macmillan & Co., 1947), 156–157.
7. Desmond Ryan, *The Story of a Success,* 102.
8. Padraic Colum, *The Irish Review,* May 1911.
9. Desmond Ryan, *The Story of a Success,* 108.
10. Desmond Ryan, *The Story of a Success,* 108.
11. See Brendán Ó Madagáin, 'Irish Vocal Music of Lament and Syllabic Verse', Robert O'Driscoll (ed.), *The Celtic Consciousness* (Dublin: Dolmen Press, 1981), 311–321.
12. Pearse, 'Specimens from an Irish Anthology', *The Irish Review* March 1911, 45.
13. Douglas Hyde, *The Religious Songs of Connacht* (1893–4), ed. Brendán Ó Conaire (Dublin: Academic Press, 1985).
14. Holloway Diaries, NLI, 7 April 1911.
15. 'Passion Play at the Abbey Theatre', *Irish Times,* 8 April 1911.
16. The first tableaux vivants by Inghinide na hÉireann and the Celtic Literary Society took place in the Antient Concert Rooms in Easter 1901 'illustrating such legends as the Children of Lir, Brian at Clontarf, and Queen Maeve'. Margaret Ward, *Unmanageable Revolutionaries: Women and Irish Nationalism* (Dingle: Brandon Press, 1983), 55. In her autobiography Máire Nic Shiubhlaigh recalls 'producing tableaux vivants at the Antient Concert Rooms, a small theatre in Brunswick Street – "living pictures" which were very popular just then [1902] . . . showing a scene from some period in Irish history or illustrating some legend or patriotic melody. The director was Alice Milligan, who also wrote some of the plays later produced by the Company, *The Harp That Once* and *The Deliverance of Red Hugh* . . . Padraic Colum gave *The Children of Lir* and *The Saxon Shilling,* two of his first works for the theatre'. *The Splendid Years* (Dublin: James Duffy, 1935), 2–3. Colum referred to Inghinidhe na hÉireann as 'the mother of Irish theatre' and they have been credited for laying the ground for a national Irish Theatre. 'The Early Days of the Irish Theatre', *The Dublin Magazine,* 24 October 1949, 14. Many of the Abbey Theatre's fine actors came out of Inghinidhe na hÉireann, for example Sara Allgood, Mary Quinn and Máire Nic Shiubhlaigh.
17. Padraic Colum, *Three Plays* (Dublin: Allen Figgis, 1963), 2.
18. The play was due to be re-performed in Easter 1914, but larger political events conspired against its production. Therefore the 1911 production of *An Páis* remained the only staging of the play.
19. Pearse, *An Macaomh,* Vol. II, No. 2, May 1913.
20. Padraic Colum, 'Editorial', *The Irish Review,* May 1911.
21. While the *Passion Play* was the first Irish language version of this tale at the Abbey Theatre it was not the only retelling of medieval mystery or morality tales staged at the theatre. Under the directorship of Nugent Monck the Abbey staged a series of English medieval plays also in 1911.
22. Desmond Ryan, *The Story of a Success,* 108; Padraic Colum, *The Irish Review,* May 1911; Joseph Holloway, Holloway Diaries, NLI, 7 April 1911.
23. F. K. Goff, 'Passion Play in Dublin', *Irish Times,* 7 April 1911. For reading on the censorship of biblical scenes in theatres, see Samuel Hynes, *The Edwardian Turn of Mind* (Oxford: Oxford University Press, 1968).

24. Herbert Sussman, *Victorian Masculinities: Manhood and Masculine Poetics in Early Victorian Literature and Art* (Cambridge: Cambridge University Press, 1995), 111–172.
25. Margaret Stokes' *Early Christian Art in Ireland* (Dublin, 1887) is the first publication to advocate the adaptation of early Christian forms into a modern Celtic style, which became a feature of Celtic revivalism.
26. Michel Foucault, *Discipline and Punish: The Birth of the Prison* (London: Penguin, 1991), 141–42.
27. For a summary of the events which led to Colmcille's exile from Ireland, see Douglas Hyde's *A Literary History of Ireland,* 175–78.
28. The phrase is accredited to Colmcille and comes from his poem 'Tá aoibhinn bheith i mBinn Eadair', known in English as 'Delights in Eirinn'. It appears in a number of different forms, according to the translator. In Mary Brigid Pearse's *The Home Life of Pádraig Pearse* she quotes the inspirational lines as 'If death comes suddenly to me, it will be because of the great love I bear the Gael'. Dr Reeve's translation of Adamnán's *Life of St Columba* (Dublin: Irish Archaeological and Celtic Society, 1857) quotes the lines as 'Take my blessing with thee to the West/Broken is my heart in my breast:/Should sudden death overtake me/It is for my great love of the Gaedhil'. George Sigerson has a translation in *Bards of the Gael and Gall* (London 1897, repr. 1907 and 1925 with a preface by Douglas Hyde) that reads: 'Should a quick death be my bale/'Tis for great love of the Gael'.
29. During the 1870s the interest in Irish antiquities produced a number of editions and translations of the life of Colmcille from various sources. Dr Reeves (later the Bishop of Down) had already published, in conjunction with the Irish Archaeological Society, an edited translation of Adamnán's *Life* in 1857, which was well received by audiences already interested in medievalism. Adamnán's *Life* was extensively republished throughout the latter half of the nineteenth century. Editions appeared in 1860, 1871, 1874, 1877, 1893, 1895 and 1897. See listings in Richard Irvine Best, *A Bibliography of Irish Philology (1913–14)* (National Library of Ireland, 1942).
30. John O'Donovan's translations of the poems were published by the Irish Archaeological Society in 1846. J. O. B. Crowe's edition appeared before Whitley Stokes' more famous ones; Crowe's *Amra Coluim Cille* was published by the Royal Irish Academy in 1871. Whitley Stokes' *The Amra Choluimb Cille* was published in London in 1872 and his 'The Bodleian Amra Choluimb Cille' in the 1899 edition of the *Revue Celtique.* The Marquess of Bute published an edition of the *Altus of St Columba* in 1882 while in 1898 Robert Atkinson's edition of the *Amra Coluim Cille* was published by the Henry Bradshaw Society in London.
31. Loughrea Cathedral in Galway contains the Dun Emer Guild tapestries, including one of St Colmcille, which were designed by Jack and Mary Yeats and embroidered by Lily Yeats and her assistants in 1903. Letterkenny Cathedral has an intricately painted vault depicting St Adamnán and St Colmcille dated *c.*1891. St Colmcille is particularly well represented in stained glass. Harry Clarke's windows in the Honan Chapel, Cork (*c.*1916), secured his reputation as the leading stained-glass artist in Ireland. Each of Clarke's windows depicts a full-length figure surrounded by Christian iconography and Celtic symbolism, resulting in a highly decorative effect.
32. Hyde, *A Literary History of Ireland,* 179.
33. Rev. John Boyle, *Cuimhne Colmcille*, ed. E. Maguire (Dublin: M. Gill & Sons, 1898), 82.

34. See Alex G. Scholes, *Education for Empire Settlement* (London: Longmans Green, 1932), which discusses the degree of illiteracy in Ireland during the nineteenth century. See also Robert Fortner, 'The Culture of Hope and the Culture of Despair: The Print Media and Nineteenth Century Irish Emigration', *Éire-Ireland* Vol. 13, No. 3 (Autumn 1978). For an excellent account of the psychological position of the 'native' speaker as debased, see Albert Memmi, *The Coloniser and the Colonised* (London: Earthscan Publications, 1990).

35. Tomás Bán Ó Concheanain, one of the first Gaelic League organizers in the West of Ireland, a regular visitor to St Enda's (his nephew was a pupil there) and a friend of J. M. Synge's, reported in *An Claidheamh Soluis* in 1899 that he met a man on Achill who told him that he 'had heard tell that Irish could be got into print but this is the first time [I] have seen it', quoted in Pádraig Ó Fearáil, *The Story of Conradh na Gaeilge* (Dublin: Clódhanna Teoranta, Conradh na Gaeilge, 1975), 15.

36. Douglas Hyde records the shame he witnessed, as late as 1901, of young people who lapsed into, or were caught, speaking Irish. 'In Sligo . . . I went into a house to wait for a train and there was a pretty little girl at the fireside . . . and, after her first shyness, she began talking Irish very nicely to me, and we were having a pleasant conversation when a dirty little unwashed red-headed brother stuck in his nose, out of a door and . . . said (imitating) "Now Mary, isn't that a credit for ye?" and not a word could I get out of Mary from that time on . . . I went home and thought over it, I swear to you that I cried, because I saw it was the tragedy of a nation in a nutshell'. Hyde, 'The Gaelic Revival', Lecture in Carnegie Hall, 26 November 1905, reprinted in Breandán Ó Conaire (ed.), *Douglas Hyde: Language Lore and Lyrics* (Dublin: Irish Academic Press, 1986), 186. *An Claidheamh Soluis* records in 1902 that people in Spiddal felt that Irish was not an appropriate language with which to address a priest or a well-dressed man or woman. An Timtire na Mumhan, 'Organiser's Reports', *An Claidheamh Soluis,* 5 April 1902. In a later, 1903, piece an old woman from the Gaeltacht is quoted as claiming it is 'a disgrace' to speak Irish since it is only for those 'who do be living out in the wild part of the country'. L. Ní Mhagnusa, 'Notes', *An Claidheamh Soluis,* 25 April 1903. Even after bilingual teaching had been introduced to Irish-speaking areas in 1904, reports from the Department of Education as late as 1911 show the steady and wilful decline of Irish as a spoken language in the intervening years. Inspectors for the Cork, Letterkenny and Ulster Irish-speaking regions were all agreed that 'there seems to be very little local interest in the language revival. Many of the parents consider it a sheer waste of time for their children to learn Irish' (General Report on Irish, *Report of the Intermediate Education Board for Ireland,* British Parliamentary Papers (1911), 134–135). The Inspector for Letterkenny observed that 'the parents, as a body, display no desire to have the language taught to their children' (Mr O'Carroll, *General Report on Irish,* 134), while the Inspector for the Galway region noted that 'it is exceedingly disappointing to find on close enquiry in the Gaeltacht that English is the language most highly favoured. The parents speak Irish beautifully, but never seem to do so to their children, when they know sufficient English to serve their purpose' (W. J. Kelly, *General Report on Irish,* 135).

37. Preface, *Cuimhne Colmcille,* 1.

38. Cardinal Logue, 'The Presentation Brothers School and the Education Question', *Cuimhne Colmcille,* 143–146.

39. *The Freeman's Journal* (4 June 1897); *The Derry Journal* (6, 9 June, 1897) published extensive details with photographs of illuminated manuscripts and sites of eccle-

siastical significance. *The Liverpool Catholic Herald* (9 June 1897) carried details of speeches and dignitaries.

40. Hyde, *A Literary History of Ireland*, 180.
41. Speech by Cardinal Logue, *Cuimhne Colmcille*, 59.
42. Thomas Carlyle, *Past and Present* (London, 1843).
43. For in-depth discussions of these and other Victorian responses to medievalism and monasticism, see Herbert Sussman, 'Artistic Manhood: The Pre-Raphaelite Brotherhood', *Victorian Masculinities: Manhood and Masculine Poetics in Early Victorian Literature and Art* (Cambridge: Cambridge University Press, 1995), 111–172.
44. David Hilliard, 'UnEnglish and Unmanly: Anglo-Catholicism and Homosexuality', *Victorian Studies*, Vol. 25 (Winter 1982), 180–210.
45. Peter Coveney, *The Image of Childhood* (London: Penguin, 1957).
46. For example, Dante Gabriel Rossetti's *The Passover in the Holy Family: Gathering Bitter Herbs*.
47. The publication of Thomas Hughes' *The Manliness of Christ* in 1879 did much to reconcile traditional concepts of Jesus within 'normative' bourgeois Victorian culture.
48. For contemporary accounts of 'The Association of the Holy Childhood' in Ireland, see M. H., 'The Holy Childhood', *Irish Ecclesiastical Record*. 3rd series, Vol. XII (June 1881), and C. J., 'Evangelism by Little Ones', *Irish Ecclesiastical Record*, 3rd series, Vol. XIII (March 1892).

4 Divine Boys

1. Carolyn Steadman, *Strange Dislocations: Childhood and the Idea of Human Interiority, 1780–1930* (London: Virago, 1995), 10–11.
2. For example, the early work of W. B. Yeats; see Declan Kiberd, *Inventing Ireland: The Literature of the Modern Nation* (London: Vintage, 1996), 103.
3. For a good introduction to the relationship between primitivism and modernism, see Colin Rhodes' *Primitivism and Modern Art* (London: Thames and Hudson, 1994).
4. Declan Kiberd, *Inventing Ireland*, 104.
5. Steadman, *Strange Dislocations*, 182.
6. *The Lost Saint* was performed a month later on 24 April 1909 at the Banba Hall as part of the Dublin feis; it is unclear if the play was performed by students of St Enda's.
7. 'Padraic Mac Piarais on the Old Heroes and the New Students', *The Irish Nation*, 27 March 1909.
8. Among those who attended were Sir John Rhys, Eoin MacNeill, W. B. Yeats, Edward Martyn, Stephen Gwynn, D. P. Moran, W. P. Ryan, Padraic Colum, Margaret Hayden, Agnes O'Farrelly, the Count and Countess Markievicz, and Mr and Mrs Standish O'Grady.
9. W. B. Yeats, *Samhain*, 1902.
10. Joseph Holloway, *Impressions of a Playgoer*, April 1910 (on the later production in the Abbey Theatre).
11. The identity of the illustrator 'Gear' is unknown.
12. Pearse, 'By Way of Comment', December 1909.
13. 'The Plays at St Enda's', *An Claidheamh Soluis*, 12 February 1910.
14. Programme notes to 1910 production in Cullenswood House.

15. 'Sgoil Éanna Players', *An Claidheamh Soluis,* 16 April 1910.
16. 'Sgoil Éanna Players', *An Claidheamh Soluis,* 16 April 1910.
17. Joseph Holloway, *Impressions of a Playgoer,* April 1910.
18. 'Sgoil Éanna Players', *An Claidheamh Soluis,* 16 April 1910.
19. See Prospectus, St Enda's School, 1908–1909. The Pearse brothers were well versed in the fine arts. Their father James Pearse had been a monumental sculptor whose High Altar for the Rotunda won an award at the 1882 Dublin Exhibition. See James Pearse's entry in Theo Snoddy, *Dictionary of Irish Artists – 20th Century* (Dublin: Wolfhound Press, 1995), 389.
20. The school's first premises at Cullenswood House boasted a stained-glass window from Sarah Purser's *An Túr Gloine.* The panel, which was at the front door, depicted a triad of candles to illustrate truth, knowledge and wisdom. George Russell donated a mystical symbolist picture *The Sword of Light* featuring a young couple peering into a Celtic twilight. Jack Yeats contributed a pen-and-ink drawing, *The Man That Buried Raftery,* executed in 1900 and either bought by, or given to, Pearse for the school. The drawing went missing from St Enda's after 1916. However, a few years ago the present curator of the Pearse Museum, Pat Cooke, saw the drawing in a fine-art auction-house window. With the aid of the friends of the museum he purchased it and it now hangs in Pearse's study at the Hermitage. Raftery, a blind Connacht poet, had died in 1835 but the story of his life and his many compositions were still extant in oral narrative. Douglas Hyde is generally credited with compiling his work in the volume *Songs Ascribed to Raftery* (1903). Father Mícheál MacGrail, one of the custodians of Cullenswood House, recalls that restorers found handpainted Celtic wallpaper, which they think probably dates to the period when St Enda's occupied the building (Conversation with Father Mícheál MacGrail, October 1996).
21. Other artworks included Jack and George Morrow's friezes, which were also designed to highlight the tradition of Celtic masculinity that was embraced by the school. Internationally acclaimed designers from Belfast, the Morrow Brothers were commissioned to design friezes executed in ancient Irish script to run throughout the rooms in the building. A past pupil, Milo McGarry, recalls that the classrooms were decorated with the names of famous Irishmen, from Colmcille to Eoghan O'Growney. Milo McGarry, 'Memories of Sgoil Éanna', *Capuchin Annual* (1930), 35. The Morrows also illustrated a panel of Cúchulainn taking arms as a young boy and inscribed with Pearse's personal motto: 'I care not though I were to live but one day and one night provided my fame and my deeds live after me.' The Morrow friezes and panel along with Purser's stained glass were stolen when Cullenswood House was vandalized during the 1960s and their whereabouts are now unknown.
22. Beatrice Glenavy, *Today We Will Only Gossip* (London: 1964), 91. The painting was reproduced in the 1907 Christmas supplement to *An Claidheamh Soluis.*
23. 'I had painted an allegorical picture . . . of Cathleen Ní Houlihan . . . Some time later I met one of the boys from the school and he told me that this picture had inspired him "to die for Ireland!" I was shocked at the thought that my rather banal and sentimental picture might, like Helen's face, launch ships and burn towers.' Beatrice Glenavy, *Today We Will Only Gossip,* 91.
24. 'And the child grew, and waxed strong in spirit, and was in the deserts until the day of his shewing unto Israel'. St Luke 1, 80.

25. *An Macaomh* was also, of course, the title of the school magazine, envisaged by Pearse as a literary review containing contributions from those connected with St Enda's. *An Macaomh* featured poems, plays and artistic illustrations from prominent revivalist figures. There was also another school magazine, mostly for in-house reading, which was called *An Scoláire* or *The Scholar*, illustrating rather neatly the twin identities of scholar/warrior which the school promoted.
26. Undated letter excerpted in Séamus Ó Buachalla, *A Significant Irish Educationalist: The Educational Writings of P. H. Pearse* (Dublin and Cork: Mercier Press, 1980), 314.
27. 'The Irish Speaking Child', *An Claidheamh Soluis*, 5 January 1907.
28. 'Lá Faoin Tuath', *An Claidheamh Soluis*, 26 April 1902.
29. See 'Lullaby of A Woman of the Mountain', in Pearse, *Selected Poems* (Dublin: New Island Books, 1993).
30. 'Folklore and the Zeitgeist', *An Claidheamh Soluis*, 16 May 1906.
31. Séamus Ó Buachalla, *The Literary Writings of Patrick Pearse* (Dublin and Cork: Mercier Press, 1979).
32. Mary Brigid Pearse recalls how young Patrick liked to wear his mother's long nightdress and pretend to serve Mass in *The Home Life of Pádraig Pearse* (Dublin and Cork: Mercier Press, 1934), 50–51.
33. 'The Irish-Speaking Child', *An Claidheamh Soluis*, 5 January 1907
34. 'The Irish Speaking Child', *An Claidheamh Soluis*, 5 January 1907.
35. 'The Irish Speaking Child', *An Claidheamh Soluis*, 5 January 1907.
36. The first Prospectus declared that the most important preparation for life was 'the profession and practice of Religion', and that the school would not shirk its duties in providing its boys with a religious and moral education. *Prospectus*, St Enda's School, 1909.
37. Joseph Campbell, Preface to *The Man-Child* (London: Loch Press Booklets, 1907).
38. Norah Saunders and A. A. Kelly, *Joseph Campbell, Poet and Nationalist 1879–1944* (Dublin: Wolfound Press, 1988), 43.
39. Campbell's literary roots are varied and draw from many sources; scattered throughout the collection are quotations from Arnold, Nietzsche, Carlyle, Ruskin, Whitman, Emerson, St Chrysostom and the book of Psalms.
40. Norah Saunders and A. A. Kelly, *Joseph Campbell*, 43.
41. In founding the Irish Theatre, Martyn, MacDonagh and Plunkett hoped to replace the Abbey Theatre as *the* Irish literary theatre. Their aim was to produce Irish-language plays, plays in English by Irish authors other than 'peasant' plays, and plays translated into English from other foreign languages. The Hardwicke Street Hall was owned by the Plunkett family. See Johann Norstedt, *Thomas MacDonagh: A Critical Biography* (Charlottesville: University Press of Virginia, 1980), 127–128.
42. The phrase is W. B. Yeats'. Pearse refers to it in *An Macaomh* (Vol. 2, No. 2, May 1913), mentioning a lecture by Yeats on Rabindranath Tagore in which Yeats spoke highly of St Enda's School. Tagore was born in Bengal in 1861 and came to the attention of western readers when he won the Nobel Prize for Literature in 1913. He was already a familiar figure to many intellectuals as an outstanding poet, storyteller, playwright, painter, composer, philosopher and educational reformer. He was of particular interest to Irish cultural nationalists, since he pioneered the revival of traditional dance and the Bengali language. He founded a

school at Bolpur based along traditional Indian lines in 1901, which later developed into an international institution called Visva-Bharati. The school had much in common with the nationalist principles of St Enda's. He was knighted in 1915 and later renounced his knighthood in protest at British policy in the Punjab. Tagore died in 1941. For further reading see B. C. Chakravorty, *Rabindranath Tagore: His Mind and His Art* (New Delhi: 1971). For a comparative study between Tagore and Celtic mysticism see Abinash Chandra Bose, *Three Mystic Poets: A Study of William Butler Yeats, AE, and Rabindranath Tagore* (Norwood Editions, 1977).

43. Ruth Dudley Edwards, *Patrick Pearse: The Triumph of Failure,* 142.
44. Louis Le Roux, *Patrick H. Pearse* (translated and adapted by Desmond Ryan; Dublin: Phoenix, 1932), 93.
45. Pearse, *An Macaomh,* Vol. 2, No. 2 (May 1913).
46. 'Dublin Happenings', *Evening Herald,* 17 June 1912.
47. 'St Enda's College', *Irish Times,* 17 June 1912.
48. Pearse, 'By Way of Comment', *An Macaomh,* Vol. 2, No. 2 (May 1913).
49. Reported in *Dublin Evening Mail,* 'A St Enda's Play in Bengal', 2 September 1915.
50. 'A St Enda's Play in Bengal', the *Dublin Evening Mail,* 2 September 1915.
51. Ruth Dudley Edwards, *Patrick Pearse: The Triumph of Failure,* 232.

5 Imperial Romanticism

1. Pearse, 'My Childhood and Youth', in Mary Brigid Pearse (ed.), *The Home Life of Pádraig Pearse* (Cork: Mercier Press, 1934), 12–15.
2. Sean Farrell Moran's psychological study of Patrick Pearse suggests that the Pearses did not have a particularly happy childhood. His arguments are convincing and involve insightful readings of the memories of the Pearse children. See 'The Making of a National Hero', *Patrick Pearse and the Politics of Redemption: The Mind of the Easter Rising, 1916* (Washington DC: The Catholic University of America Press, 1994), 22–51.
3. Mary Brigid Pearse, *The Home Life of Pádraig Pearse,* 15.
4. 'Notes', *Fáinne an Lae,* 5 March 1898.
5. Pearse, 'Our Heritage of Chivalry', *An Claidheamh Soluis,* 14 November 1908.
6. Desmond Ryan, 'Pearse, St Enda's College, and the Hound of Ulster', *Threshold.* Vol. 1, Autumn 1957, 55.
7. Pádraig Óg Ó Conaire, 'Cuimhní Scoil Éanna' ('Memories of St Enda's'), *Cuimhní na bPiarsach* (Memories of the Pearses) (Dublin: 1958).
8. Ryan, 'A Retrospect', *A Story of a Success,* 90.
9. Stephen McKenna, quoted in Desmond Ryan, *Remembering Sion,* 58.
10. Ryan, 'A Retrospect', *A Story of a Success,* 90.
11. 'By Way of Comment', *An Macaomh,* Vol. 1, No. 1, Midsummer 1909.
12. 'By Way of Comment', *An Macaomh,* Vol. 1, No. 1, Midsummer 1909.
13. 'Report', *Fáinne an Lae,* 14 January 1899.
14. A body of scholarship exists on attempts to make Christianity 'manly'; some of this has already been documented in previous chapters. However, the foundation of the Salvation Army in 1865 neatly demonstrates the tensions felt between Christianity and manliness. The Salvation Army's borrowing of military language, its use of uniforms and recruiting drives may be seen as an attempt to map Christianity onto prevailing conceptions of imperial manliness. See Pamela J. Walker, 'I Live But Not Yet I For Christ Liveth in Me: Men and Masculinity in the Sal-

vation Army, 1865–90', in Michael Roper and John Tosh (eds.), *Manful Assertions* (London and New York: Routledge, 1991) 92–112.

15. For a discussion of European themes on chivalry, see Mark Girouard, *The Return to Camelot: Chivalry and the English Gentleman* (New Haven: Yale University Press, 1981).
16. Debra N. Mancoff, *The Arthurian Revival in Victorian Art* (New York: Garland, 1990), 35.
17. Mancoff, *The Arthurian Revival in Victorian Art* (Aldershot: Scolar Press, 1995), 41.
18. Joseph Kestner, *Masculinities in Victorian Painting,* (Aldershot: Scholar Press, 1995) 95.
19. Jeffrey Richards, 'Passing the Love of Women: Manly Love and Victorian Society' in J. A. Mangan and James Walvin (eds.), *Manliness and Morality* (New York: St Martin's Press, 1987), 113.
20. Roger Casement, 'Chivalry', *The Fianna Handbook* (Dublin: Central Committee of Na Fianna Éireann, 1909; repr., 1914).
21. See Karl Beckson on parallels made between the collapse of the ancient Roman Empire and fears for the future of the British Empire at the end of the nineteenth century, *London in the 1890s: A Cultural History* (New York and London: W. W. Norton & Company, 1992). See also Samuel Hynes, 'The Decline and Fall of the Tory Empire', *The Edwardian Turn of Mind* (London: Oxford University Press, 1968), 24–27.
22. Karl Beckson, *London in the 1890s: A Cultural History,* 285.
23. For an in-depth discussion on the influence of Carlyle on O'Grady, see Edward A. Hagan, 'History of Ireland: The Heroic Period', *High Nonsensical Words: A Study of the Works of Standish James O'Grady* (New York: The Whitson Publishing Company, 1986).
24. Æ, 'The Dramatic Treatment of Heroic Literature', *United Irishman,* 3 May 1902.
25. F. S. L. Lyons, *Ireland Since the Famine* (London: Fontana, 1973), 235.
26. Malcolm Brown, *The Politics of Irish Literature: From Thomas Davis to W. B. Yeats* (Seattle: University of Washington Press, 1972), 318.
27. There is a conscious determination on O'Grady's part to present a coherent 'story' from extant historical manuscripts. He states quite categorically that 'the treatment to which I have myself adopted consists in the reduction to its artistic elements of the whole of that heroic history taken together' with a keen regard for 'the light shed by the discoveries of modern archaeologians' and 'the actual language of the bards'. O'Grady, 'Introduction', *History of Ireland,* Vol. 1, x. Where Eugene O'Curry had laboured over the exegesis of ancient manuscripts, O'Grady was concerned with formulating the ancient tales in a manner which would be palatable and, more importantly, *recognizable* to a contemporary audience.
28. Pearse, 'The Murder Machine', *Political Writings and Speeches,* 37.
29. Pearse, 'The Murder Machine', *Political Writings and Speeches,* 38.
30. Pearse, 'The Murder Machine', *Political Writings and Speeches,* 41.
31. Pearse, 'The Murder Machine', *Political Writings and Speeches,* 43.
32. Pearse, 'From a Hermitage', *Political Writings and Speeches,* 205.
33. Pearse, 'The Duty of the Schools', *An Claidheamh Soluis,* 7 September 1907.
34. In *On Heroes* Carlyle praised the Teutonic valour and integrity of Martin Luther; in *The Roman and the Teuton* (1864) Charles Kingsley stressed the superiority of the Teutonic Aryan. Joseph Kestner documents how Teutonic culture also influenced

figurative painting and representations of masculinity. See Kestner, *Masculinities in Victorian Painting,* 12–15.

35. Walter Houghton, *The Victorian Frame of Mind* (New Haven and London: Yale University Press, 1957), 316.
36. See Charles Osborne, *The Complete Operas of Wagner* (London: Victor Gollancz, 1992), 140–141.
37. *Der Ring* was made up of four distinct operas, *Das Reingold, Die Walkure, Siegfried* and *Gotterdammerung. Das Rheingold* was first performed in 1869, *Die Walkure* in 1870 and both *Siegfried* and *Gotterdammerung* as part of the first complete *Ring* cycle in 1876.
38. Louis Le Roux, *Patrick H. Pearse* (trans. by Desmond Ryan; Dublin: Phoenix Publishing Company Ltd., 1932), 222–24.
39. Pearse, 'The Schools', *An Claidheamh Soluis,* 7 March 1908.
40. For a history of Pearse's involvement with the Pan-Celtic Movement and the subsequent debate over the place of pan-Celticism in the Gaelic League, see Ruth Dudley Edwards, *Patrick Pearse: The Triumph of Failure,* 31–36.
41. Denis Gwynn, *Edward Martyn and the Irish Revival* (London: Jonathan Cape, 1930).
42. Denis Gwynn, *Edward Martyn and the Irish Revival,* 48.
43. Stoddard Martin, *From Wagner to the Waste Land: A Study of the Relationship of Wagner to English Literature* (London and Basingstoke: Macmillan, 1982), 121.
44. Stoddard Martin's source for this information is from Alfred Lowenberg's *Annals of Opera* (Geneva: 1955), which is now out of print. See *From Wagner to the Waste Land,* 121.
45. Martin, 'Yeats', *Wagner to the Waste Land,* 121.
46. David Sears, *Cuimní na bPiarsach: Memories of the Brothers Pearse,* ed. by Brothers Pearse Commemoration Committee (Dublin: 1966); reprinted from *The Cross* (May 1917).
47. M. B. Pearse (ed.), *The Home Life of Pádraig Pearse.* (Cork: Mercier Press, 1934), 91.
48. Denis Gywnn, *Edward Martyn and the Irish Revival,* 320.
49. Denis Gywnn, *Edward Martyn and the Irish Revival,* 18.
50. See Nicola Gordon Bowe (ed.), *Art and the National Dream: The Search for Vernacular Expression in Turn of the Century Design* (Dublin: Irish Academic Press, 1993).
51. For an in-depth exploration of the personal and professional friendship between the men, see Peter Faulkner, *William Morris and W. B. Yeats* (Dublin: 1962).
52. 'The Bishops and the Language', *An Claidheamh Soluis,* 30 January 1909.
53. Widar Halén, *Dragons from the North* (Dublin and Bergen: 1995).
54. McKenna, 'Pageants', *Freeman's Journal,* 23 June 1909.
55. Philip O'Leary, 'What Stalked Through the Post Office: Pearse's Cúchulainn', Pearse Museum Archive, 26.
56. O'Leary notes that, although Pearse's knowledge of Irish literature may have been impressive, he actually refers to a very limited number of texts and 'that in virtually every instance it is possible to trace the translation he used'. However, this is not particularly revealing or shocking, since very few of Pearse's contemporaries would have had any mastery of the ancient texts that were beginning to be published in popular form for the first time. O'Leary, 'What Stalked Through the Post Office?', 25.
57. Stephen McKenna (pseud. Martin Daly), *Memories of the Dead* (Dublin: 1916), 19.
58. David Greene, *Writing in Irish Today* (Dublin: Mercier Press, 1972), 19.

59. O'Leary, 'What Stalked Through the Post Office?', 25.
60. Eleanor Hull (1860–1935) was a prolific compiler and editor in literature. After her 1898 edition of *The Cúchulainn Saga* she produced *The Silver Bough in Irish Legend* (1901); *The Saga Book of the Viking Club* (1903); *Pagan Ireland* (1904); *The Story of Deirdre* (1904); *Early Christian Ireland* (1905); *A Textbook of Irish Literature to the Sixteenth Century* (1906); *Cúchulainn the Hound of Ulster* (1909); *The Poem Book of the Gael: Translations from Irish Gaelic Poetry into English Prose and Verse* (1912); and *The Northmen in Britain* (1913). She was Honorary Secretary of the Irish Texts Society for almost thirty years.
61. Letter from Eleanor Hull to Pearse, undated, *c.*1906, Pearse Papers, MS 21,054, Folder 5, National Library of Ireland.
62. Lady Augusta Gregory, *Cuchulainn of Muirthemne: The Story of the Men of the Red Branch of Ulster* (Dublin: 1902; repr. Gerarrd's Cross: Colin Smythe, 1970), and *Gods and Fighting Men* (London: John Murray, 1904). There were a number of books telling and retelling the Cúchulainn saga but not all of them were for a popular audience. Amongst these are Alfred Nutt, *Cuchulainn: The Irish Achilles* (1900), William Ridgeway, *The First Shaping of the Cuchulainn Saga* (1905), and Arthur Leahy, *The Sick Bed of Cuchulainn* (1905). W. B. Yeats's *On Baile's Strand* (London: A. H. Bullen, 1904) was based on the death of Cúchulainn. In the 1930s W. M. Crofton composed two operas on the Ulster cycle based on the structure of the *Ring* operas: the first opera was called *Cúchulainn: A Opera in Four Acts* and the second *The Wooing of Emer: An Opera in Four Acts.* Both operas were published in Dublin by the Talbot Press in 1930.
63. Margaret (Mary) Hutton was a scholar and member of the Gaelic League Belfast Executive. She lectured at Ard-Scoil Uladh in Belfast and met Pearse through the League. They became firm friends, as is evidenced by the warm correspondence between them, in addition to her unstinting financial aid to St Enda's. After her husband died in 1912 she moved to Dublin and was a regular contributor to the cultural life of St Enda's.
64. 'Annála na Sgoile 1908–1909', *An Macaomh,* Vol. 1, No. 1 (Midsummer 1909).
65. For a discussion of the post-1916 appropriation of Cúchulainn, from Oliver Sheppard to loyalist murals, see John Turpin. 'Cúchulainn lives on', *CIRCA Art Magazine,* No. 69 (Autumn 1994).
66. For further reading on nationalism as a project of modernity, see Partha Chatterjee, 'The Nationalist Elite', *The Nation and Its Fragments* (Princeton: Princeton University Press, 1993), 35–75.
67. 'Cúchulainn at Sgoil Éanna', *An Claidheamh Soluis,* 3 July 1909.
68. O'Leary, 'What Stalked Through the Post Office?', 27.
69. O'Leary, 'What Stalked Through the Post Office?', 27.
70. See Joseph Bristow, *Empire Boys: Adventures in a Man's World* (London: Harper Collins, 1991).
71. 'By Way of Comment', *An Macaomh,* Vol. 1, No. 1 (Midsummer 1909).
72. 'By Way of Comment', *An Macaomh,* Vol. 2, No. 1 (Christmas 1910).
73. 'By Way of Comment', *An Macaomh,* Vol. 2, No. 1 (Christmas 1910).
74. 'By Way of Comment', *An Macaomh,* Vol. 1, No. 1 (Midsummer 1909).
75. 'By Way of Comment', *An Macaomh,* Vol. 1, No. 1 (Midsummer 1909).
76. 'By Way of Comment', *An Macaomh,* Vol. 1, No. 1 (Midsummer 1909).
77. The art historians John Turpin and Belinda Loftus have both commented on the post-1916 popular and commercial appropriation of Sheppard's image of Cúchu-

lainn, from army medals, which have obvious reference points to the nationalist past, to business trophies, which have little to do with his status as nationalist hero. John Turpin, 'Cúchulainn Lives On', *CIRCA Art Magazine.* No. 69 (Autumn 1994), 6, and Belinda Loftus, 'In Search of a Useful Theory', *CIRCA Art Magazine,* No. 40 (Summer 1988).

6 Literary Revivals

1. Among the most popular editions of the tales of the ancient Fianna in circulation were works by Standish O'Grady, *Finn and His Companions* (London: Fisher Unwin, 1892); P. W. Joyce, *Old Celtic Romances* (1894), which was republished by Pearse in *Sgeal Fiannaidheachta* (Dublin: Gaelic League Publications, 1908); David Comyn issued a school's edition entitled *The Youthful Exploits of Finn* (Dublin: 1896); Lady Gregory, *Gods and Fighting Men* (Dublin: John Murray; New York: Scribners: 1904); A. H. Leahy, *Heroic Romances of Ireland* (London: 1905–6); and T. W. Rolleston, *The High Deeds of Finn* (London: George Harrap, 1910).
2. A very short survey includes a report of a public meeting condemning the popularity of English popular literature, 'The Schools and the Nation', *An Claidheamh Soluis,* 17 May 1900. Agnes O'Farrelly decried the 'cancer' of anglicization and the degenerating influence of cosmopolitan culture in 'The Reign of Humbug', *Gaelic League Pamphlet* No. 10 (1901). A letter from Eleanor Hull to Douglas Hyde in the same year also laments the 'debasing influence of unwholesome English sensational fiction', 'The Irish Language and Irish Intermediate Education III: Dr Hyde's Evidence', *Gaelic League Pamphlet* No. 13 (1901). See also Reverend Henebry, 'The Irish Language and Irish Intermediate Education IX', *Gaelic League Pamphlet* No. 19 (1901); Eoin MacNeill, 'Editorial', *An Claidheamh Soluis*, 8 February 1902; C. J. O'Hehir, 'The Problem of Nationality', *Studies,* 2 (1913); R. Fullerton, 'What Is the Good of It: A Word to Our Young Priests', *Catholic Bulletin* (1914), No. 4; *The Prudence of St Patrick's Irish Policy* (Dublin: O'Brien and Ards, 1916).
3. Stephen Brown, 'Irish Historical Fiction', *Studies,* 5 (1916), 82–95.
4. For example Kathryn Castle, *Britannia's Children: Reading Colonialism through Children's Books and Magazines* (Manchester: Manchester University Press, 1996), and John McKenzie (ed.), *Imperialism and Popular Culture* (Manchester: Manchester University Press, 1986). Norman Vance's work on literature for juveniles makes clear the investment of Christian publishing societies in promoting particular concepts of 'manliness' which constitute, in part, the imperial call to adventure and the need for manly duty, bravery and heroism. See *The Sinews of the Spirit: The Ideal of Christian Manliness in Victorian Literature and Religious Thought* (Cambridge: Cambridge University Press, 1985).
5. Stephen Brown, 'Irish Fiction for Boys', *Studies,* 7 (1918), 469–472, 662.
6. For details on the contents of these magazines, see Kathryn Castle, *Britannia's Children,* Chaps. 3 and 4.
7. A 1915 article in an Irish paper for boys decries the influence of English publications on Irish boys. See 'Killing Irish Nationalism', *Fianna,* Vol. 1, No. 2 (March 1915).
8. Apart from Standish O'Grady's works, some of the books for children that were on offer were Eleanor Hull, *Cúchulainn: The Hound of Ulster* (Dublin: Harrap, 1909); Mrs Stephen Gwynn, *Stories from Irish History Told for Children,* illustrated by Arthur Donnelly and George Morrow (Dublin and Cork: Browne & Nolan,

1904); Ella Young, *Celtic Wonder Tales*, illustrated by Maud Gonne (Dublin: Maunsel, 1910). As appropriate reading matter for children, Stephen Brown recommended: Joseph Jacobs, *Celtic Fairy Tales*, illustrated by J. D. Batten (London: David Nutt, 1892); T. W. Rolleston, *The High Deeds of Finn*, illustrated by Stephen Reid (London: Harrap, 1910); Charles Squire, *The Boy Hero of Erin* (1907); Alice Furlong, *Tales of Fairy Folks, Queens and Heroes* (1909); and Elizabeth Grierson's illustrated *Children's Book of Celtic Stories* (1908). See S. Brown, 'Irish Fiction for Boys', *Studies*, 7 (1918), 670. See also Máire West, 'Kings, Heroes and Warriors: Aspects of Children's Literature in Ireland in the era of emergent Nationalism', *Bulletin of John Rylands University Library of Manchester (BJLR)*, Vol. 76, No. 3 (Autumn, 1994), 165–184.

9. Standish O'Grady, *Lost on Du Carrig: Or 'Twixt Earth and Ocean* (London and Paris: Cassell, 1894); *The Chain of Gold: A Boy's Tale of Adventure* (London: Unwin, 1895); *The Coming Of Cuculain* (London: Methuen, 1894); *Finn and His Companions*, illustrations by Jack B. Yeats (London: Fisher Unwin, 1892); and *The Flight of the Eagle* (London: Lawrence & Bullen, 1892; repr. Dublin: Talbot Press, n.d.).
10. Máire West, 'Kings, Heroes and Warriors', *BJLR*, 180.
11. Padraic Colum, *A Boy in Eirinn* (Dublin: 1913). Colum also wrote another book for children, *The King of Ireland's Son* (New York: 1916). Its publication in New York in 1916 secured Colum's reputation as an outstanding writer of children's literature in the United States.
12. 'Killing Irish Nationalism', *Fianna*, Vol. 1, No. 2 (March 1915).
13. One tale, 'The Prince Who Got Fed Up', tells the story of a country boy who is wooed by a princess. On the eve of his wedding the moon speaks to him and tells him that a life on the land can offer him more beauty, satisfaction and riches than any woman can. He gets on his horse and heads for home. *Fianna*, Vol. 2, No. 7 (January 1916).
14. Masters at the school who appear in *The Wandering Hawk* include Dr Doody, Peter Slattery, Frank Burke and Brian Joyce, while amongst the pupils the O'Doherty, Clery and Sweeney brothers all appear at different points. As was usual with Pearse, the story has a lengthy dramatis personae with as many boys' names as possible mentioned.
15. Joseph Sweeney, 'In the GPO: The Fighting Men', in F. X Martin (ed.), *The Easter Rising: 1916 and University College, Dublin* (Dublin: Browne and Nolan, 1966), 100.
16. Pearse, 'The Fianna of Fionn', *Fianna Éireann Handbook* (Dublin: Central Committee of Na Fianna Éireann, 1909; repr. 1914), 157.
17. 'By Way of Comment', *An Macaomh*, Vol. 2, No. 3 (Christmas 1910).
18. 'By Way of Comment', *An Macaomh*, Vol. 2, No. 3 (Christmas 1910).
19. 'By Way of Comment', *An Macaomh*, Vol. 2, No. 3 (Christmas 1910).
20. Desmond Ryan, *A Man Called Pearse* (London and Dublin: Maunsel Press, 1919), 47.
21. David Sears, *Cuimhni na bPiarsach: Memories of the Brothers Pearse*, ed. by Pearse Brothers Commemoration Committee (Dublin: 1966); repr. from *The Cross* (May 1917). According to Sears, Willie, as well as Patrick, 'greatly believed in the instincts of children and maintained that boys were much nobler and more honourable than men: that they were often right when men were wrong' (29).
22. 'Féile Éanna', programme notes, 20, 21, 22 March, 1909.
23. Kenneth Reddin, 'A Man Called Pearse', *Studies* (June 1943), 243.

24. Pearse, 'St Enda's', *An Craobh Ruadh* (May 1913).
25. Desmond Ryan, *A Man Called Pearse,* 82.
26. Desmond Ryan, *A Man Called Pearse,* 82.
27. 'Padraic Mac Piarais on the Old Heroes and the New Students', *The Irish Nation (and Peasant),* (27 March 1909).
28. 'School Annals', *An Macaomh,* Vol. 1, No. 1 (Midsummer 1909).
29. Quoted by Pearse in *An Macaomh,* Vol. 1, No. 1 (Midsummer 1909).
30. 'Féile Éanna', programme notes, 20, 21, and 22 March 1909.
31. W. P. Ryan, quoted in *An Macaomh,* Vol. 1, No. 1 (Midsummer 1909).
32. 'Fionn and His Companions in Dublin', *An Claidheamh Soluis,* 27 March 1909.
33. The dramatic tradition of the tableau vivants as a form of highly theatricalized display were very popular in nationalist circles from the late nineteenth century. The subject matter of such displays were often scenes enacted from Ireland's historical and/or mythical past. Margaret Ward notes the first production of tableaux vivants by Inghinide na hÉireann and the Celtic Literary Society in the Antient Concert Rooms in Easter 1901 'illustrating such legends as the Children of Lir, Brian at Clontarf, and Queen Maeve'. *Unmanageable Revolutionaries: Women and Irish Nationalism* (Dingle: Brandon Press, 1983), 55. In her autobiography, *The Splendid Years,* Máire Nic Shiubhlaigh recalls 'producing tableaux vivants at the Antient Concert Rooms, a small theatre in Brunswick Street – "living pictures" which were very popular just then [1902], showing a scene from some period in Irish history or illustrating some legend or patriotic melody: William Rooney's *Dear Dark Head* or something out of Moore's *Rich and Rare* in which would appear a lady, richly bejewelled and garbed in silks, wooed by a glittering Sir Knight to the accompaniment of appropriate choral music. The director was Alice Milligan, who also wrote some of the plays later produced by the Company, *The Harp That Once* and *The Deliverance of Red Hugh* and some members of the Celtic Literary Society contributed to pieces of their own in the years that followed: Padraic Colum gave *The Children of Lir* and *The Saxon Shilling,* two of his first works for the theatre'. *The Splendid Years* (Dublin: James Duffy & Co. Ltd., 1935), 2–3. Colum had referred to Inghinidhe na hÉireann as 'the mother of Irish theatre' and the group have been credited with popularizing the tradition of the tableaux vivants in nationalist circles and for laying the ground for a national Irish Theatre. 'The Early Days of the Irish Theatre', *Dublin Magazine,* 24 October 1949, page 14. Many of the Abbey Theatre's fine actors came out of Inghinidhe na hÉireann, for example, Sara Allgood, Mary Quinn and Máire Nic Shiubhlaigh. Brenna Katz Clarke argues that the tableaux vivants were designed to compete with 'vulgar' English entertainments and music hall and were the first contemporary dramatic attempts to represent rural Ireland and peasant life; *The Emergence of the Peasant Play at the Abbey Theatre* (Theatre and Dramatic Studies No. 12; UK: Bowker Publishing Company, 1987), 15–17. Clarke comments on W. B. Yeats's enthusiastic response to the stylized and ritualistic pieces he saw in 1901, documented in his autobiography, and how they made him assess his own work: 'I came away with my head on fire. I wanted to hear my own unfinished *Baile's Strand,* to hear Greek tragedy, spoken with a Dublin accent'. *The Emergence of the Peasant Play,* 18. For a discussion of the popularity of colonial tribal displays see in particular Ben Shephard, 'Showbizz Imperialism: The Case of Peter Lobengula', in John McKenzie (ed.), *Imperialism and Popular Culture* (Manchester: Manchester University Press, 1986), 94–111.

34. Shephard, 'Showbizz Imperialism', 99–100. Between 1910 and 1913 a Matabele warrior, an 'actor' in the African tableau, married an Irish woman and fathered five children. The story was something of a sensation in the British papers, sparking debates on miscegenation and immorality. It is unlikely that either the case or knowledge of the existence of 'tribal shows' were unknown in Ireland.
35. Letter from Fionntain Ua Murchadha to Br Allen, dated 14 June 1960, Br Allen Collection, Dublin.
36. Milo McGarry, 'Memories of Sgoil Éanna', *Capuchin Annual (*1930).
37. Milo McGarry, 'Memories of Sgoil Éanna', *Capuchin Annual* (1930).
38. Programme notes, *The St Enda's Fete,* 9–13 June 1913.
39. Sean O'Casey, 'In This Tent, the Republicans' *Drums Under the Windows* (9–13 June 1913 collected in *Autobiographies 1*; New York: Carroll & Graft, 1984), 618.
40. Sean O'Casey, 'In This Tent, the Republicans', 621.
41. Sean O'Casey, 'In This Tent, the Republicans', 622.
42. Sean O'Casey, 'In This Tent, the Republicans', 622–23.
43. 'Fionn and His Companions in Dublin', *An Claidheamh Soluis,* 27 March 1909.

7 Sport and Physical Culture

1. W. F. Mandle, *The GAA and Irish Nationalist Politics 1884–1924* (London: Christopher Helm; Dublin: Gill and Macmillan, 1987), 14.
2. J. A. Mangan, 'Ethics and Ethnocentricity: Imperial Education and British Tropical Africa', in W. J. Baker and J. A. Mangan (eds.), *Sport in Africa: Essays in Social History* (London and New York: Routledge, 1987), 139.
3. Brian Stoddart, 'Sport, Cultural Imperialism, and Colonial Response in the British Empire', *Comparative Studies in Society and History,* Vol. XXX (1988), 650.
4. In 1881 Michael Cusack wrote an article for *Irish Sportsman* outlining the moral and physical benefits of sport to national morale. See Marcus de Búrca, *The GAA: A History of the Gaelic Athletic Association* (Dublin: Cumann Lúthchleas Gael, 1980), on Cusack's call for a revitalization of physical fitness (14–15), and Derek Birley, *Sport and the Making of Britain,* on Archbishop Croke's advocacy of Gaelic games as a moral necessity in the fight against English degeneracy in 1889 (281–282).
5. W. F. Mandle, *The GAA and Irish Nationalist Politics 1884–1924,* 14.
6. See Alan Bairner, 'Ireland, Sport and Empire', in Keith Jeffrey (ed.), *An Irish Empire? Aspects of Ireland and the British Empire* (Manchester and New York: Manchester University Press, 1996), 58–59.
7. The use of cricket as a pedagogical tool to teach national and colonial subjects about 'Englishness' is discussed by Derek Birley in his book, *Sport and the Making of Britain,* especially Chapter 15, 'The Missionary Spirit: Imperial Fiddlestick', pages 327–41. Cricket societies and working men's clubs can be seen as an attempt to reinforce a grassroots, and especially working-class, cultural identity as well as being the product of social, educational and welfare reform. For a discussion of the use of sport as a colonizing force, see J. A. Mangan, 'Britain's Chief Spiritual Export: Imperial Sport as Moral Metaphor, Political Symbol and Cultural Bond', in J. A. Mangan (ed.), *The Cultural Bond: Sport, Empire, Society* (London: Frank Cass, 1992), 1–10.
8. W. F. Mandle, 'To Test the Pulse of a Nation', *The GAA and Irish Nationalist Politics 1884–1924,* 5.

9. Many of the pieces published in *Irish Sportsman* also appeared in *United Ireland* and *United Irishman* (edited by Richard Pigott). See Marcus de Búrca, *The GAA,* pages 19–21.
10. Between 1898 (the centenary of the 1798 Rising) and 1899 (the beginning of the Boer War) there was an explosion of popular nationalism which helped to boost membership of the GAA and the Gaelic League. The 1798 Commemorations resulted in a number of public events, memorial matches, the erection of public statues and plaques, theatrical productions, pageants, visits to historic sites, and lectures and discussions, while widespread opposition to the Boer War focused popular opinion on the ills of British imperialism. W. F. Mandle notes that during the Boer War the GAA provocatively used Boer names for teams in competition. *The GAA and Irish Nationalist Politics,* 160.
11. See Marcus de Búrca, *The GAA: A History of the Gaelic Athletic Association*, 4.
12. W. F. Mandle, *The GAA and Irish Nationalist Politics 1884–1924,* 15.
13. *Eiriu,* Vol. VIII (1915), 128.
14. De Búrca, *The GAA,* 3.
15. The popular conception of hurling as an especially nationalist game with impeccable historical credentials is illustrated by the wording of an advertisement for sportswear at Whelan & Son, who were situated in the GAA House in Dublin. It also reveals the increasing militancy of GAA members: 'When comes the day/as come it must/That England's rule of greed and lust/Shall lie, all broken, in the dust/We'll still have IRISH HURLING MEN'. Cumann na mBan Programme for Aeridheacht and Military Display, 8 August 1915, in Fairview. (Dublin: Gaelic Press, 1915).
16. For further reading on British Army and other reports on physical and moral decline see Samuel Hynes, 'The Decline and Fall of Tory England', in *The Edwardian Turn of Mind* (London: Oxford University Press, 1968), at pages 15–53.
17. Samuel Hynes, *The Edwardian Turn of Mind,* 30–34.
18. Samuel Hynes, *The Edwardian Turn of Mind,* 30–31.
19. J. Story, 'Physical Deterioration and a Remedy', *Dublin Journal of Medical Science* (June 1909).
20. J. Story, 'Physical Deterioration and a Remedy'.
21. M. E. Sadler, *Special Report on Preparatory Schools for Boys: Their Place in English Secondary Education* (London: His Majesty's Stationery Office, 1900).
22. J. Story, 'Medical Inspection of Schools and School Children'. Address to the Statistical and Social Inquiry Society of Ireland, 1912.
23. Joanna Bourke, *Dismembering the Male: Men's Bodies, Britain and the Great War* (London: Reaktion Books, 1996), 179.
24. Joanna Bourke, *Dismembering the Male,* 179.
25. See Michael Rosenthal, *The Character Factory: Baden-Powell and the Origins of the Boy-Scout Movement* (New York: Pantheon, 1986).
26. J. M. Barrie's (1860–1937) *Peter Pan* was first staged in London in 1904, in which Dion Boucicault's daughter, Nina, played the part of Peter. *Peter Pan* was first published as a book in 1911.
27. H. W. Gibson published a book called *Boyology or Boy Analysis* in 1918. See Mark Seltzer, 'The Love Master: The Anthropology of Boys', *Bodies and Machines* (London and New York: Routledge, 1992), 150.
28. Seth Koven, 'From Rough Lads to Hooligans: Boy Life, National Culture and Social Reform', *Nationalisms and Sexualities* eds. Andrew Parker, Mary Russo,

Doris Sommer and Patricia Yeager (London and New York: Routledge, 1992), 376.

29. The American Boy Scout Movement developed out of a similar youth movement, the Woodcraft movement, which was influenced by Baden-Powell and established by Ernest Thompson Seton, who authored the first *Boy Scouts of America* handbook in 1910. For a history and analysis of the American Boy Scout Movement, see Mark Seltzer 'The Love-Master'. See also David Macleod, *Building Character in the American Boy: The Boy Scouts, YMCA, and their Forerunners, 1870–1920* (Madison: University of Wisconsin Press, 1983).
30. 'Thoughts Aroused on Seeing a Boy Scout', *The Irish Nation,* 19 June 1909.
31. 'Thoughts Aroused on Seeing a Boy Scout', *The Irish Nation,* 19 June 1909.
32. Margaret Skinnider, *Doing My Bit for Ireland* (New York: Century, 1917), 15.
33. Margaret Skinnider, *Doing My Bit for Ireland,* 15.
34. *Fianna Éireann Handbook* (Dublin: 1914).
35. Margaret Skinnider, *Doing My Bit for Ireland,* 15.
36. The Fianna had a President (Constance Markievicz), two Vice-Presidents (Bulmer Hobson and Joseph Robinson), an Honorary Secretary and Assistant, a Central Council, a Congress of Members, an Honorary Treasurer, District Councils, Branches (i.e. troops) and *sluaighte,* which were sections of eight boys each.
37. The first verse reads: 'Draw the sword ye Irish men/The sword is mightier than the pen/Fight the good old fight again/To crush the old transgressor'. *Fianna Handbook* (1909; repr. 1914).
38. *The Constitution of na Fianna Éireann* (1909, amended in 1912).
39. The 1914 *Fianna Handbook* describes the uniforms of the Fianna as: 'green slouch hat, olive green shirt (double-breasted, brass buttons, no pockets on out-side of shirt, shoulder straps); dark breeches and puttees or kilts with saffron *brat* caught at left shoulder with brooch. With the kilts a jersey of a dark green colour may be worn instead of the shirt.'
40. *The Constitution of na Fianna Éireann* (1909).
41. The rising/setting sun is a commonly used symbol in revivalist imagery and Markievicz used it to effect when she designed the masthead for the socialist feminist newspaper *Bean na hÉireann* in 1908. See Nicola Gordon Bowe and Elizabeth Cumming, *The Arts and Crafts Movements in Dublin and Edinburgh, 1885–1925.* (Dublin: Irish Academic Press, 1997).
42. Constance Markievicz, 'Introduction', *The Fianna Handbook* (Dublin: 1909; repr. 1914).
43. Michael D. Blanch, 'Imperialism, Nationalism and Organised Youth', in J. Clarke, C. Critcher, and R. Johnson (eds.), *Working Class Culture* (London, 1979).
44. Circular Letter to St Enda's Past Pupils from Fionntain Ua Murchadha after an Easter 1960 School Reunion; Brother Allen Collection, Dublin.
45. Letter from Fionntain Ua Murchadha to St Enda's Past Pupils detailing the former chief of the Fianna Éireann, Eamonn Martin's, directive; 1960, Brother Allen Collection, Dublin.
46. 'Annála na Sgoile', 24 November 1910, *An Macaomh,* Vol. 2, No. 1 (Christmas 1910).
47. Ryan, *The Man Called Pearse,* 193.
48. Frank O'Connor, *An Only Child* (London: Macmillan, 1961), 124.
49. 'Physical and Intellectual Forces', *The Irish Homestead,* 6 December 1913.
50. 'Physical and Intellectual Forces', *The Irish Homestead,* 6 December 1913.

51. Prospectus, *St Enda's School,* 1908–09.
52. Pearse, *A Story of a Success,* 8.
53. W. F. Mandle, *The GAA and Irish Nationalist Politics,* 17.
54. Ryan, *The Story of a Success,* 36.
55. School Annals, *An Macaomh,* Vol. 1, No. 1 (Midsummer 1909).
56. 'By Way of Comment', *An Macaomh,* December 1909.
57. 'St Enda's School Gardens and Pleasure Grounds', *Irish Gardening,* Vol. VI, No. 60 (February 1911), 27.
58. 'By Way of Comment', *An Macaomh,* Vol. 1, No. 3 (Christmas 1910).
59. 'By Way of Comment', *An Macaomh,* Vol. 2, No. 3 (Christmas 1910).
60. 'By Way of Comment', *An Macaomh,* Vol. 1, No. 3 (Christmas 1910).
61. 'By Way of Comment', *An Macaomh,* Vol. 1, No. 3 (Christmas 1910).
62. 'By Way of Comment', *An Macaomh,* Vol. 1, No. 3 (Christmas 1910).
63. 'By Way of Comment', *An Macaomh.* Vol. 2, No. 2 (Christmas 1910).

8 The Erotics of Boyhood

1. Henry Scott Tuke and Frederick Walker were two of the best-known serious painters of boys bathing. Tuke's paintings *August Blue* (1894), *Ruby Gold and Malachite* (1901) and *The Diving Place* (1907) are all typical depictions of nude boys at play, swimming, fishing and boating. See Joseph Kestner, 'The Male Nude', *Masculinities in Victorian Painting,* 235–89
2. Paul Fussell, *The Great War and Modern Memory,* 283.
3. Paul Fussell, *The Great War and Modern Memory,* 284.
4. See Kenneth Dutton, *The Perfectible Body: The Western Ideal of Physical Development* (London: Cassell, 1995).
5. Paul Fussell, *The Great War and Modern Memory,* 305.
6. See Paul Fussell, *The Great War and Modern Memory,* 305–06, for an in-depth discussion of bathing imagery in literary fiction. See also Brian Reade (ed.), *Sexual Heretics: Male Homosexuality from 1850 to 1900* (New York: Coward McCann, 1971), at page 13 for a discussion of pederastic bathing verses. Joseph Kestner, *Masculinities and Victorian Painting,* discusses fine-art bathing imagery and its homoerotic connotations, 260–67.
7. Paul Fussell, *The Great War and Modern Memory,* 285.
8. See, for example, Linda Dowling, *Hellenism and Homosexuality in Victorian Oxford* (Ithaca and London: Cornell University Press, 1994), and Stefan Collini, *Public Moralists, Political Thought and Intellectual Life in Britain 1850–1930* (New York and Oxford: Oxford University Press, 1991).
9. 'In First Century Ireland' formed the text of a lecture Pearse gave to the Metropolitan School of Art in April 1906. It was later expanded into a series of three lectures delivered to *An Ard Chraobh* or Head Branch of the Gaelic League in 1907. It was subsequently reprinted in *An Claidheamh Soluis* on 21 December 1907 and published as a pamphlet entitled 'In First Century Ireland' by the Talbot Press, Dublin and Cork, 1907.
10. Patrick W. Joyce, *A Social History of Ancient Ireland,* 2 vols. (London: 1903; repr. Dublin: 1913).
11. Pearse, 'In First Century Ireland', 16.
12. See Hyde, 'Irish Folklore', in Breandán Ó Conaire (ed.), *Douglas Hyde: Language, Lore and Lyrics* (Dublin: Irish Academic Press), 94–95.

13. 'The Necessity for De-Anglicising Ireland' (1892), repr. in Ó Conaire, *Douglas Hyde: Language, Lore and Lyrics,* 155.
14. T. W. Rolleston, 'Alliances with the Greeks', *Celtic Myths and Legends* (repr. London: Senate, 1995), 22.
15. Linda Dowling, *Hellenism and Homosexuality in Victorian Oxford.*
16. Joseph Kestner, *Masculinities in Victorian Painting,* 248.
17. For a discussion of the role of the ephebe in Greek culture, see Jean Pierre Vernant, *Mortals and Immortals* (Princeton, New Jersey: Princeton University Press, 1991). Pierre Vidal-Naquet's 1896 study, *The Black Hunter,* is the authoritative Victorian text on the significance of the ephebe to contemporary codes of masculinity.
18. Joseph Kestner, *Masculinities in Victorian Painting,* 248.
19. Joseph Kestner, *Masculinities in Victorian Painting,* 249. The pedagogic relationship between man and adolescent is best explored in both Plato's *Symposium* and his *Phaedrus.*
20. Pearse, 'Some Aspects of Irish Literature', lecture delivered to the National Literary Society, 9 December 1912, reprinted in *Collected Works of Padraic Pearse: Songs of the Irish Rebels* (Dublin: Phoenix Publishing Company, Ltd., *c.*1923), 131–58.
21. Pearse, 'In First Century Ireland', 20.
22. Pearse, 'In First Century Ireland', 27.
23. Pearse, 'In First Century Ireland', 27.
24. Pearse, in 'In First Century Ireland', comments on the vogue amongst Irish speakers for sleeping nude as the ancient Gaels did (27).
25. Pearse, 'In First Century Ireland', 32.
26. Pearse, 'In First Century Ireland', 32.
27. Pearse, 'In First Century Ireland', 33.
28. Pearse, 'In First Century Ireland', 33.
29. Pearse, 'In First Century Ireland', 33.
30. Pearse Papers MSS 21,054, Folder 4.
31. Ruth Dudley Edwards, *Patrick Pearse: The Triumph of Failure,* 126.
32. Desmond Ryan, *Remembering Sion: A Chronicle of Storm and Quiet* (Edinburgh: 1934), 97. Ryan quotes a line from Pearse's poem 'I Have Not Garnered Gold', 'In love I found but quiet that withered my life', which he maintains is a reference to the thwarted future of his love for Nicolls.
33. Editorial, *An Claidheamh Soluis,* 21 August 1909.
34. See Ruth Dudley Edwards, *Patrick Pearse: The Triumph of Failure,* 52–54 and 126–128.
35. Elizabeth Butler Cullingford, 'Thinking of Her . . . as . . . Ireland: Yeats, Pearse and Heaney'. *Textual Practice,* Vol. 4, No. 1 (1990), 1–21.
36. Dermot Bolger (ed.), *Padraic Pearse: Selected Poems* (Dublin: New Island Books, 1993), introduction by Eugene McCabe, 8. Éibhear Walshe (ed.), *Sex Nation and Dissent in Irish Writing* (Cork: Cork University Press, 1997).
37. Sean Farrell Moran, *Patrick Pearse and the Politics of Redemption,* 112.
38. Michel Foucault, *The History of Sexuality. Volume 1* (London: Penguin, 1978).
39. On the construction of modern homosexual identity, see Jeffrey Weekes, *Against Nature: Essays on History, Sexuality and Identity* (London: Rivers Oram Press, 1991).
40. L. Ua Gallchobhair, 'The Children of P. H. Pearse', *Irish Monthly* (March 1922), 120–124.
41. L. Ua Gallchobhair, 'The Children of P. H. Pearse', 122.
42. Eugene McCabe, 'Introduction', *Padraic Pearse: Selected Poems,* 16.

43. Ruth Dudley Edwards, *Patrick Pearse: The Triumph of Failure*, 127.
44. Éibhear Walshe, 'Introduction', *Sex Nation and Dissent in Irish Writing*, 4.
45. Paul Fussell, *The Great War and Modern Memory*, 272.
46. Paul Fussell, *The Great War and Modern Memory*, 281–82.
47. Paul Fussell, *The Great War and Modern Memory*, 282.
48. Paul Fussell, *The Great War and Modern Memory*, 283.
49. 'By Way of Comment', *An Macaomh*, Vol. 1, No. 2 (Midsummer 1909).
50. 'By Way of Comment', *An Macaomh*, Vol. 1, No. 2 (Midsummer 1909).
51. 'By Way of Comment', *An Macaomh*, Vol. 1, No. 2 (Midsummer 1909).
52. Paul Fussell, *The Great War and Modern Memory*, 278.
53. Paul Fussell, 'Soldier Boys', *The Great War and Modern Memory*. For example, Fussell observes that the first edition of John Addington Symonds' *Sexual Inversion* (1896) included a chapter entitled 'The Love of Soldiers and Related Matters'. Fussell, 278–309.
54. 'By Way of Comment', *An Macaomh*, Vol. 2, No. 4 (May 1913).
55. 'By Way of Comment', *An Macaomh*, Vol. 2, No. 4 (May 1913).
56. *Fianna*, No. 6 (December 1915), 16.
57. Elizabeth Butler Cullingford, 'Thinking about Her . . . as . . . Ireland: Yeats, Pearse and Heaney', 14.
58. Abigail Solomon-Godeau, *Male Trouble: A Crisis in Representation* (London: Thames and Hudson, 1997), 11.
59. Abigail Solomon-Godeau, *Male Trouble*, 11. Solomon-Godeau is informed by Eve Kosofsky Sedgwick's work on homosociality and relationships between men; *Between Men: English Literature and Male Homosocial Desire* (New York: 1985).
60. Abigail Solomon-Godeau, *Male Trouble*, 11.
61. Mary Colum, *Life and the Dream*, 151–155.
62. Mary Brigid Pearse, *The Home Life of Pádraig Pearse*, 40. Sean Farrell Moran claims that Pearse's frequent 'female' wanderings took him into the area of 'Monto', well known in Dublin for prostitution, and Farrell Moran suggests that Pearse's sexual curiosity was not as dormant as has perhaps been commonly assumed. However, sexual curiosity and sexual experience are not one and the same thing. Furthermore, there is nothing to indicate that Pearse was initiated into either hetero- or homosexual experiences as a result of his night-time wanderings. *Patrick Pearse and The Poltics of Redemption*, 48–49.
63. Desmond Ryan, *The Man Called Pearse*, 202.
64. Sean Farrell Moran, *Patrick Pearse and the Politics of Redemption*, 114.
65. The question of Pearse's sexuality was raised as being an issue of interest in the public debate on the letters page of the *Irish Times* (Aug/Sept 2000). Arising directly out of the public interest in Pearse evidenced by the many letters to the newspaper, Stephen Carson made a documentary entitled *Pearse – Fanatic Heart* (Mint Productions, 2001) for RTÉ television. One of the topics addressed by contributors was the question of Pearse's sexuality. Both contributors on this matter (Ruth Dudley Edwards and myself) were in agreement as to Pearse's sublimated homosexuality and the homoerotic tendencies of Pearse's work.

9 'What if the Dream Come True?'

1. For a detailed account of the financial affairs of St Enda's and St Ita's during this time, see Ruth Dudley Edwards, *Patrick Pearse: The Triumph of Failure*, 144–52.

2. Ruth Dudley Edwards, *Patrick Pearse: The Triumph of Failure,* 189.
3. Ruth Dudley Edwards, *Patrick Pearse: The Triumph of Failure,* 197.
4. Desmond Ryan, *Remembering Sion,* 167.
5. Desmond Ryan, *Remembering Sion,* 123.
6. Desmond Ryan, *Remembering Sion,* 124.
7. Padraic Colum, 'Padraic Pearse – the Poet', *The Irish Rebellion of 1916 and Its Martyrs* (New York: The Devin-Adair Company, 1916), 284.
8. Joseph Sweeney, 'In the GPO: The Fighting Men', 98. The group consisted of Joe Sweeney, Frank Burke, Eamonn Bulfin, Desmond Ryan, Fintan Murphy, Brian Joyce, Conor McGinley, John Kilgallon, Eunan McGinley and David Sears.
9. Joseph Sweeney, 'In the GPO: The Fighting Men', 96.
10. Joseph McDonagh made the film *Willy Reilly and the Colleen Bawn* in the grounds of St Enda's in 1920. The film is based on William Carleton's 1855 novel *Willy Reilly and his dear Colleen Bawn.* The use of St Enda's as a location was intended to underline the film's nationalist reference points. See Kevin Rockett, Luke Gibbons and John Hill, *Cinema and Ireland* (London: Croom Helm, 1987), 23–29.
11. Ruth Dudley Edwards, *Patrick Pearse: The Triumph of Failure,* 331.
12. Ruth Dudley Edwards, *Patrick Pearse: The Triumph of Failure,* 333.
13. Margaret Ward, *Unmanageable Revolutionaries: Women and Irish Nationalism* (Dingle: Brandon Press, 1983), 202.
14. See Ruth Dudley Edwards, 'The Political Legacy', *Patrick Pearse: The Triumph of Failure,* 323–28.
15. Desmond Ryan, *Remembering Sion,* 125–26.
16. Ruth Dudley Edwards, *Patrick Pearse: The Triumph of Failure,* 339–40.
17. Ruth Dudley Edwards, *Patrick Pearse: The Triumph of Failure,* 340.
18. L. Ua Gallchobhair, 'The Children of P. H. Pearse', *Irish Monthly* (March 1922), 120–124.
19. 'Department of Education Notes for Teachers', quoted in Ruth Dudley Edwards, *Patrick Pearse: The Triumph of Failure,* 341.
20. Kenneth Reddin, 'A Man Called Pearse', *Studies* (June 1943), 241–51.
21. Milo McGarry, 'Memories of Sgoil Éanna', *Capuchin Annual* (1930), 35–41.
22. Denis Gwynn, 'Patrick Pearse', *Dublin Review* (Jan–March 1923).
23. Denis Gwynn, 'Patrick Pearse', 93.
24. Desmond Ryan, *Remembering Sion,* 161.
25. W. B. Yeats, 'Easter 1916', *Collected Poems* (Basingstoke: Macmillan, 1982), 202–03.
26. W. B. Yeats, 'Three Songs to the One Burden', *Collected Poems,* 371.
27. Elizabeth, Countess of Fingall, *Seventy Years Young* (Dublin: Lilliput Press, 1991), 376.
28. See Ruth Dudley Edwards, *The Triumph of Failure,* for an assessment of Pearse's political legacy and a synopsis of the differing views of Pearse's contribution to Irish political life, 335–44.

Index